Acclaim for *Toil and Transcendence*
by Rev. Charles P. Connor, S.T.L., Ph.D.

In Toil and Transcendence: Catholicism in 20th-Century America,
Father Connor has provided an insightful and accurate portrait
of Catholic life in the United States based on firmly established
facts and a keen sense of the relationship between the Church and
currents in society and politics of the time. His discussion of the
personalities of prominent churchmen and influential people in
American society manifests his uniquely astute grasp of the transi-
tions in the twentieth-century Catholic experience.

Father Connor's fidelity to scholarship is equaled only by his
love for the Church and his quest for a clear exposition of the
struggles and triumphs of past generations of Catholics in America.
A masterpiece that will light the path for the Church in the future!
A must-read for any student of Catholic history!

—Most Rev. William J. Waltersheid, D.D., S.T.L.
Auxiliary Bishop of Pittsburgh

Toil and Transcendence: Catholicism in 20th-Century America is truly
a remarkable work—a carefully researched and engaging study
of United States Catholicism in the twentieth century. I highly
recommend this book. A monumental gift to the Church!

—Most Rev. Joseph C. Bambera, D.D., J.C.L.
Bishop of Scranton

Father Connor's final installment on American Church history
provides an insightful overview of the significant persons and
events, both in the Church and in society, that helped shape the
life of Catholics in the United States in the twentieth century. It

is a useful resource both for those who have a special interest in Church history as well as for Catholics who want to learn more about the life of the Church in these momentous years.

—Most Rev. Joseph M. Siegel, D.D., S.T.L.
Bishop of Evansville, Indiana

The story of U.S. Catholicism in the twentieth century provides an essential reference for understanding and confronting the challenges we face in the twenty-first century. In the words of Pope Saint John XXIII, "History is the best of professors." I highly recommend Catholic American historian Father Connor's excellently researched and engaging account of persons and events that make up the history of the Catholic Church in the United States in the twentieth century. Thank you, Father Connor, for helping us understand our past so as to move intelligently and confidently into the future in accomplishing our evangelizing mission in a culture significantly shaped by the events and movements of the past century.

—Most Rev. Kevin C. Rhoades, D.D., S.T.L., J.C.L.
Bishop of Fort Wayne–South Bend

In this extraordinary survey of the American Catholic experience in the last century, Father Charles Connor once again demonstrates his keen sensibility to the ongoing Catholic struggle in a civil context often suspicious and even antagonistic toward Catholicism and its values. In this work, he clearly shows his prowess as an accomplished historian and a man of faith who sees history as a reality not only defined by the actions of men and women, but always within the context of God's Divine Providence. *Toil and Transcendence: Catholicism in 20th-Century America* is a valuable study of our Catholic contribution and struggle in the past, which helps us intuit our place in the future of a turbulent "postmodern"

America. It is a "must-read" for those who truly wish to understand the American Catholic experience.

—Most Rev. Peter B. Wells, D.D., J.C.D.
Apostolic Nuncio to South Africa

Father Connor takes seriously George Santayana's famous quote, "Those who cannot remember the past are condemned to repeat it." In *Toil and Transcendence*, Father Connor eloquently remembers the history of American Catholicism in the twentieth century through the turbulent times of war, economic boom and bust, and the growth of Catholic education. He writes of the struggle against anti-Catholicism, the lives of great churchmen such as Cardinals Gibbons and Spellman, dissent over *Humanae Vitae*, and finally the alliance of a conservative president and a saintly pope, which changed history.

I know that with the scholarly skill of Father Connor, this final book in his trilogy of American Church history will not only serve us well in remembering the past but will also, with the Holy Spirit to guide us, forge a brighter and even better future for Catholicism in the United States. I highly recommend this book.

—Rev. Msgr. Andrew R. Baker, S.T.D.
Rector, Mount St. Mary's Seminary, Emmitsburg, MD

We've been waiting for Father Connor's next volume in his tantalizing history of Catholicism in America, and our patience has paid off! He brings us home, from the "teenage" Church of the 1880s, to the "adult" one of recent memory. Did you ever ask, "How'd we get here?" Well, let this historian tell you.

—Timothy Michael Cardinal Dolan
Archbishop of New York

I have known Father Connor since our days as seminarians at the Pontifical North American College and have always found his love of history and the Catholic Faith to be inspirational. He has combined this passion into another work that I am sure will enlighten and enhance the reader's knowledge of and appreciation for the experience of the Church in the twentieth century. I have no doubt that Father Connor's trilogy will serve as a great contribution to those who wish to learn more about the Catholic Church and Her history in the United States and hopefully inspire many to grow in their faith as well.

—Most Rev. James F. Checchio, D.D., J.C.D., M.B.A.
Bishop of Metuchen

In the third volume of his trilogy, *Toil and Transcendence*, Father Connor recounts afresh the story of the Church in the late-nineteenth and twentieth centuries. In so doing, he helps us understand both our heritage as Catholics in America and also the current opportunities and challenges the Church is facing. I highly recommend Father Connor's trilogy to anyone who wants to appreciate more deeply the Church in the United States.

—Most Rev. William E. Lori, S.T.D.
Archbishop of Baltimore

I am delighted that Father Connor has published the fruits of his research and reflection on the experience of the Catholic Church in the United States in the twentieth century. Contemporary historical research too often neglects the influence of the spiritual dimension of human life. In following the life of the Church through this remarkable century of change, Father Connor's study of the unique role of the Catholic Church in this period will add greatly to this continuing reflection. Though his research is focused on the Church's life in the United States, the narrative touches aspects that are common to the Church in other countries of North America, Western Europe, and elsewhere. I am confident that his book will add greatly to the ongoing reflection of the Church's contemporary experience.

—Most Rev. Michael Mulhall
Archbishop of Kingston, Ontario

Toil and Transcendence is an essential resource for the library of anyone interested in the history of the Church in the United States from the end of the First Vatican Council through the 1980s. Father Connor's work is a truly valuable contribution to the study of American Catholicism during this period!

—Most Rev. Frank J. Dewane
Bishop of the Diocese of Venice in Florida

∞

Toil and Transcendence

Also by Rev. Charles P. Connor:

Pioneer Priests and Makeshift Altars
A History of Catholicism in the Thirteen Colonies

Faith and Fury
The Rise of Catholicism during the Civil War

Rev. Charles P. Connor, S.T.L., Ph.D.

Toil and Transcendence

Catholicism in 20th-Century America

EWTN PUBLISHING, INC.

Irondale, Alabama

EWTN Publishing, Inc.
5817 Old Leeds Road, Irondale, AL 35210

Distributed by Sophia Institute Press, Box 5284, Manchester, NH 03108.

paperback ISBN 978-1-68278-142-5
ebook ISBN 978-1-68278-143-2
Library of Congress Control Number: 2020945802

Contents

∝

Foreword

Preaching at the funeral of the eminent Church historian Reverend Marvin O'Connell at the University of Notre Dame, Professor Wilson Miscamble, C.S.C., quoted Father O'Connell as having observed that history has "a special role in the life of the Christian people, and so does the historian." He noted that Father O'Connell considered the historian to be a veritable "midwife to our faith."

With the publication of *Toil and Transcendence: Catholicism in 20th-Century America*, Father Charles Connor vividly illustrates the special role that a Church historian can play in the life of God's people and establishes himself as a true "midwife to our faith." His careful historical research and presentation draws the reader deeper into the mystery of Christ and His Church and reflects Father Connor's years of experience as a professor of systematic theology and Church history at Mount St. Mary's Seminary and University in Emmitsburg, Maryland. With a Ph.D. in history from Fordham University and impressive credentials in theology and philosophy, Father Connor clearly has all the necessary scientific tools for his "trade" as a Church historian. It is apparent from *Toil and Transcendence*, however, that it is his love for the Church that animates his work and gives purpose to his labors.

Toil and Transcendence

I met Father Connor some thirty-five years ago in Rome when he was just beginning his theological studies in preparation for the priesthood. I was inspired by his ability to articulate how his study of Church history had led him to say yes to the Lord's call, illustrating the abovementioned nexus between Church history and faith. It was an honor to gather with his family and many friends in Saint Peter's Cathedral in Scranton in 1990 when Dr. Connor joyfully became Father Connor.

For even the best of historians, the task of chronicling the contemporary age can be challenging. When the historian is writing about events of which there is personal recall, it is sometimes difficult to maintain the objectivity that is necessary for clear analysis. Moreover, the work of the contemporary historian at times suffers from the lack of an established body of other historical scholarship. In *Toil and Transcendance*, however, Father Connor proves himself up to the challenge of writing about the Church in the twentieth century.

While focusing on the major, salient events and persons who shaped the story of U.S. Catholicism in the twentieth century, Father Connor wisely begins his study a few decades before the turn of the century. By beginning with the close of the First Vatican Council and the promulgation of *Pastor Aeternus*, the decree on papal infallibility, he is able to root his examination firmly in the broader context of the events that were affecting the Church universal just as the Church in the United States began to arrive at a new prominence, with the appointment of Her first cardinals in America and with the need to address pressing social issues emerging in American society.

Though appreciating the importance of developments in the global Church, and the ways in which the twentieth-century successors of Saint Peter have related to the Church in the United States, Father Connor appropriately highlights throughout his study the significant events, movements, and developments that were particular to the experience of U.S. Catholics. His nuanced understanding of the dominant currents in American political and economic history, as well as trends in secular society, contributes considerable insight to his explication of the events and personalities that defined the American ecclesial experience in the last century.

Father Connor captures masterfully the personalities and contributions of the leaders who shaped American Church history in this period. It is not surprising that, as a professor teaching in the archdiocese once headed by James Cardinal Gibbons, Father Connor demonstrates in particular a deep understanding of Cardinal Gibbons's oversize impact not only on the Church in the premier see of Baltimore but also throughout the United States, as well as more globally, on Catholic social teaching. I am especially delighted, moreover, to see that my larger-than-life predecessor, Archbishop John Ireland, also figures prominently in Father Connor's study of the first decades of the twentieth century.

Going far beyond a study of the handful of individuals who are regularly singled out for their contribution to the Church in the twentieth century, Father Connor weaves a broader tapestry that emphasizes the trends and connections that continue to have relevance for our experience of the Church in the twenty-first century. Those who are today examining issues of religious liberty and prejudice; or exploring the challenges of welcoming immigrants, asserting the dignity of all human life and protecting the rights, of the vulnerable; or assessing the appropriate impact of faith on public service and its relevance to debate in the public square will all find insights in *Toil and Transcendance*.

The history of the Church in twentieth-century America is ultimately a story of remarkable faith, generous service, and courageous adherence to the teachings of Jesus Christ, all in a rapidly changing social context. May Father Connor's engaging and meaningful study inspire us to work with similar conviction and creativity to meet the challenges of the present day.

—Most Rev. Bernard A. Hebda, J.C.L., J.D.
Archbishop of Minneapolis–Saint Paul, Minnesota

∞

Toil and Transcendence

1

∞

Prelude: The Late Nineteenth Century

A Long-Expected Council

Historians have traditionally designated 1877 as the close of our
nation's period of Reconstruction, when the last federal troops of
occupation left the former Confederate States of America. Shortly
before this, the Catholic bishops of the world had gathered in the
Eternal City of Rome for the First Council of the Vatican. With
the American mind preoccupied with the future of the reunified
nation, one wonders how much concern was given to the events
that had transpired in Rome. Many Catholics in the United States,
though, did fear another wave of anti-Catholic persecution and
violence due to the promulgation of the doctrine of papal infallibility. These were indeed interesting years in which to be a
Catholic in America.

The First Vatican Council, unlike its successor nine decades
later, was essentially a European council. The global concerns facing
the fathers of Vatican II were nonexistent in the 1870s, and the
debates among the bishops, as well as the documents produced,
reflected Europe's contemporary problems. The effects of the Enlightenment upon modern thought and the devastation wrought
by the French Revolution were serious concerns to be addressed,
as were the influence of new philosophers such as Kant and Hegel.
Political liberalism, long a concern to the Church in Europe, and

the continuous problems faced by the pope as political leader of the Papal States, were also at the forefront.

Best remembered, however, is the debate over, and subsequent declaration of, the doctrine of papal infallibility, which is the belief that when the Holy Father speaks *ex cathedra* — literally, from the chair — on matters of faith and morals, he is preserved from error by the specific working of the Holy Spirit. The Council Fathers engaged in much spirited debate on this teaching, both among the American bishops and their European counterparts. Rochester's Bishop Bernard McQuaid once said that, among his episcopal colleagues, the matter of infallibility was very little spoken of. Though that may have been the case, McQuaid himself, while he ultimately accepted the dogma, was until the end opposed to its promulgation. His major reason for opposing it expressed a notion of collegiality often found among American prelates: "Somehow or other it was in my head that the Bishops ought to be consulted."[1]

The American bishops were divided between opportunists and inopportunists — that is, those who felt the time for promulgation was appropriate and those who did not. Many, that is, felt the doctrine was true and definable but that the time was not right for such a strong pronouncement. America had witnessed more than two and a half centuries of anti-Catholic bigotry. With the latest outburst following Lincoln's assassination, many of the bishops felt that promulgating infallibility would fan the flames. Other bishops felt just as strongly that, even so, a strong affirmation of the Catholic Faith was far more important than any worldly or political concerns. These included the Franco-Americans from

[1]   Frederick J. Zwierlein, *The Life and Letters of Bishop McQuaid*, 3 vols. (Rochester, NY: 1926), 2:63, cited in Gerald P. Fogarty, S.J., *The Vatican and the American Hierarchy from 1870 to 1965* (Collegeville, MN: Liturgical Press, 1982), 1.

Prelude: The Late Nineteenth Century

New England as well as those from the Pacific Northwest and the Gulf Coast. Bishop Michael Heiss, a native of Bavaria who served as bishop of La Crosse, Wisconsin, along with Baltimore-born William Henry Elder of Natchez, Mississippi, joined the voices of those calling for a formal definition.[2]

Most conspicuous among the inopportunists was the Dublin-born archbishop of Saint Louis, Peter Richard Kenrick. His objections ran deeper than timing, though: He could find nothing in Scripture or Tradition that convinced him that a universal definition of infallibility was plausible. It surely was a topic on which theologians were free to debate, on his reading, but bishops gathered in such solemn convocations were tasked with preserving and defending the Faith rather than dividing into camps over legitimate theologial diversity. In the end, some fifty-five bishops left the council early to avoid casting a negative vote in the presence of the Holy Father, Pius IX. And so the vote was overwhelming in favor of the definition of papal infallibility, and the reception of this decision in the episcopacy, especially among those with reservations, was laudatory. Kenrick, one of the more conspicuous opponents, stated publicly:

> The motive of my submission is simply and singly the authority of the Catholic Church. That submission is a most reasonable obedience, because of the necessity of obeying an authority established by God; and having the guaranty of Our Divine Savior's perpetual assistance is in itself evidence, and cannot be gainsaid by anyone who professes to recognize Jesus Christ as his Savior and his God. Simply and singly on that authority I yield obedience and full and

[2] James Hennesey, S.J., *American Catholics: A History of the Roman Catholic Community in the United States* (New York: Oxford University Press, 1981), 169.

unreserved submission to the definition the character of which there can be no doubt as emanating from the Council, and subsequentially accepted by the greater part even of those who were in the minority on that occasion.[3]

Growth Spurt

Since the original suffragan sees of Boston, Philadelphia, New York, and Bardstown, Kentucky, had been carved from Baltimore in 1808, the physical growth of the Church had been little short of remarkable. This necessitated the creation of several new dioceses and provinces.[4] Compared with the growth of other religious groups, Catholicism can rightfully be viewed as an American success story. One historian has estimated that while Catholic immigration had increased rapidly in the pre–Civil War years,

> giant strides in membership took place in the decades that followed. The four million Catholics of 1870 increased to six million in 1880. Ten years later the total was nine million, and in 1900 it was twelve million. By 1920 every sixth person and every third church member was a Roman Catholic.[5]

Immigration would transform Catholicism in the United States. Until the 1890s, most immigrants had come from Northern and Western Europe. Newer groups in the late nineteenth and early twentieth centuries, following the Irish and Germans of midcentury,

---

[3] Fogarty, *The Vatican and the American Hierarchy*, 4.

[4] An ecclesiastical province is simply a geographical area headed by a metropolitan archbishop in his archdiocese, containing within it any number of dioceses.

[5] Winthrop S. Hudson, *Religion in America: An Historical Account of the Development of American Religious Life* (New York: Charles Scribner's Sons, 1965), 247.

included Italians, Polish, and Hungarians. Still later we see very significant numbers of Lithuanians, Bohemians, Slovaks, Croats, and Slovenes.

Over a million Catholics poured into the country in each decade between 1880 and 1920 and over two million in the years 1901–1910. Catholic population grew from 6,259,000 in 1880 to 16,363,000 in 1910 in a national population that went from 75,995,000 to 91,972,000. Some Czechs and Germans became farmers, but most Catholics settled in eastern and midwestern cities. In 1890, four of every five people in greater New York City were either immigrants or children of immigrants. The Irish preferred the east; Germans headed for cities in the Cincinnati–St. Louis–Milwaukee triangle. Italians recreated in city neighborhoods something of the village atmosphere they had left behind.[6]

A very significant appointment for the Church in the United States, considering its growth and advancing maturity, was John McCloskey as the nation's first cardinal in 1875. Born in Brooklyn in 1810, the son of Irish immigrants from County Derry studied at Mount St. Mary's College in Emmitsburg, Maryland, and in later years returned there to train for the priesthood. In 1834, he was ordained a priest in St. Patrick's Old Cathedral in New York City, after which he served briefly as a seminary professor and then as president of St. John's College, later Fordham University, in the Bronx. McCloskey was named coadjutor bishop of New York in 1843, later moved to Albany, and then returned to New York as its archbishop in 1864. Fifteen years later, he dedicated St. Patrick's Cathedral on Fifth Avenue, begun under his predecessor, Archbishop John Hughes. McCloskey would serve twenty-one

---

6   Hennesey, *American Catholics*, 173.

years as archbishop of New York and likely received the red hat for several reasons:

> In terms of size, his see was the most important in the United States. It had, moreover, weathered the waves of immigrants flowing through its port and the storms of nativism occasioned by their arrival; it had created a parochial school system, second to none in the country, to preserve the faith of Catholic children; and, in general, the diocese was well administered.[7]

New Thinking

Bishops returning from the Vatican Council presided over a Church that had significantly grown — and much more was to come. At the same time, the Church was part of a nation with a great and growing intellectual diversity. Most people today take for granted the existence of the political theory of Karl Marx, the science of evolution linked to Charles Darwin, and the philosophy of Hegel. From these formative sources evolved much of modern thought. Significant for America especially was the British sociologist Herbert Spencer, who argued that a "pure competitive society ... would produce by the workings of the natural law of the survival of the fittest the most progressive and abundant economy known to the world."[8] Spencer's most ardent disciple in the United States was William Graham Sumner, a professor of sociology at Yale whose underlying premise was that the social order "is fixed by laws of nature precisely analogous to those of the physical order."[9]

[7] Fogarty, The Vatican and the American Hierarchy, 9.
[8] George E. Mowry, The Era of Theodore Roosevelt and the Birth of Modern America: 1900–1912 (New York: Harper & Row, 1958), 17.
[9] Ibid., 20.

Such theories, in the minds of many, indicated that the social structure in America was completely justifiable as it stood. Those who accumulated tremendous wealth were "the fittest" and deserved nothing less than whatever they could accumulate; the "dregs of society," which was a popular term, were simply the least "fit" and deserved nothing more than whatever meager existence they could eke out. The class structure of haves and have-nots was supported in the highest sociological circles; the thinking behind it was closely related to the Calvinistic ethic brought to these shores by the Puritans and enshrined, at least by implication, in America's foundational documents, which were written by inheritors of the Enlightenment and the Protestant Reformation.

This existing order, however, came to be challenged by a newer strain of thought, particularly in sociology, but also in other areas of America's mainstream. In 1883, sociologist Lester Ward of Dartmouth produced his *Dynamic Sociology*, in which he argued that social evolution had nothing to do with natural law, but rather an individual's intellectual capacity to think about and produce change. Man was using environmental forces to his own advantage, Ward contended, and, as such, he was "not only the inheritor of change ... [but] also the creator of it, fully capable of rational planning and social engineering."[10]

Economics was also a field strongly affected by the new thinking. Scholars such as Richard T. Ely of Johns Hopkins University asserted that man was no longer the passive recipient of change; he was the maker of it. Following from this, these thinkers believed

---

[10] Ibid., 21. Interestingly, Mowry also notes that the flowering of this new era of social studies brought about, in other disciplines, such publications as the *Political Science Quarterly*, the *Quarterly Review of Economics*, the *Annals of the American Academy of Political and Social Sciences*, the *Journal of Political Economy*, and the *American Historical Review*. Ibid., 20.

9

the state, "as an educational and ethical agency is an indispensable condition to human progress."[11] Juridically, Oliver Wendell Holmes Jr. published his *Common Law* in 1881. He argued against the well-established idea that law was based upon "nearly immutable principles, and that it changed, if at all, by a process of rigorous logical extrapolations from such principles."[12] Instead, he stated that the basis of law was human experience and the material and intellectual environment man found himself in in any given period. As such, law became "one of the felt necessities of the times, evolving from the prevalent moral and political theories from economic rationalizations, and even from the unconscious prejudices which judges shared with their fellow men."[13]

Finally, religion in America in the later decades of the nineteenth century became much imbued with a spirit of liberalism. The nature of this has been well defined as

> a point of view which, like the adjective "liberal" as we commonly use it, denotes both a certain generosity or charitableness toward divergent opinions and a desire for intellectual "liberty". Liberal theologians wished to "liberate" religion from obscurantism and creedal bondage so as to give man's moral and rational powers larger scope.... With regard to human nature, they emphasized man's freedom and his natural capacity for altruistic action. Sin, therefore

---

[11] Ibid., 22. Curiously, Ely would become the mentor of the doctoral dissertation of Monsignor John A. Ryan, longtime faculty member at the Catholic University of America, who came as close as any American thinker to developing a Catholic position of political economy.

[12] Ibid., 23.

[13] Ibid. Holmes went on to define truth as the system of his own limitations, whereas absolute truth he preferred to leave to "those who are better equipped."

was construed chiefly as error and limitation which education in morals and the example of Jesus could mitigate, or else as the product of underprivilege which social reform could correct. Original Sin or human depravity was denied or almost defined out of existence.... Ethical imperatives became central to the Christian witness, and the Sermon on the Mount was often regarded as the heart and core of the Bible. On the other hand, liberals tended to slight traditional dogma and the sacraments.

Perhaps the single most important fact about liberals on the American religious scene is that they

led the Protestant churches into the world of modern science, scholarship, philosophy, and global knowledge. They domesticated modern religious ideas. They forced a confrontation between traditional orthodoxies and the new grounds for religious skepticism exposed during the nineteenth century, and thus carried forward what the Enlightenment had begun.[14]

Even more significant was what has been called the Social Gospel, which was a submovement within American religious liberalism. Based on a spirit of optimism and hope that prevailed in the country until events such as the First World War and the Great Depression of the 1930s shattered such illusions, the phenomenon found its inspiration in works such as *If Christ Came to Chicago* by the British journalist and reformer William T. Stead, and especially *In His Steps*, written by a Congregationalist minister from Kansas, Charles M. Sheldon. The latter was an imaginary look at a town trying to act as Christ had in His earthly life. Noble as

---

[14] Sydney E. Ahlstrom, *A Religious History of the American People*, 2 vols. (Garden City, NY: Doubleday, 1975), 1:243, 248.

such sentiments were, the Social Gospel's existence and passion for reform could also be seen as an attempt

> to abolish the devil and hell and deny original sin ... an extravagant fete for this pious generation, but to obtain the Kingdom of God on earth, to secularize heaven, was obviously an even greater task.[15]

In the early 1880s, a minister in Cincinnati named Reverend Josiah Strong organized a group of Congregational and Methodist ministers to discuss the churches' relation to the secular world. He was joined by well-known contemporaries Lyman Abbott, Washington Gladden, and Professor Richard T. Ely. They began, in 1887, the Evangelical Alliance, which subsequentially evolved into the Brotherhood of the Kingdom. Varying degrees of commitment to social and economic change were to be found within its ranks; the best remembered were the more moderate elements favoring economic reforms, but not the overthrow of capitalism. For his part, Josiah Strong

> was the dynamo, the revivalist, the organizer, and altogether the most irrepressible spirit of the Social Gospel movement. Though of orthodox upbringing ... he came to regard the new industrial city as the central crisis for the nation and the church. In 1885 ... he expounded his views in what was almost certainly the most influential Social Gospel book of the nineteenth century, *Our Country: Its Possible Future and Its present Crisis.*[16]

Further indictments of the prevailing order were to be found in such works as Henry George's *Progress and Poverty*, advocating single

---

[15] Mowry, *Era of Theodore Roosevelt*, 27–28.
[16] Ahlstrom, *Religious History*, 265.

tax theory that many identified as socialistic, though it became a blueprint for reform thought for the next several decades.[17] Edward Bellamy's *Looking Backward*, a utopian novel read by thousands of Americans, and Henry Demarest Lloyd's *Wealth against Commonwealth*, a muckraking journalist's indictment of the Standard Oil company, were other contemporary works that strongly influenced the American mindset.

Postwar Politics

Other issues of significance faced the country in the nineteenth century's final decades. One has been called the "bloody shirt," after a Massachusetts congressman presented to his colleagues a bloodstained shirt belonging to an Ohio carpetbagger[18] who had been beaten and flogged by terrorists in Mississippi. He meant to show that those who had taken the South out of the union and had precipitated the Civil War had been Democrats and that their violent descendants were still loyal Democrats. If such people were ever to gain control, he argued, they could well undo all the work accomplished at great sacrifice during the war years:

> "Every man that endeavored to tear down the old flag", a Republican orator proclaimed in 1876, "was a Democrat. Every man that tried to destroy this nation was a Democrat.... The man that assassinated Abraham Lincoln was a Democrat.... Soldiers, every scar you have on your

---

[17] George's theory, and especially his run for mayor of New York City, attracted the strong support of a priest of the Archdiocese of New York, Father Edward McGlynn; this was wrought with complications for McGlynn personally and the Church nationally.

[18] The term "carpetbagger" refers to persons from the Northern states who went to the South after the Civil War to profit in any fashion from the Reconstruction.

heroic bodies was given you by a Democrat." Naturally every scoundrel or incompetent who sought office under the Republican banner waved the bloody shirt in order to divert the attention of Northern voters from his own shortcomings but the technique worked so well that many decent candidates could not resist the temptation to employ it in close races.[19]

The tariff was another burning issue in post–Civil War politics. Aside from extreme political liberals, most favored some form of protectionism—manufacturers, for sure, but also a majority of workers who felt sure that their wages would decrease if goods produced by cheap foreign labor were allowed to enter the country. "Whatever college professors may say about the virtues of free trade and international competition," a young congressman from Ohio named William McKinley observed, "the school of experience teaches that protection is necessary if America is to prosper."[20]

Currency reform was a third area of national concern, and it came about owing to the printing of Civil War greenbacks because the government could not meet its obligations by taxing or borrowing. People had little confidence in this currency, especially now that the war was over, and many feared that, given another set of trying economic circumstances, the government might well put more in circulation, diluting its value. A strong sentiment developed for withdrawing the greenbacks from circulation and getting back to a gold bullion standard.

Finally, civil service reform was much on citizens' minds. With the rise of industrialization, the country was becoming more complex

---

[19] John A. Garraty, *The American Nation: A History of the United States*, 2 vols. (New York: Harper & Row, 1966), 2:181.

[20] Ibid., 182.

to run; the bureaucracy exploded; the government payroll expanded; and the number of federal employees kept multiplying. Because of this, opportunities for corruption flourished:

> When reformers, most of them eminently respectable and conservative men, suggested establishing even the most modest kind of professional, nonpartisan civil service, politicians of both parties subjected them to every kind of insult and ridicule, although both the Democratic and Republican parties regularly wrote civil service reform planks into their platforms.[21]

The late-nineteenth-century presidents have often been described as somewhat nondescript; while they were solid citizens and stalwart in their patriotism, few are remembered in the way chief executives such as Abraham Lincoln or Theodore Roosevelt have been. Rutherford Hayes, often termed "His Accidency" or "His Fraudelency" because of the controversial and convoluted election of 1876 that brought him to the White House, was followed by James A. Garfield of Ohio, only the second president in the nation's history to be assassinated. His vice president, Chester A. Arthur of New York, completed the term and headed an administration remembered for the enactment of a significant civil service reform bill. Arthur, in turn, was followed by a conservative gold-standard Democrat from New Jersey, Grover Cleveland, who is the only president to have served two nonconsecutive terms, between which came the presidency of Indiana's Benjamin Harrison, son of an earlier president, William Henry Harrison. Finally, Ohio's William McKinley brought the century to a close and, just briefly into his second term, became the third victim of assassination. All might be termed safe, conservative leaders who presided

---

[21] Ibid., 184.

over a generally prosperous American economy and maintained the ship of state safely.

Gibbons of Baltimore

It was in this political, social, and economic scene that the Church of the late nineteenth century operated, even as it was, in a sense, separate from it. The hard balance of engagement fell largely to the ninth archbishop of Baltimore, the nation's premier see, James Cardinal Gibbons. His forty-four-year episcopacy, from 1877 until 1921, defined American Catholicism, and it was to Gibbons, as *primus inter pares* (first among equals), that the hierarchy and laity looked for leadership.

He was born in Baltimore in 1834, the fourth of six children of Thomas and Bridget Walsh Gibbons, immigrants from County Mayo, Ireland. After falling ill with tuberculosis when James was only five, the elder Gibbons moved the family back to Ireland in the hope his health would improve. Thomas died in 1847, and to this day in the parish graveyard in Ballinrobe, County Mayo, there is an old, rusted iron fence with an inscription reading "affectionately given by Very Rev. James Gibbons, Vicar Apostolic of North Carolina." Six years after his father's death, the future cardinal's mother moved the family back to the United States, settling in New Orleans. The fourteen years young Gibbons lived in Ireland would endear him to the land of his ancestors for the rest of his life.

Gibbons's call to the priesthood came early, after he listened to a sermon preached by the famed convert priest Clarence Walworth. He entered St. Charles College in Ellicott City, Maryland, studying for the archdiocese of his birth, and took his theology at St. Mary's Seminary, Baltimore, where he attained a brilliant academic record. He was ordained to the priesthood on June 30, 1861, in the Baltimore cathedral by Archbishop Francis Patrick Kenrick. As a young priest, he was given the typical parochial assignments and served as one of the chaplains at Fort McHenry during the Civil War. Soon named secretary to Archbishop Martin J. Spalding, he did much of the preparatory work for the Second Plenary Council of Baltimore in 1866, and, when the council fathers recommended the creation of an apostolic vicariate in North Carolina, Gibbons, after only seven years of priestly life, was chosen to lead it. He was consecrated at age thirty-four, becoming the youngest bishop in the United States.

The vicariate had fewer than seven hundred Catholics when Gibbons arrived, and he set out, on horseback, to cover his new territory: the entire state of North Carolina. Though he did build churches, befriend Protestants, and win converts, his best remembered accomplishment was his apologetical work, *Faith of Our Fathers*, written in down-to-earth language for all to understand and appreciate. Not only did the book explain the Catholic Faith to those who did not understand it, but it went far to break down the prejudices of those who were quick to oppose it.

> The volume was something more than apologetics, however. In a manner reminiscent of Isaac Hecker, the young Bishop aspired to attract Protestants to the Catholic Church. Noting that Scripture speaks of Christ's Church" by the beautiful title of bride or spouse of Christ", Gibbons underlined his point: "and the Christian law admits of only one wife". He went on: "With all due respect for my dissenting brethren, truth compels me to say that this unity of doctrine and government is not to be found in the Protestant sects, taken collectively or separately.... Where then shall we find this essential unity of faith and government? I answer, confidently, no where save in the Catholic Church."[22]

---

[22]   Cited in Russell Shaw, *Catholics In America* (San Francisco: Ignatius Press, 2016), 64. Isaac Hecker was a famed nineteenth-century

Toil and Transcendence

At the age of thirty-five years, four months, Gibbons was the youngest bishop in attendance at the First Vatican Council. He went on to become bishop of Richmond, Virginia, and finally was appointed coadjutor to James Roosevelt Bayley in Baltimore, who died only months later, leaving the see to Gibbons. Nine years later, he would become the nation's second cardinal and, in 1903, the first American to participate in a papal conclave. Just a few days before his death in March 1921, the British author, convert, and apologist G. K. Chesterton was visiting the city of Baltimore. As Chesterton related the story in *What I Saw in America*, the ailing prelate had designated two priests to call on Chesterton at his hotel to extend sincere greetings and to have a cordial visit in the cardinal's absence. When Chesterton heard of Gibbons's death shortly thereafter, he used the example of such kindness as an illustration of the cardinal's greatness. Far removed from this British defender of the Faith, however, was H. L. Mencken, the "sage of Baltimore," who rarely had much positive to write or report about the Catholic Church, or religion in general. And so Mencken's observation on Gibbons's death is noteworthy:

> More presidents than one sought the counsel of Cardinal Gibbons ... a man of the highest sagacity, a politician in

convert who came from transcendentalism, through several religious experiences, to the Catholic Faith. He was ordained a Redemptorist priest and did considerable work among German Catholics in several cities. He was convinced, after much thought, travel, and prayer, that the United States, as a nation, could be converted, en masse, to Catholicism. The lack of ardor among some of his Redemptorist superiors led him to request a release from his vows so that he could form his own religious community, the Society of Saint Paul, or Paulists, as they came to be known. For generations, the Paulists did remarkable work throughout the United States in winning hundreds, if not thousands, to the Catholic Faith.

the best sense". There was "no record," the Sage added, of the late prelate's having "ever led the Church into a bog or up a blind alley."[23]

Knights of Labor

These sentiments about the cardinal were the result of a life of true service to his Church and his nation. One of the first episodes that brought him to national attention was the emergence of the Knights of Labor and its overwhelming Catholic membership. The Noble and Holy Order of the Knights of Labor, as it was officially called, was founded in Philadelphia in 1869 by Uriah S. Stephens, and it included all branches of honorable toil. In the first decade of its existence, membership hit twenty-eight thousand; by 1880, it had reached one hundred thousand. Only a few years later, 20 percent of the nation's labor force, or eight hundred thousand workingmen, were affiliated. The Knights filled a vacuum created by the demise of a former national labor organization and fulfilled the desire of most working men for such an institution.

Stephens was replaced as Grand Master Workman in 1879 by Terence V. Powderly, a Catholic who would figure prominently in relations with his Church and Her leaders. The Knights could be described as a diverse organization whose belief was that the more types of labor were represented, the greater would be the diversity of opinion. The only groups excluded from membership were bankers, land speculators, lawyers, liquor dealers, and gamblers. Its members included low-skilled workers, railroad workers, steel workers, and immigrants. Politically, the Knights were generally associated with independents and third-party movements, though they were also favorable to pro-labor planks in the Democratic or

[23] Cited in ibid., 62.

Republican platforms. On the national level, the union opposed strikes, referring to them as barbaric; on the local level, however, greater freedom of opinion prevailed, and it was not uncommon to see local chapters of the Knights actively supporting all sorts of work stoppages.

The primary demands of the Knights were for the eight-hour workday, an end to child and convict labor, and a graduated income tax. They accepted women and Blacks into membership and, with their close ties to the Irish Land League, tried to bring together Catholic and Protestant Irish-born workers.[24] The greatest stumbling block, at least for the Catholic Church — to which the great majority of the Knights belonged — was the secrecy of its organization, a factor strongly reminiscent of European Freemasonry.

In 1738, Pope Clement XII had condemned Freemasonry, and from then on, Catholic membership in societies hostile to the Church was strictly forbidden. It became a serious concern in the United States, when, in the late nineteenth century, Americans "turned with furious zeal to the creation of secret societies cut to their own pattern."[25] The American bishops who gathered for the Third Plenary Council of Baltimore recognized this problem and addressed it. They began with the thought that men will naturally band together to carry out laudable purposes, or evil ones, depending on the circumstances and the men. Weakened human nature can easily be taken up with one side of a question and develop it with passionate intensity while leaving the other side of the question barely considered. Therefore, the Council Fathers underscored

---

[24] The Irish Land League was a political organization in the late nineteenth century that sought to help poor tenant farmers. Its primary aim was to abolish landlordism in Ireland and enable tenant farmers to own the land they worked on.

[25] Arthur M. Schlesinger, *The Rise of the City, 1878–1898* (New York: Macmillan, 1933), 288.

the fact that every Catholic must rely on the teaching authority of the Church as the surest solution to any difficulty — because Christ, in His Spirit, dwells fully in the Church that He Himself began and will guide until the end of time.

With this in mind, the bishops reminded the Catholic faithful that Pope Leo XIII had recently shown that the Masonic guilds, especially in Europe, while originally organized to sanctify "trades and tradesmen with the blessings of religion," had deviated far from their original purposes to "array themselves in avowed hostility against Christianity, and against the Catholic Church as its embodiment." They have substituted, the pope averred, a "world-wide fraternity of their own for the universal brotherhood of Jesus Christ." This substitution implied an attempt to replace supernaturally revealed religion with pure naturalism.

> There is one characteristic which is always a strong presumption against a society, and that is secrecy. Our Divine Lord Himself has laid down the rule: "Every one that doth evil, hateth the light and cometh not to the light, that his works may not be reproved. But he that doth truth cometh to the light that his works may be made manifest, because they are done in God." When, therefore associations veil themselves in secrecy and darkness, the presumption is against them, and it rests with them to prove that there is nothing evil in them. But if any society's obligation be such as to bind its members to secrecy, even when rightly questioned by competent authority, then such a society puts itself outside the limits of approval, and no one can be a member of it and at the same time be admitted to the sacraments of the Catholic Church.[26]

[26]   *The Pastoral Letter of the Third Plenary Council of Baltimore on Forbidden Societies*, December 7, 1884, cited in John Tracy Ellis, *Documents of American Catholic History* (Milwaukee: Bruce, 1956), 435–436.

Toil and Transcendence

There were many reasons for such concern. There was a serious depression in the country in 1873, and as it deepened, increasing unemployment gave rise to riots and violence, as typified by the great railroad strikes of the 1870s. Meanwhile the rate of immigration into the United States showed no signs of decreasing, and the fact that most newcomers secured employment in mines, factories, railroads, and so on contributed to the American hierarchy's concern about labor and labor groups. The railroad strikes also gave way to even greater disturbances, especially the Haymarket Square Riot in Chicago in 1886.[27] In addition, the Molly Maguires, a secret organization, were causing serious disturbance in the coal fields of Pennsylvania.[28]

None of this was foreign to the cardinal of Baltimore. He had grown up in a family of modest means; his father knew what it meant to work to support his wife and six children, and after his death, it had become necessary for his son to go to work to help support his mother and his siblings. Many years later, while serving

[27] The Haymarket Square Riot was the aftermath of a bombing that took place at a labor demonstration on May 4, 1886. It began as a peaceful rally in support of workers striking for an eight-hour workday on the day after police killed one worker and injured several others. Then an unknown person threw a dynamite bomb at the police as they tried to disperse the meeting, and the bomb blast and ensuing gunfire resulted in the deaths of seven police officers and at least four civilians; dozens of others were wounded.

[28] The Molly Maguires were a nineteenth-century secret society active in Ireland, Liverpool, and parts of the Eastern United States. They were best known for their activism among Irish-American and Irish immigrant coal miners in Pennsylvania. After a series of often violent conflicts, twenty suspected members of the Molly Maguires were convicted of murder and other crimes and were executed by hanging in 1877 and 1878. Their history remains part of local Pennsylvania lore.

as vicar apostolic of North Carolina, he preached a sermon titled "Man Born to Work: or, Necessity and Dignity of Labor." In it, one senses his true feelings. Gibbons's biographer writes:

> "I would rather grasp the soiled hand of the honest artisan, than touch the soft, kid-gloved hand of the dandy." [Gibbons] stated that he had three admonitions to give to the men who composed his congregation. He would have them avoid idleness and be as much ashamed to be called an idler as they would a thief; second, the preacher urged his listeners to take an active and personal interest in the business of their employers; and third, he counseled the laborers to be content in the state and city where Providence had placed them and not to be beguiled into moving from place to place since, as he said, "a strolling family gather very few coins or greenbacks in their perambulating wheel of fortune."[29]

Gibbons's biographer went on to say that "it was in the guise of a problem directly related to the secret societies that James Gibbons earned one of his most striking claims to fame and to an enduring place in the esteem of his fellow Americans of all religious beliefs."[30] The labor leader with whom the cardinal would have the most contact was his coreligionist, at least for the greater part of his life.

Terence V. Powderly was born in Carbondale, Pennsylvania, to Irish immigrant parents from Drogheda, County Louth. He was educated in local schools, began work on the railroad at thirteen, and by seventeen was a machinist with a local master mechanic.

---

[29] John Tracy Ellis, *The Life of James Cardinal Gibbons, Archbishop of Baltimore, 1834–1921*, 2 vols. (Milwaukee: Bruce, 1952), 1:489.

[30] Ibid., 486.

Toil and Transcendence

In 1871, he joined the Machinists and Blacksmiths International Union and encountered the Church's fear of such groups when he attempted to attend Sunday Mass at Saint Peter's Cathedral in Scranton:

> The usher in charge at the entrance laid his hand on my shoulder, turned me around, and shoved me to the steps leading to the street. I knew the man quite well ... and it occurred to me at first that he was joking. I attempted to walk around him when he again intercepted me, and said that if I did not go away peaceably he would use force to compel me to do so. Realizing that he was in earnest and not wishing to create a scene, I walked toward the door, he following close behind me. At the door I asked for an explanation, and received this answer: "I have my orders and you cannot come in here today or any other day until you quit the masons".[31]

Powderly did acknowledge that the pin he wore as a member of the Machinists and Blacksmiths Union could bear some resemblance to that of the masons. When the charge was made, however, Powderly had no knowledge whatever of the Masonic order, and the first thought that came into his mind was that the gentleman must have been referring to some organization of stone masons. Sometime later, he went to confession to a priest at Saint Peter's Cathedral who recognized him — and who had been tipped off, incorrectly, that Powderly was a Mason. The priest became very angry, threatened to "horsewhip" Powderly if he did not leave them, and, according to Powderly, spoke so

---

[31] Terence V. Powderly, *The Path I Trod: The Autobiography of Terence V. Powderly* (New York: Columbia University Press, 1940), 318.

loudly that "every person in the church could hear him." Powderly, obviously no shrinking violet, recounts the remainder of the episode:

> Had it been a shopmate who used violent language toward me I might not have acted as I did, but here was a man from whom I expected better things. Remember, that as a Catholic about to make preparation to receive the sacrament, I tried to believe that priest represented God, and that my confession would be made to God rather than the priest. When he ended his tirade, I arose, stepped out of the confessional, and, instead of leaving the church, as, perhaps, I should have done, said in a tone loud enough for listeners to hear—yes, I wanted them to hear it: "I didn't come here to make my confession to all these people and you have no right to talk that way to me. I can't give you what you deserve here, but if you come outside of this church, I'll give you the damnedest thrashing you ever got." ... He said no more, and I left the church.[32]

By 1878 Powderly had been elected mayor of Scranton on the Greenback Labor ticket. He would go on to serve three two-year terms as the city's chief executive and was to have, again by his own accounts, some rather unpleasant encounters with Bishop William O'Hara, the first bishop of Scranton. On one occasion, returning from a political gathering in Philadelphia on a Sunday evening, he received notice that the bishop wished to see him at the episcopal residence. Powderly claimed O'Hara had "called me out" from the altar that morning and had "in effect, excommunicated

---

[32] Ibid., 319. The priest was Father Richard Hennessy, who, if the account given is accurate, told the future labor leader, "You are damn'd; your soul will roast in hell unless you quit that society."

me by warning the people of the congregation to have nothing to do with me in [the] future."[33] According to the mayor's account, the bishop admonished the cathedral congregation:

> I warn you against these pernicious secret societies; they are devised by designing men to dupe the unwary and draw them into their toils for the purpose of using them as tools for their own personal advancement. We have one instance of it in this city in a man who has hoodwinked the workingman into electing him Mayor. He is a busybody and a slanderer. He has circulated the rumor that I have approved of one of these secret societies; I have not even considered it. He is a fraud, an imposter, and I warn you against his scheming. Beware of being misled by such a character. Have nothing to do with him.[34]

Powderly also described a meeting with Bishop O'Hara in which the prelate is supposed to have referred to him as a "bad man, a scoundrel" who had lied about the bishop, and for which he was to beg O'Hara's pardon by getting down on his knees. When Powderly refused, the bishop "poured on me a torrent of invective and abuse such as I never listened to before." A second time the bishop insisted he get down on his knees and beg pardon, and a second time the Mayor refused. When the bishop finally ordered him to leave his house, Powderly responded obstinately:

> "No, I shall not leave your house, I cannot; it is not your house. My father and mother came to this valley in 1829,

---

[33] Ibid., 320. The editors of Powderly's memoir are careful to note that contrary to what the author says, "he was not excommunicated, either technically or 'in effect.'"

[34] Ibid. This statement, according to Powderly, was carried by the Associated Press.

and ever since then, they and their children have been paying into the church. In the Cathedral across the lot there is money of mine, part of my earnings are in that convent across the street and money of mine is invested in this house. There's not one cent of yours in it; it is not your house; you, sir, are but a tenant here. You weren't known here when this building was erected; you are here as a servant of God. Even though you had a million dollars in it, I'll not stir a foot from it until you retract the abuse you have heaped on my head tonight.... You are the most vindictive, unreasoning man I ever met. I'll not leave your house." He turned from me and left the room.[35]

The next morning, the bishop's priest secretary called on the mayor and informed him that the bishop wished to see him immediately. To that, the mayor handed the priest his business card and told him that at whatever hour the bishop felt convenient, he would meet him; he had no intention of returning to the cathedral rectory and encountering the same abuse. The priest, a Father Dunn, informed the mayor that if he did not come, the bishop would publicly castigate him from the altar again the following Sunday. "Tell Bishop O'Hara if he denounces me next Sunday from the altar, he will answer for it next Monday in the courts."[36]

Powderly obsessed in his memoir over how a man of God could have handed out such treatment. But Powderly's own attitude is just as much in need of examining. In the nineteenth century, it would have been unthinkable to speak to a bishop of the Church in such tones, regardless of what station one occupied in life. If there was any unreasonableness on the part of the bishop, it surely was equaled by the mayor's. Furthermore, in view of Powderly's

[35] Ibid., 320–322.
[36] Ibid., 323.

exaggerated statement of his excommunication, one wonders to what extent details might have been amplified in his autobiography. One wonders, too, if Cardinal Gibbons was made fully aware of the events that transpired in Scranton.

To his credit, Powderly felt it was in the best interests of the Knights of Labor to eliminate at least some elements of its secrecy. He succeeded at a general assembly of the Knights in Detroit in 1881 in having the organization's name made public, in dropping certain ritualistic elements from its initiation ceremony, and in having its secret oath replaced by what they called a "word of honor."

One year prior to the Third Plenary Council, the American archbishops were summoned to Rome. In the course of that gathering, Cardinal Gibbons, along with the archbishop of Chicago, Patrick A. Feehan, spoke with officials of the Propaganda[37] and told them that most workingmen's groups proposed no reason for condemnation or ecclesiastical prohibition. It was especially significant to get such a view across to curial officials because of events that had recently transpired in the Church in Canada. The Knights of Labor had grown significantly there, and, alarmed by the group's secrecy and strength in numbers, the archbishop of Quebec, Elzéar-Alexandre Taschereau,[38] had succeeded in securing from the Holy Office[39] a directive describing the Knights of Labor as a society that "ought to be considered among those prohibited by the Holy See."[40]

---

[37] Today called the Congregation for the Evangelization of Peoples, this is the congregation of the Roman Curia responsible for missionary work and related activities. The United States was considered mission territory until 1911.

[38] Elzéar-Alexandre Taschereau (1820–1898) served as archbishop of Quebec from 1871 until his death in 1898. He was the first Canadian cardinal, elevated by Pope Leo XIII in 1886.

[39] The Holy Office was the term for what is now the Congregation for the Doctrine of the Faith.

[40] Ellis, Life of Gibbons, 1:492.

There would undoubtedly be those in the American hierarchy who would have favored such a declaration,[41] but Cardinal Gibbons, for one, wanted to make certain it did not occur in the United States.

Gibbons had met with Powderly at great length prior to an important meeting of the American archbishops held in Gibbons's residence in Baltimore in October 1886. The cardinal told his episcopal confreres of the further concessions Powderly had promised to make to the order's constitution, and, while certain prelates were strongly in favor of condemning the Knights, Gibbons's view prevailed. A rough draft of the meeting's minutes reflects his position:

> Labor has rights as well as capital. We should not condemn labor and let capital go free—we should regard condemnation of K. of L. as disastrous for the Church—We should send documents to Rome and if objectionable features are eliminated K. of L should be tolerated, should not be condemned—We have controlling influence over them; if they are condemned, a secret organization will follow in their wake and over that we will have no control.[42]

Early in 1887, Gibbons received word from Rome that he was to be elevated to cardinal, the second American to be so named up to that time.[43] He conferred with some episcopal colleagues before sailing and, once arrived in the Eternal City, called on a number of key officials in the Holy Office and Propaganda to persuade them that official condemnation of the Knights of Labor would be

---

[41] One of the best examples would be James Augustine Healy, bishop of Portland, Maine, a staunch foe of the Knights, bordering so close to his New England diocese.

[42] Minutes of the meeting of the archbishops on the secret societies, Baltimore, October 28, 1886. Cited in Ellis, *Life of Gibbons*, 1:503.

[43] The first American cardinal, as noted, was John McCloskey of New York.

very detrimental to the Church in the United States. The official statement was dated February 20, 1887, and has been described by the major historian of this question as "the most important single factor in the settlement of the case."[44]

In presenting his case, the cardinal began by emphasizing his adherence to the various encyclicals of Pope Leo XIII on the evils growing in modern society, as well as their remedies. He said that in the constitution of the Knights of Labor, along with their many laws and declarations, there could be found statements of which the Church would not approve; at the same time, none could be found that were worthy of condemnation. Their laws of secrecy in no way hindered Catholic members from disclosing to the proper ecclesiastical authorities any business that would be necessary for such authorities to know, even outside the sacrament of penance. Members made no promise of blind obedience, Gibbons noted, and the organization did not profess hostility to the Church or to organized religion. Finally, as regards Powderly, their Grand Master Workman,

> in sending me a copy of their constitutions, says he is a catholic from the bottom of his heart; that he practices his religion faithfully and receives the sacraments regularly; that he belongs to no Masonic or other society condemned by the Church; that he knows of nothing in the association of the Knights of Labor contrary to the laws of the Church.[45]

[44] Henry J. Browne, *The Catholic Church and the Knights of Labor* (Washington, D.C.: Catholic University of America Press, 1949), 239.
[45] "Cardinal Gibbons Defends the Knights of Labor (1887)," in Mark Massa, S.J., ed., *American Catholic History: A Documentary Reader* (New York: New York University Press, 2008), 133.

The cardinal then acknowledged the prevailing social evils and public injustices and that "monopolies on the part of both individuals and corporations have already called forth not only the complaints of our working classes, but also the opposition of our public men and legislators."[46] Gibbons argued that an organization of all interested persons is the most efficient means to attain any public end. This kind of thinking, totally compatible with the genius of America, needed to be stressed. Further, he said, Catholic workingmen across America simply did not see the Knights of Labor as related to Freemasonry and would not affiliate with a lodge out of obedience to the Holy See.

The prelate's final considerations dealt with answering typical objections to the Knights. For example, it was said that Catholics joining the labor group would mix with Protestants, to the peril of their faith. The cardinal replied that in American society, the strict separation of religions in social affairs was not possible; on the contrary, Catholics in the United States, unlike many of their European counterparts, did not look on the Church as a "hostile stepmother," but rather, were "intelligent, well instructed, devoted children."[47] Nor did Gibbons accept the argument that confraternities under the direction of priests throughout the country might better unite Catholic workingmen. "We find in our country that the presence of clergy would not be advisable where our citizens, without distinction of religious belief, come together in regard to their industrial interests alone."[48] Also refuted was the argument that such labor organizations might expose Catholics to the evil influences of atheists, communists, and anarchists. There people could be met almost daily in America, Gibbons argued,

---

[46] Ibid., 134.
[47] Ibid., 135.
[48] Ibid.

and Catholics were able to meet such thinking with "good sense and firmness."[49]

Finally, the European (and especially Roman) mind associated labor associations with strikes and violence. To this point, Gibbons gave three responses: strikes were not the invention of the Knights of Labor, but almost always the natural result of employee grievances against injustices: In struggles of the "poor and indignant multitudes" against "hard and obstinate monopoly," anger and violence are often "as inevitable as they are regrettable." The laws and authorities of the Knights of Labor, far from encouraging such outbursts, "exercise a powerful influence to hinder it, and to keep strikes within the limits of good order and legitimate action."[50]

The cardinal's most respected biographer felt that

in every respect the Gibbons memorial on the Knights of Labor was a remarkable document. Not only did it display a deep sympathy with the just claims of the workingman to organize and for Catholics to join such organizations, but it showed as well that the Cardinal understood thoroughly the temper of the age in which he lived. His shrewd observations about the strength of the masses ... his keen insight into the psychology of the American people in their dislike for orders given by simple fiat ... and the manner in which he drew out the implications of all these factors for the future welfare of the Catholic Church in the American Republic, stamped Gibbons as a man who possessed a knowledge and understanding of his country and its conditions that was truly admirable.[51]

[49] Ibid., 135–136.
[50] Ibid., 136.
[51] Ellis, *Life of Gibbons*, 1:510.

As for Terence Powderly, his altercations with Bishop O'Hara of Scranton, Father Daniel O'Connor of St. Joseph's parish in Girardville, Pennsylvania, and Bishop James A. Healy of Portland, Maine, show a side of a man who, though avowedly Catholic, had a temperament toward the hierarchy not typical of a layman of his era. His reminiscence of Cardinal Gibbons's contribution to the Knights of Labor was only the comment that he deserved credit for his work, and a brief summation from the ending paragraphs of his memorial in their behalf. He eventually left Scranton to become commissioner general of immigration, by appointment of President William McKinley.

Some felt he received the appointment because he was, in fact, a Mason. On one occasion, some members of the Knights of Columbus called on him in his Washington office, described the purposes of the Knights, and left him an application for membership. He recalls in his memoirs that whenever he went to a town in advance of brewing labor troubles, he invariably sought out a man with a Masonic emblem on his lapel, thinking that sort of man would give him an honest assessment of the situation. From this he came to believe that the Masonic order must be based on sound principles, and he never filled out the membership application for the Knights of Columbus.

> I have since then taken all the degrees in the York and Scottish rites of freemasonry except the 33rd, and at every step have expectantly looked forward to the next to ascertain why the church is opposed to freemasonry. I have not yet found a good and sufficient reason for that opposition.[52]

Powderly went on to confess that he had been raised believing the Catholic Church to be of divine origin but that the events of

---

[52] Powderly, *The Path I Trod*, 371.

his life had caused him to question that teaching. He said he had known some marvelous Catholic priests, but just as many wonderful Protestants and Jews. Some of the most vindictive, vengeful, arrogant, and intolerable men he had ever met had been Catholic priests, but they were this way because they were men, not because they were clerics. He said his idea of a priest was not that of a person "following an iron rule in governing from above, but of one who governs himself wisely in temper, speech and conduct, and who unfolds the teachings of religion in wisdom, charity and kindness."[53]

At the end of his life, Powderly had to admit that

> while the treatment I was subjected to—and I have not told a tenth of it—shook my belief in the Catholic Church, my faith in the goodness of God was never disturbed. On the contrary, the more I reflected on the conduct of churchmen, the more convinced did I become that such as these could not fairly, honestly, truthfully, or lovingly represent God. A man who could not deal patiently with a fellow man, could not or would not give one kind word to that fellow man, could not, cannot represent Him who gave His life for that man.... My belief in the existence and goodness of God gave flat denial to the claim of a mortal to stand in His place or act for Him on earth.[54]

---

[53] Ibid., 372.

[54] Ibid., 372–373. Though Powderly in his memoirs does not clearly state that he formally left the Catholic Church, his comments point in that direction. Contemporary press accounts of his funeral in 1924 indicate only the performance of a Masonic service at his grave in Washington's Rock Creek Cemetery. In addition, on his gravestone, the dates of his birth and death are followed by a large Masonic inscription.

Negative as Powderly's story may have been, the outcome of the entire episode of the Knights of Labor showed the Church's favorable disposition toward the rights of labor and proved Cardinal Gibbons a friend of the workingman. Indeed, Gibbons's work was influential in drafting the celebrated 1891 papal encyclical *Rerum Novarum*. Written by Pope Leo XIII, this letter to the universal Church discussed the relationship and mutual duties between labor and capital, as well as government and its citizens. The pope was primarily concerned with the need for some correction of the misery and injustice burdening the working class. It supported the right of labor to form unions, rejected socialism as well as unrestricted capitalism, and affirmed the right to private property. The encyclical has been considered a foundational text of modern Catholic social teaching, and Baltimore's cardinal, it is believed, exerted much influence over it.

A Catholic Bloc

Further proof that Catholics were coming into their own in the late nineteenth century could be found in the presidential election campaign of 1884. The race pitted New York's Democratic governor Grover Cleveland against the U.S. Senator from Maine, Republican James G. Blaine. Despite some allegations of corrupt activities while he was Speaker of the House,[55] Catholics that year

---

[55] In 1869, Blaine was speaker of the House of Representatives when a bill involving a land grant came up. There was a deadlocked vote over the bill, which would have granted land to the Little Rock and Fort Smith Railroad. Blaine broke the tie and later wrote to the railroad reminding them how they had secured their land. In gratitude, the railroad made him a bond salesman with a commission. At the end of his correspondence, Blaine admonished railroad officials to burn the letter. A clerk named Mulligan in the House of Representatives found the letter, though, and demanded

tended to favor Blaine because his mother and two sisters were Catholics. Grover Cleveland, on the other hand, had had an affair with a young woman in Buffalo years earlier who now claimed he was the father of her child. While Cleveland admitted to the affair, he was publicly noncommittal about whether the child was his. In any event, he agreed to pay for the child's education to a certain age.

Given such a serious indiscretion, it appeared certain that Blaine would get a large percentage of the Catholic vote. Shortly before election day, though, Blaine was in New York campaigning and staying at the Fifth Avenue Hotel. At the end of a grueling day, he was headed upstairs to go to bed when he was approached by the Revered Dr. Samuel D. Burchard, pastor of the Presbyterian Church at Thirty-Sixth Street and Madison Avenue, asking him to sign what Blaine believed to be simply a patriotic statement stressing traditional American values. Blaine hastily scanned and signed the document, not realizing it also contained an accusation against the Democrats as the party of "rum, Romanism and rebellion." Catholics, faced with a choice between personal immorality or a direct attack on their religion, chose the former, voted the Democrat ticket en masse, and, as heavy a bloc as they were in New York state, carried it for Cleveland, giving him the election. Surely, by 1884, the Catholic vote could not be taken for granted.[56]

$30,000 of Blaine, or he would give the letter to the Democrats. The Republicans, for their part, hired detectives to find anything they could about Grover Cleveland, unearthing a story that he may well have fathered an illegitimate child years earlier in Buffalo, a town where he also had served as mayor.

[56] Catholic opinion, though not condoning Cleveland's private life, was softened a bit by his willingness to pay for the child's education. Such munificence made it considerably easier for many to return to their traditional political allegiance.

Prelude: The Late Nineteenth Century

A Catholic University for America

As the century progressed, a number of additional Catholic bishops emerged on the scene to join Cardinal Gibbons in a genuine embrace of American culture. Prominent among them was John Lancaster Spalding, the first bishop of Peoria, Illinois. Born in Lebanon, Kentucky, in 1840, he was the descendant of a Southern Maryland Catholic family who had joined the large Catholic migration to Kentucky decades earlier. Educated at Mount Saint Mary's Seminary in Emmitsburg, Maryland, and at the Catholic University of Louvain in Belgium, he rose quickly as a leading intellectual in the American hierarchy. As early as 1884, he preached a sermon at the Third Plenary Council of Baltimore in which he lamented the lack of national influence and intellectual leadership in the Catholic Church in the United States.

> As the devotion of American Catholics to this country and its free institutions, as shown not on battlefields alone, but in our whole bearing and conduct, convinces all but the unreasonable of the depth and sincerity of our patriotism, so when our zeal for intellectual excellence shall have raised up men who will take place among the first writers and thinkers of their day their very presence will become the most persuasive of arguments to teach the world that no best gift is at war with the spirit of Catholic faith, and that, while the humblest mind may feel its force, the lofty genius of Augustine, of Dante, and of Bossuet is upborne and strengthened by the splendor of its truth. But if we are to be intellectually the equals of others, we must have with them equal advantages of education; and so long as we look rather to the multiplying of schools and seminaries than to the creation of a real university, our progress will be slow and uncertain,

because a university is the great ordinary means to the best cultivation of mind.[57]

In the mind of many historians, Spalding paved the way for the establishment of the Catholic University of America with this sermon. Within four days of the council's opening, a young millionaire heiress from New York City informed Cardinal Gibbons of her intention to give $300,000 for the establishment of a national Catholic university.[58]

The offer came just a few days before Spalding's sermon and immediately heightened debate among the council fathers about the advisability of a national Catholic university. The matter was referred to a committee of bishops, who advised that Miss Mary Gwendoline Caldwell's gift be accepted, plans begun, and a formal request for acceptance sent to Rome.[59] The Holy See approved the initial request, and the bishops of the United States committed themselves to establish a national university.

[57] "Bishop Spalding on the Intellectual Weakness Among American Catholics, November 16, 1884," in Ellis, *Documents*, 431–432.

[58] Mary Gwendoline Caldwell was born in Louisville, Kentucky, in 1863 and died in New York City in 1909. She and her younger sister, Mary Elizabeth, were the daughters of William Shakespeare and Mary Eliza Breckenridge Caldwell. They moved to New York City with their father following their mother's death. While there, they made the acquaintance of John Lancaster Spalding, then serving in the Archdiocese of New York on leave from the Diocese of Louisville. Mary Gwendoline later married the Marquis Monstiers-Merinville in Paris, with then-Bishop Spalding officiating. Some years later, she received Notre Dame's famed Laetare Medal, though prior to her death, she renounced Catholicism She and her sister, who also married European royalty, are buried in Cave Hill Cemetery, Louisville.

[59] The committee consisted of Archbishops Corrigan of New York, Kenrick of Saint Louis, Alemany of San Francisco, Ryan of Philadelphia, and Spalding.

Prelude: The Late Nineteenth Century

In January 1885, a meeting of the bishops' committee recommended purchasing Seton Hall College in South Orange, New Jersey, and transforming it into the desired national entity. Miss Caldwell, when informed, did not approve of New Jersey, but favored the nation's captial. It would take much time and animated debate among the bishops before a site was chosen. By the spring of 1885, some were becoming restive, especially Archbishop John Ireland of Saint Paul, Minnesota, another of the powerful "Americanizers" as they came to be called.[60] Writing to Gibbons, he pressed the Baltimore prelate to act:

> You will please bear with me if I ask what is being done with our university project? I am afraid that with our delay the interest felt in it through the country will be lost. Already two of those whom we expected to be chief benefactors have died; others may pass away. I may not understand things in my remote quarter of the country; but it does seem to me it were better if we were showing some signs of life.[61]

---

[60] John Ireland was the third bishop and first archbishop of Saint Paul, Minnesota. He was born in County Kilkenny, Ireland, in 1838, and his family immigrated to the United States, settling in Saint Paul in 1848. He was educated in France, ordained in 1861, served in the Fifth Minnesota Regiment in the Civil War, and later was named pastor of St. Paul's Cathedral. He became coadjutor archbishop of Saint Paul in 1875 and its ordinary in 1884. He served as bishop and later archbishop until his death in 1918. A friend of Presidents William McKinley and Theodore Roosevelt, he was a staunch Republican at a time when few of his coreligionists were. He firmly believed in the colonization of the Irish in rural America and established several Irish colonies in Minnesota for immigrants arriving in Eastern port cities. He was also a strong proponent of the establishment of the Catholic University of America.

[61] Cited in Marvin R. O'Connell, *John Ireland and the American Catholic Church* (Saint Paul: Minnesota Historical Society Press, 1988), 210.

Toil and Transcendence

Gibbons himself favored Philadelphia as the university's location; he disliked his own city because the Sulpicians already had
educational institutions there. The Jesuits at Georgetown feared
another institution of similar academic standing so close, while
opinion in New York, the leading city in wealth and population,
favored nearby Seton Hall. Some felt the city of Washington too
distracting for students; others felt it too southern. It appears to
have been the strong push of Archbishop Ireland and Bishop Spalding, along with the strong preference of Miss Caldwell, the chief
benefactoress, that carried the day for Washington.

Interestingly, one who strongly favored the idea of a national
Catholic University was Cardinal John Henry Newman in England.

> Newman stated that at a time when the Catholics of the
> old world had so much to depress and trouble them the
> circular on the prospective university for the new world
> had rejoiced the hearts ... "of all well educated Catholics
> in these Islands."[62]

Pope Leo XIII was known to favor the project, and when Cardinal
Gibbons received a letter from him in the late fall of 1885, he proudly
read it to his fellow bishops assembled for a committee meeting. Yet
another item of importance was the choice of a rector for the new
school; the committee had favored Spalding, but when he declined,
they chose John J. Keane, bishop of Richmond. Keane was initially
reluctant, perhaps because Gibbons had said that the rector should
pattern his work on that of the legendary Daniel Coit Gilman, president of Johns Hopkins University in Baltimore, and all that he was
doing to build up his school. In the end, Keane accepted.[63]

[62] Ellis, *Life of Gibbons*, 1:396.
[63] John J. Keane was born in Ballyshannon, County Donegal, Ireland
in 1839. His family immigrated to the United States when he was
seven. He was ordained for the Archdiocese of Baltimore in 1866,

By the spring of 1887, Gibbons had received a papal brief from Leo XIII giving hearty approval to the establishment of the Catholic university. The cornerstone of Caldwell Hall, the university's first building, was laid on May 24, 1888. On the invitation of Gibbons, President Grover Cleveland, along with several members of his cabinet, attended and mingled with some thirty-one bishops. Bishop Spalding spoke on the occasion, admitting candidly that in the United States bigotry was far from dead, for "where there is a question of religion, of society, of politics, even the fairest minds fail to see things as they are, and the multitude ... will never become impartial." The tendency of the age, however, was opposed to such prejudice, and, "as we lose faith in the efficacy of persecution, we perceive more clearly that true religion can neither be defended nor propagated by violence and intolerance."[64] Nonetheless, the greatest significance of American Catholic history, said Spalding, is to be found in the fact that "our example proves that the Church can thrive, where it is neither protected nor persecuted, but simply left to itself to manage its own affairs and to do its work." [65] Within this sort of climate, Spalding laid out what the new university could achieve:

> became a curate at St. Patrick's Church in Washington, D.C., and was instrumental in founding the Catholic Total Abstinence Union of America. He became bishop of Richmond when he was thirty-eight and followed as Catholic University's first rector. Removed because of the progressive stands he took on various issues, he went to Rome, where he was appointed by Pope Leo XIII as a canon at Saint John Lateran Basilica, assistant at the Pontifical Throne, and a counselor to the congregation Propaganda Fide. In 1900, the pope named him fourth bishop and second archbishop of Dubuque, Iowa.

[64] *An Address Delivered at the Laying of the Cornerstone of the Catholic University at Washington, D.C., May 24, 1888, by J. L. Spalding, Bishop Of Peoria* (Peoria, IL: B. Cremer & Bros. 1888), 6.

[65] Ibid., 7.

A true university will be the home both of ancient wisdom and of new learning; it will teach the best that is known and encourage research; it will stimulate thought, refine taste and awaken the love of excellence; it will be at once a scientific institute, a school of culture and a training ground for the business of life; it will educate the minds that give direction to the age; it will be a nursery of ideas, a center of influence.[66]

In March 1889, the year of the centennial of the establishment of the American hierarchy, Leo XIII issued his apostolic letter *Magni Nobis* to Cardinal Gibbons and the American bishops, giving his final approval to the university in Washington. The formal opening was set to coincide with the celebration of the centennial, and, at the same time, the first Catholic Lay Congress was scheduled to be held at Baltimore. Though initially reluctant to support such a gathering, Gibbons finally acquiesced, and the lay participants, often well-known names among American Catholics, delivered papers on many of the most significant issues of the day.

Archbishop Francesco Satolli, a professor of theology in the College of the Propaganda in Rome who had recently been conse-crated archbishop of Lepanto, was chosen to represent the pope at the official opening of Catholic University's Caldwell Hall. Prior to the event, Gibbons published a pastoral letter on the significance of the upcoming celebrations, praising the nation's first bishop, John Carroll, on how he had so well adapted the Church to the Ameri-can setting. This proved, according to Gibbons, "that the Catholic religion adapted itself to all times and places and circumstances, and this without any compromise of principle."[67]

---

[66] Ibid., 17–18.
[67] Ellis, *Life of Gibbons*, 1:416.

Prelude: The Late Nineteenth Century

On Wednesday, November 13, 1889, Gibbons dedicated Caldwell Hall; there followed a solemn pontifical Mass in the chapel, and after Mass a dinner was served to assembled guests, including President Benjamin Harrison and three members of his cabinet. A short time later, Gibbons wrote to the pope, telling him that

> the president of the United States, the Vice-president, the Secretary of State, and several members of the Cabinet made it a point to honor this festivity with their presence, and the applause which burst forth when Your health was proposed and which followed the answer of Mgr. Satolli to this toast, as well as that which greeted the President, manifest greatly that the love of the Church and the love of the country are indissolubly united in the hearts of the faithful.[68]

As the years passed, Gibbons's interest in the Catholic University deepened, and he never let pass an opportunity to advance its cause before the American Catholic public. This was not based on a keen interest in academia; Gibbons, after all, though he excelled in his studies in St. Charles College and St. Mary's Seminary, had received no more formal academic training than any other priest of the age, either in philosophy or theology. Rather, his attachment to the university was based on his unrelenting efforts for the school's establishment, along with his belief in the university's enhancement of a genuine American Catholic culture.

Charles Herbermann,[69] Catholic writer and editor, wrote the most complete account of Catholic University's original faculty

---

[68] Ibid., 421.

[69] Herbermann, a German Catholic immigrant who arrived in the United States in 1851, graduated from St. Francis Xavier College in New York City, became a professor and librarian at the College of the City of New York, and for more than a half century was involved in Catholic activities. He was president of the United

in the *American Catholic Quarterly Review*, just one month before
the school's opening. He provided biographical sketches of each
faculty member, describing, for example, professor of dogmatic
theology Monsignor Joseph Schroeder as "a Roman trained priest
who had been selected by Archbishop Krementz of Cologne to fill
the chair of Matthias J. Scheeben in his seminary." A man who
had been prominent in supporting the anti-slavery movement in
Africa, he was the author of the volume *Liberalism in Theology and
History* and had contributed to numerous European periodicals.
Henri Hyvernat was "appointed to teach scripture and oriental
languages," and Charles Warren Stoddard was "a newspaperman,
author and world traveler" who had converted to the Catholic Faith
and had taught English at Notre Dame. Irish-born Abbe John B.
Hogan, the director of the divinity college, had been superior of
Saint John's Seminary, Brighton, Massachusetts.

Joseph Pohle, thirty-eight years of age, had taken doctorates in
philosophy and theology at the Gregorian University in Rome and
had been kept out of Germany by Bismarck's Kulturkampf. During
these years, he had "taught in Switzerland and in the seminary of
the Diocese of Leeds in England." Swiss-born Sebastian Messmer,
a future bishop of Charleston, South Carolina, who compiled the
papers of his predecessor, Bishop John England, would be the university's canon lawyer. Trained at the University of Innsbruck, he
had been in America since 1871, teaching dogma at Seton Hall.
Thomas Bouquillon, educated in the Catholic University of Louvain in Belgium and previously a teacher at the Catholic Institute
in Lille, would be professor of moral theology. Church history would
be taught by the Paulist Augustine Hewit, "one of the original
band who helped Isaac Hecker found the Paulists in 1858." He had

States Catholic Historical Society and later became editor in chief
of the *Catholic Encyclopedia* in 1905.

graduated from Amherst College, went to Hartford Theological Seminary, wrote his autobiography, and became a convert in 1846. Hewit's fellow Paulist George M. Searle would teach astronomy and physics. "English born and Harvard graduate of 1857," he had taught at the Naval Academy in Annapolis and served as assistant at the Harvard observatory. He became a Catholic in 1862 and had published a volume titled *Elements of Geometry*. A Sulpician, Alexis Orban, was to fill the post of librarian temporarily. Finally, in response to the argument that the initial faculty comprised so many foreigners because the pope did not trust American scholarship, Herbermann replied that the real reason was that many of the finest American minds had already been snatched up in episcopal appointments.[70]

The Problem of Georgism

Another question for Cardinal Gibbons during these years was that of a possible condemnation of the writings of Henry George, an immensely popular writer whom some felt leaned too close to socialism and whose field was political economy. His basic philosophy was based on a belief that individuals should own the value they produce themselves, but the economic value derived *from land* should belong equally to all members of society. He became especially known for his book *Progress and Poverty*, which sold millions of copies worldwide, perhaps more than any American book

---

[70] John Tracy Ellis, *The Formative Years of the Catholic University of America* (Washington, D.C.: American Catholic Historical Association, 1946), 371–373. Ellis treats the development of the idea of the university, the Third Plenary Council of Baltimore and preliminary steps, the university's site, Roman negotiations, Bishop Keane's early years, the final preparations, and the school's final opening.

up to that time. In it, George espoused his single land tax theory, and by 1886, he was a popular third-party candidate for mayor of New York City, coming in second—ahead of Theodore Roosevelt.

Many in the Church felt that George's works should be condemned for their resemblance to socialism, and it was an issue to which Gibbons gave serious thought. In the end, he decided against such a course and, when in Rome, presented his case against condemnation to the Holy Office. He began by telling Congregation officials that George himself did not personally develop the theories he put forth; he was strongly influenced by social scientist Herbert Spencer and political economist John Stuart Mill. Also, upon examination, George's writings could not be categorized as pure socialism or communism because, as Gibbons noted from another author, these are defined as "the abolition of private property and the collectivization of all goods in the hands of the state."[71] On the contrary, George neither taught nor desired this. Rather, "he maintains the absolute ownership of all the fruits of human energy and industry, even when they amount to great riches acquired either by labor or heredity."[72] It is only on land that he would wish to limit the *supremum dominium* of the state, and even this, Gibbons noted, was open to qualifications.

> In a country such as the United States, by no means a land of "doctrinaires and visionaries", speculative theory would not be dangerous, nor are such hypotheses usually long lived. By applying a principle of morality that would advise "not to pronounce a sentence the consequences of which would

---

[71] "Cardinal Gibbons Opposes the Works of Henry George, February 25, 1887," in Ellis, *Documents*, 474. The work Gibbons was quoting from was written by a Father Valentine Steccanella and published by the Propaganda Press in 1882.

[72] Ibid., 474–475.

probably be adverse rather than favorable to the good end proposed", Gibbons rested his case, and, in the end, was listened to.[73]

The real difficulty with George was his involvement with a priest of the Archdiocese of New York, Father Edward McGlynn, pastor of St. Stephen's Church. He was born in New York City to Irish immigrant parents from County Donegal, studied in Rome—first at the College of the Propaganda and later at the North American College—and was ordained to the priesthood in Rome in 1860. He had taken doctorates in philosophy and theology in the Eternal City and, upon his arrival home, was first assigned to St. Joseph's parish in Greenwich Village. Through the years, he became known for taking controversial stands, such as his opposition to parochial schools on the view that public schools were good enough for all American children. He maintained rather close friendships with Protestant clergymen, once speaking at Henry Ward Beecher's church, though the latter was an outspoken opponent of Catholicism.

McGlynn first met Henry George in 1882 and, four years later, actively campaigned for him in the race for mayor of New York City. In September 1886, the archbishop of New York, Michael Augustine Corrigan, forbade him to speak on behalf of George's candidacy. An engagement had already been set up, and McGlynn replied that to back out would be imprudent, but he would refrain for the remainder of the campaign. He was suspended from priestly duties for two weeks but on election day made the rounds of the city's polling places with George and Terence V. Powderly.

In November, the archbishop issued a pastoral letter in the *New York Freemen's Journal* condemning any theories that would violate a person's right to private property and, toward the end of that month,

---

[73] Ibid., 475–476.

a second suspension was imposed on McGlynn. He was eventually summoned to Rome to explain his views but refused to go; at this, he was excommunicated. He continued giving lectures sponsored by an anti-poverty society in the city, and the archbishop declared it a sin for any Catholic to attend his lectures.[74] Meanwhile, Corrigan was convinced that Cardinal Gibbons was interfering in Rome on McGlynn's behalf, which merely accentuated the rift between liberal and conservative prelates. The McGlynn episode ended some years later when the papal representative lifted the excommunication, and McGlynn eventually lived out his years queietly as a pastor in Newburgh.[75]

Educational Controversies

Yet another interesting chapter in United States Catholic history occurred when the colorful archbishop of Saint Paul, John Ireland, devised his famous Faribault Plan, a valiant attempt to secure state finances for the operation of parochial schools in the towns of Faribault and Stillwater, Minnesota. The story began with Ireland's address to the National Education Association of the United States, which held their annual convention in Saint

[74] Michael Augustine Corrigan (1839–1902) served as the third archbishop of New York, from 1885 until his death. Born to Irish immigrant parents in Newark, he studied at Mount St. Mary's Seminary and became a member of the first class at Rome's North American College. Ordained in 1864, he joined the faculty at Seton Hall College and eventually became its president, then bishop of Newark. He and Bishop Bernard McQuaid of Rochester became the two leading conservative leaders of the American hierarchy, often opposing the Americanizing views of such prelates as Gibbons and John Ireland.

[75] For more on this topic see Hennesey, *American Catholics*, 189–190. Coincidentally, both Father McGlynn and Bishop John L. Spalding offered eulogies at the funeral of Henry George.

Paul in July 1890. He began by profusely praising the nation's free public schools:

> Free schools!... Blest indeed is the nation whose vales and hillsides they adorn, and blest the generations upon whose souls are poured their treasures. No task is more legitimate than that which is levied in order to dispel mental darkness and build up within the nation's bosom intelligent manhood and womanhood.[76]

Having dutifully lauded the system, he immediately launched into a criticism of public schools for making no provision for the teaching of religion — even trying to eliminate it from the minds of young students. He believed it common knowledge that there was great dissatisfaction throughout the country because of this lack of religious training. It was no honor to America, he felt,

> that ten million of its people were forced by law to pay taxes for the support of schools to which their conscience does not give approval; that they were ... compelled by their zeal for the religious instruction of their children to build schools of their own and to pay their own teachers. It was no honor to the American republic that she, more than any other nation, was eager to keep religion away from the schools. No nation went in this direction as far as ours. It was a terrible experiment upon which we had entered; the very life of our civilization and our country was at stake.[77]

The outcry was tremendous, becoming so intense throughout the country that word of it reached Rome, and Cardinal Gibbons

---

[76] James H. Moynihan, *The Life of Archbishop John Ireland* (New York: Harper & Brothers, 1953), 79.

[77] Ibid., 80–81.

was asked to intervene and to solicit an explanation from his friend in Saint Paul. With his theological training in France, Ireland wrote his response in French, telling Vatican officials that he felt compelled to explain to his countrymen the real Catholic grievances against the public school system and to help eliminate the anger existing between Catholics and non-Catholics, due, he felt, to exaggerations on the part of the former and prejudice on the part of the latter.

This seemed to soothe matters somewhat, until two further events occurred: the implementation of Ireland's educational theories in his archdiocese and the publication of a pamphlet on education, titled *Education, to Whom Does It Belong?*, by Dr. Thomas Bouquillon, a professor of moral theology at the Catholic University of America.

> The Archbishop's proposal, known since as the *Faribault Plan*, used the parochial school building of Immaculate Conception parish in that city to impart secular knowledge during the school day; its character as a parochial school was limited to the period before the school's formal opening, and after its afternoon closing. In this way, the parish would be relieved of the burden of supporting the school. The school would retain its own teachers, and the children would attend Mass and receive religious instruction before and after regular school hours. The Faribault School Board accepted this proposal in August, 1891, and a similar such agreement was reached with the School Board in the town of Stillwater in October of the same year.[78]

[78] Moynihan maintains that the plan was an attempt to solve one of the most serious problems besetting the Church in America in the last decade of the nineteenth century: Of 2,200,000 Catholic children in the United States, no more than 725,000 were enrolled

Bouquillon's pamphlet recognized every man's right to communicate truth, a right that belonged not only to individuals but also to "individuals collected in legitimate association and fitted to teach." Parents have the initial right to teach, followed by the civil authority, since, "for the promotion of the common good, knowledge is a prime necessity." As for the Church, She had the absolute right to teach supernatural truths, but, in the area of the natural sciences Her "duty of imparting is [merely] indirect."[79] A Jesuit priest, Rene Holaind, gave a stinging reply in a work titled *The Parent First*, strongly supporting the concept of the parents' right to choose the sort of education their children would receive. Holaind hastily wrote this reply lest Bouquillon's views might exert too much influence on the thinking of the American bishops — although that never happened.

These disputes were dividing Catholics from their fellow Americans. With this in mind, Monsignor Denis O'Connell, rector of the North American College in Rome and the American bishops' chief informant in the Eternal City, wrote to Ireland, strongly encouraging him to come to Rome to plead his case. It could be said that, prior to his departure, the majority of American bishops were supportive of the archbishop of Saint Paul. Cardinal Gibbons, in correspondence to Monsignor O'Connell, summarized the 1891 meeting of the U.S. bishops, noting that Ireland had expressed a willingness to discontinue his plan if his brother bishops so advised, though no such advice was forthcoming, since "the advantage is all on his side." Ireland answered several questions, and the result

in Catholic schools. (In New York City, it was only 42,000 of 150,000.) He raises the question of how one and one-half million Catholic children could be given religious instruction or have contact with a priest or a religious sister. Ibid., 85.

[79] Ibid., 86.

among the bishops was said to be "a triumphant vindication of his course."[80] To this statement, however, Archbishop Corrigan of New York was quick to respond, calling Gibbons's attention to an article in a recent issue of the Jesuit publication *La Civiltà Cattolica*, from which could be taken the conclusion that all bishops in the United States were in favor of the Faribault Plan. Corrigan, clearly expressing his displeasure, reminded Gibbons that "no reference to such approval is found" in the meeting, adding that his own memory was strengthened by another bishop who wrote to him that an explanation of the plan had been given, but "no opinion of its merits was asked at St. Louis."[81]

Shortly after his arrival in Rome, Ireland was granted a private audience with Pope Leo XIII, who received him very cordially and allowed him to summarize events up to that point, as well as other areas of concern in the American Church. While there, Ireland submitted a much-read memorial in his own defense. He noted that the chief enemies of his plan were "Protestant bigots, certain Catholic clergymen, and some foreign Catholics who were bent on guarding their native languages in their primary schools." Only 26 percent of Catholic children around the United States attended parochial schools, he stated, and yet these schools, to be successful, should be "gratuitous, and on a par with public schools." This was impossible, his memorial read, because of the poverty of most American parishes, while the government school "with its unlimited endowments is increasing in every perfection that money can command."

He reminded those willing to listen that the Sacred Congregation of the Propaganda required each parochial school to be "at least not inferior to the schools of the state." To the optimistic view

80 O'Connell, *John Ireland*, 338.
81 Ibid., 338–339.

expressed in some quarters that the American people in the late nineteenth century were moving in the direction of acceptance of government aid for private schools, Ireland responded that "we are further today from state aid for purely confessional schools than ever we were before." This, said the archbishop, was because of the extremely heterogeneous makeup of the American public, coming from fatherlands with very diverse opinions.[82] To this must surely be added the church-state separation enshrined in the country's foundational documents.

The memorial closed with what Ireland termed "supplementary remarks," alerting Rome to the fact that systems akin to the Faribault Plan had been put into operation in other areas of the United States, that nearly all the American archbishops had given the prelate of Saint Paul their strong endorsement, that his plan had borne up under intense scrutiny, and that all articles written in opposition, such as those published in the Jesuit *La Civiltà Cattolica*, were written in bad faith. Finally, he averred that he, John Ireland, was considered to be one of the leading bishops strongly favorable to the government of the United States, while his opponents could all be classified as inimical to all foreigners, seeing in them a serious threat to the country's rights and liberties.

In the end, the plan was short-lived:

> In Stillwater, the Board of Education had rejected the application of five nuns as teachers and thus prevented the renewal of the contract. In Faribault, a new school board, unfriendly to the system, had been elected. Father Conry appeared before the Board of Education on September 14, 1893, and said that the Catholics of Faribault could no longer consent to the assignment of two Protestant teachers to

---

[82] Moynihan, *Life of Ireland*, 91.

the old parochial school. Professor Willis West, Superintendent of Education, gave as reasons for the failure Protestant opposition to the dress of the Sisters, neglect on the part of the board to inform the people on all that had been accomplished, and the placing of Father Conry's name on the election ticket in the place of Mr. Keeley, which made the Protestants suspicious.[83]

The Nuncio

Since the inception of the American hierarchy in 1789, the Holy See had never had a representative in the United States. Up to the time of Cardinal Gibbons, the archbishops of Baltimore had served a similar function, but Rome had no full-time delegate. As early as 1853, however, things appeared to be changing. In that year, Archbishop Gaetano Bedini, nuncio to Brazil, stopped in the United States for a lengthy visit. Part of the Bedini mission was to report on the state of the Church in America, and one of his recommendations to Rome was the appointment of a permanent nuncio, a kind of ecclesial ambassador, both to strengthen the unity of the American episcopate and to deepen the American Church's loyalty to the Holy See.

The prelate chosen in 1891 was Archbishop Francesco Satolli, a former professor of Thomism in Perugia and later at the Urban College in Rome. At the time of the appointment, he was serving as president of the Pontifical Academy of Noble Ecclesiastics, which trained priests for diplomatic service. Satolli had previously visited the United States in 1889 for the centennial of the American hierarchy and had become quite familiar with the American scene.

---

[83] Ibid., 101–102. Fr. Conry was pastor of the parish. His name being placed on an election ticket for a seat on the school board aroused Protestant suspicions of some sort of clerical cabal.

Initially, the more progressive of the American bishops, and their contact in Rome, Monsignor Denis O'Connell,[84] seemed to favor such an appointment, if for no other reason than to spread the openness to liberal democracy for which Leo XIII had become known.

In a private audience with O'Connell in 1891, Leo XIII reportedly said regarding the divisions among American bishops about establishing a permanent nunciature in the United States:

> The whole evil is in this: that they do not want to have a representative of me there. If they had one of my representatives there now, that could speak to them the sentiments of the Pope, this trouble would never have happened. But for some reason of jealousy among themselves, they don't want to have my representative there tho' I would only name someone acceptable to them all. Why don't they want the Pope there? If Christ were to return again to earth, you would all rejoice to give Him a welcome. Why not then receive His Vicar?[85]

Some bishops were favorable to the idea because it would free them from the direct supervision of the Congregation of Propaganda Fide which, up till them, had overseen the American Church;

---

[84] Denis O'Connell, rector of the North American College in Rome, was born in Donoughmore, County Cork, Ireland, in 1849 and died as bishop of Richmond, Virginia, on January 1, 1927. He was raised in Columbia, South Carolina, and was ordained in 1877. He served as Cardinal Gibbons's secretary and in 1885 became rector of the seminary that was his alma mater. For the next ten years, he was the unofficial Roman contact for the American bishops. He would eventually become third rector of the Catholic University of America, auxiliary bishop of San Francisco, and seventh bishop of the Diocese of Richmond.

[85] Cited in Fogarty, *The Vatican and the American Hierarchy*, 117.

others disfavored it because it could lead to certain factions being favored over others; still another group of bishops valued the autonomy they had enjoyed since the American episcopacy was created. This only scrathces the surface of the underlying motives for or against having a Nuncio.

When Satolli arrived in the United States, he met first with New York's Archbishop Corrigan, who was not particularly friendly to his appointment; the next day, he traveled to Baltimore in a special railroad car provided by the president of the Baltimore and Ohio Railroad, on Cardinal Gibbons' request. He participated in festivities commemorating the fourth centenary of Columbus's arrival in America and met with Secretary of State John Foster, representing President Benjamin Harrison, whose wife was very ill. Satolli stressed the rapport that had traditionally existed between the Holy See and the United States government, and assured the Secretary that Pope Leo was "so much in tune with American ideals that the government would never have to fear that Catholicism and hierarchial authority would ever do anything prejudicial to those liberties established by the Constitution, but on the contrary, the liberty of the Catholic Church in these states ought to be the greatest guarantee of civil liberties and of every other good."[86]

Religious Protectionism

Satolli had more to worry about than the divisions between bishops. It has been argued that his presence as apostolic nuncio was a contributing factor in the rise of another high tide of anti-Catholicism in the form of the American Protective Association, known as the APA. Formed in 1887 by Henry F. Bowers, a "paranoid crony" of the mayor of Clinton, Iowa, who had been defeated

---

[86] Ibid., 123.

by the Irish labor vote, this secret society promised never to vote for a Catholic, never to hire a Catholic when a Protestant was available, and never to strike with a Catholic. By 1890, the movement was flourishing "from Detroit to Omaha," though it never achieved any tangible results legislatively or politically.

> It did serve to revive grass roots anti-Catholicism in many areas, especially after its reorganization under [APA president] William J. ("Whiskey Bill") Traynor during the depression of 1893. As American nationalism heightened in the 1890's, the APA emphasized the subservience of Catholics to a "foreign potentate." In 1893 Traynor even fomented a bogus "Popish Plot" by publishing a false encyclical. In its singleminded concentration on Catholicism the APA neglected other "foreigners"; it even rallied much support among Protestant immigrants.[87]

The American Protective Association not only had a tremendous membership, but it never let pass an opportunity for Catholic baiting. One such incident occurred in 1892, when Grover Cleveland was running for a second, nonconsecutive term. Cleveland had been a friend of Cardinal Gibbons for many years, and the APA took the opportunity during the campaign to circulate the rumor that during his first term, the president had installed a special telephone in his office that connected to the archbishop's residence in Baltimore. Further, they said he had placed a Catholic at the head of every major division of government; if he were reelected, one could only imagine the part Catholics would play in the administration. Cleveland received reports of these acivities from many sources, and felt compelled to reply:

---

[87] Ahlstrom, *Religious History*, 2:331–332.

I know Cardinal Gibbons and I know him to be a good citizen and first-rate American, and that his kindness of heart and toleration are in striking contrast to the fierce intolerance and vicious malignity which disgrace some who claim to be Protestants. I know a number of members of the Catholic Church who were employed in the public service during my administration, and I suppose there were many so employed. I should be ashamed of my Presbyterianism if these declarations gave ground for offence.[88]

In the off-year elections of 1894, Archbishop Ireland was the subject of attention during a visit to New York City. He had attended a rally in the city at which former President Benjamin Harrison was guest speaker. The archbishop, who sat next to the former president on the stage that evening, had wanted to attend to thank Harrison for several favors he had done for the Catholic Church in the United States, and for Ireland personally. As his visit progressed, he gave several newspapers interviews in which he was sharply critical of the corruption of Tammany Hall, an arm of the Democratic Party, maintaining that it had been repudiated by respectable Democrats and Republicans alike. Going further, the archbishop, himself a staunch Republican, castigated the Democrats for spreading stories that the Republicans were intent on persecuting Catholics in any way possible. To make their point, in fact, the Democrats had pointed to an alleged alliance between the Republicans and the American Protective Association. While Ireland admitted their anti-Catholicism, he saw in them little cause for concern. The Democrats had set up a "straw man" in the APA as a way of attracting Catholic voters:

[88] Cited in Ellis, *Life of Gibbons*, 2:507.

I hold it as certain that the Republican party has no connection with the APA and that the assertion that it does is
nothing more than a political ruse. Why then … should I
allow the Republican party, including as it does among its
adherents an immense number of Americans, among whom
are the most eminent and influential men in the country, to
be falsely accused? And why should I allow my co-religionists
to be duped by politicians? It was perfectly clear to me that
the Republicans were on the eve of a great victory and that
they would hold power for years to come. What a disaster
for the Church it would be if these victors … should believe
that Catholics are their enemies![89]

A final episode occurred during the presidential election campaign of 1896, in which the Democrats nominated William Jennings Bryan of Nebraska against William McKinley of Ohio. Satolli
was coming near the end of his time as apostolic nuncio, and it
was announced that he had been made a cardinal. The APA,
its influence waning by the end of the century, still managed to
take the occasion of Satolli's visit to Saint Louis to cause trouble,
circulating rumors that even Catholic clergy would not welcome
him. Diocesan officials, including the auxiliary bishop John Kain,
told Satolli that were he to cancel his plans, he would be playing
directly into the hands of the APA.

---

[89] Cited in O'Connell, *John Ireland*, 397. Though the Republicans did
win in New York State in the 1894 elections, Ireland's comments
brought down the wrath of Bishop Bernard McQuaid of Rochester,
who, from his pulpit, said that Ireland's political involvement was
"undignified, disgraceful to his episcopal office, and a scandal in the
eyes of all right-minded Catholics of both parties…. If Archbishop
Ireland had made himself as conspicuous in favor of the Democratic
party, he would be just as blameworthy in my estimation." Ibid.,
397–398.

Toil and Transcendence

Cardinal Gibbons replied to these happenings while the APA was meeting in Washington, D.C., where its president, William Traynor, said that "the keystone of the APA, in fact, is that a papist, no matter how liberal nominally, is not a consistent citizen of the United States."[90] Gibbons noted in his statement that it was the duty of all political parties in the United States to commit themselves to the principles of religious liberty and that Catholics could be found conspicuously in both of the country's major political parties. It was an American Catholic boast that as a religious group, they never interfered in the civil and political rights of those who differed from them in religious matters. "We demand those same rights for ourselves and nothing more, and will be content with nothing less." He continued:

> Not only is it the duty of all parties distinctly to set their faces against the false and un-American principles thrust forward of late, but much as I would regret the entire identification of any religious body as such with any political party, I am convinced that the members of a religious body whose rights, civil and religious, are attacked, will naturally and unanimously espouse the cause of the party which has the courage openly to avow the principles of the civil and religious liberty according to the constitution. Patience is a virtue, but it is not the only virtue. When pushed too far it may degenerate into pusillanimity.[91]

Papal Notice

The American Protective Association was not the only cause of difficulty for the American Church in these years. Rome continued

---

[90] Cited in Ellis, *Life of Gibbons*, 2:35–36.
[91] Ibid., 36.

to cast a very dubious eye on such secret fraternal associations as the Knights of Pythias and the Odd Fellows. The secrecy and openly Protestant membership of both these groups were a cause of concern, especially if Catholics were attracted to join them. In addition, these were years of domestic strife: The march of Coxey's Army—thousands of unemployed from all over the country—on the nation's capital in 1894 and the Pullman Car railroad strike, along with a general strike on the western railroads and the Haymarket Square Riot in Chicago in 1886, all caused Roman authorities to take notice.

Pope Leo XIII and his secretary of state, Cardinal Mariano Rampolla, were both known to favor the development of liberal democracies in many parts of Europe, but beginning to be influenced by prominent conservative Jesuit thinkers in Rome, they were less impressed by the more liberal, Americanizing prelates in the United States. Thus, it was American conservatives such as New York's Archbishop Corrigan and Rochester's Bernard McQuaid who had the pope's ear on these matters. The outcome of this was the 1895 publication of an encyclical letter from Leo to the Church in the United States, *Longinqua Oceani*.

As is so often the case with papal statements, the letter began with extensive praise for the growth and development of the Church in the United States. The pope spoke of the greatness of George Washington and especially the close friendship that had developed between the first president and John Carroll, the nation's first Catholic bishop. This was evidence that the United States "ought to be conjoined in concord and amity" with the Catholic Church. The pope then traced such institutions as the North American College for the training of American priests in the Eternal City; the development of the Catholic University of America in Washington, begun in conjunction with the centennial observance of the establishment of the American hierarchy;

and finally the opening of the Apostolic Delegation, that the Holy Father might be represented in the United States.

At the same time, the pope perceived certain difficulties. Catholics, he noted, should always prefer to associate with fellow Catholics, a course that would "be conducive to the safeguarding of their faith."

> Let this conclusion, therefore, remain firm — to shun not only those associations which have been openly condemned by the judgement of the Church, but those also which, in the opinion of intelligent men, and especially of the bishops, are regarded as suspicious and dangerous.[92]

Not only were Catholics warned about groups both suspicious and dangerous, but the traditional Protestant eyebrow was surely raised when Leo went on to assert:

> For the Church amongst you, unopposed by the Constitution and government of your nation, fettered by no hostile legislation, protected against violence by the common laws and the impartiality of the tribunals, is free to live and act without hinderance. Yet, though all this is true, it would be very erroneous to draw the conclusion that in America is to be sought the type of the most desirable status of the Church, or that it would be universally lawful or expedient for State and Church to be, as in America, dissevered and divorced.[93]

Thus, in advance of later papal and conciliar documents about modern politics, Leo XIII gave a formal endorsement of the

---

[92] Ellis, *Documents*, 516–524.
[93] Ibid., 517–518.

acceptability of American-style religious liberty while still reminding the faithful that the arrangement was not ideal.

Big Plans for the West

The idea of creating "colonies" of Catholic immigrants, especially the Irish, in the empty swaths of America came to the forefront in the late nineteenth century and is perhaps most closely associated with Archbishop John Ireland. Some decades earlier, New York's Archbishop John Hughes strongly opposed the idea of settling the Irish in remote colonies in the Midwest: He argued that it would separate them from many of their own loved ones who did not care to make such a life adjustment, and that it ran the risk of separating them from the faith, as it would be difficult to staff the communities with a sufficient number of priests. Hughes feared they could easily drift into other denominations and be lost to the Church, not to mention their descendants, for whom the Catholic Faith would become merely a distant memory of a creed to which their forebearers had once adhered. Finally, Hughes seemed convinced that those who had worked on railroads, canals, coal mines, and city labor were ill-equipped for life on the farm.

With the passage of time, however, this dynamic was changing. It was obviously an idea that Cardinal Gibbons looked on favorably. He had spent many of his early years in County Mayo in Ireland, where his parents had been born and raised. As early as 1871, while vicar apostolic of North Carolina, he returned to his native city of Baltimore to preach the Saint Patrick's Day sermon in St. Patrick's Church. Titling his sermon "The Apostolic Mission of the Irish Race," he noted that the conversion of Ireland under Saint Patrick had four characteristics: It was sudden, peaceful, abundantly spiritually fruitful, and to that point inextinguishable. He noted that any recounting of the history of the Irish that left out her religious persecutions and her triumphs of faith became a "thread-bare narrative without interest, without connection, without glory":

> Ireland without her Church and her priests would be like Rome without St. Peter's majestic dome, or like that Basilica itself without its Supreme Pontiff. Ireland without the Church would be like Jerusalem of old divested of her sacred temple and her venerable High Priest. Ireland without the Church would be like her own desecrated and ruined monasteries, stripped of her ancient glory, with altars dismantled, shorn of their interior beauty, with nothing of them left save tottering walls yielding to the decaying hand of time. In a word, the history of Ireland without her sacred traditions would be like the records of the Jewish nation with their religion left out.[94]

Some eight years later, Gibbons saw no reason why this splendid legacy should not be extended throughout the country. He subscribed for five shares of stock at $100 each in the Irish Catholic Colonization Association. The purpose of the association was exactly what Hughes had opposed decades earlier. This time, both Archbishop Ireland and Bishop John Lancaster Spalding were instrumental in its development. Also prominent in its founding was a well-known Chicago Catholic businessman, William J. Onahan.[95]

[94] Gibbons, A Retrospect of Fifty Years, 2 vols. (Baltimore: John Murphy, 1916), 1:186–187.

[95] Onahan was an Irish immigrant who settled in Chicago in the 1850s. He was a member of the city school board, president of the public library, both city collector and controller, and jury commissioner. He was the chief architect of the American Catholic Lay Congress in Baltimore in 1889, which drew 1,500 participants. Notre Dame University awarded him its prestigious Laetare Medal in 1890.

John Ireland wrote to Gibbons, enthusiastically sharing his plans for the settling of Irish Catholic farmers in Nebraska and Minnesota and concluded his missive observing that "the one name of the Archbishop of Baltimore on our list did more than fifty discourses from little Bishops of the West."[96]

Bishop Spalding described the enterprise in detail in a published work titled *The Religious Mission of the Irish People and Catholic Colonization*. Writing in 1880, Spalding painted an optimistic picture of the role of religion in the spirit of the age, linking its influence to "health, vigor and progress."[97] He felt that the Irish figured very prominently in this picture because of their strength of numbers and their strong adherence to the truths of their Faith. In this they differed significantly from the small band of English Catholics who settled Southern Maryland in the seventeenth century, among whose number were Bishop Spalding's forebearers. It was not that the latter group lacked a strong Catholic faith, but rather that they had survived from "a past age and an effete civilization." There was, he said, "no contagion in their faith, which seemed at best to nourish but a dying flame."[98] Their weakness in numbers, and the fact that they came almost totally from the upper echelons of British society, were far surpassed by the countless numbers of working people constantly entering the eastern port cities of America. Spalding painted an interesting portrait of the Irish in America in 1880:

> Our eye is ... drawn to a broad line of deep emerald green on the Atlantic seaboard, stretching from the southern point

---

[96] Ireland to Gibbons, March 2, 1880, cited in Ellis, *Life of Gibbons*, 1:194.

[97] J. L. Spalding, *The Religious Mission of the Irish People and Catholic Colonization* (New York: Catholic Publication Society, 1880), 15.

[98] Ibid., 57.

of Long Island all the way up to Maine. Here are the great cities, New York, Brooklyn, Newark, Jersey City, Albany, Hartford, New Haven, Providence, and Boston, together with the manufacturing towns of New England. South and west of this line there is a strip of green almost as large, but of somewhat lighter hue, which covers Philadelphia, and Baltimore and the coal regions of Pennsylvania. Along the southern shore of Lake Ontario there is an extensive border of green of the same shade, taking in Buffalo, Rochester, and the manufacturing towns of Western New York. The southern shore of Lake Erie has a border almost as extensive, but of lighter shade. To the south and west of Lake Michigan there is a considerable area of green of the same tint as that along Lake Erie, extending from Chicago to Milwaukee, and thence west and south towards the Mississippi River. Flecks of the same hue centre around St. Louis, Cincinnati, Kansas City, Omaha and St. Paul. Then there is a large territory, extending from New England through New York, Pennsylvania, Ohio, Indiana, Illinois, and thence along both banks of the Mississippi River into Minnesota, which is colored pea-green, and in which the density of the Irish population is ... from one to three to the square mile, while in the emerald green it is over fifteen to the square mile.[99]

Spalding traced the settlement of Irish Catholics as day laborers along the lines of canals and railroads; often when projects were completed, they took advantage of opportunities to buy land. Mathias Loras, the first bishop of Dubuque, Iowa,[100] and Joseph Crétin,

---

[99] Ibid., 108–109.
[100] Loras had been a seminary classmate of St. John Vianney, the Curé of Ars, in France.

the first bishop of Saint Paul, Minnesota, had both pioneered an interest in colonization, Spalding noted, though it fell especially to Crétin's successor, John Ireland, to take up the task. Spalding described Minnesota as a place with a "healthful climate and fertile soil" where there was "abundance of cheap land, nearly all of which ... belongs to railroad corporations."[101] It was on such land that Archbishop Ireland began to establish unique Irish Catholic colonies. A biographer observes that Ireland had a "Jeffersonian view of a class of sturdy Catholic yeomen who owned and farmed their own land and who thus gained a measure of independence and respectability unattainable by propertyless day laborers."[102]

What the Irish immigrant needed for his share in the American dream, Ireland felt, was his own parcel of land that could be worked, enlarged, and passed on to future generations. Unsurprisingly, the first order of business in these colonies was the construction of a church and the raising of a parish. The parish priest became the leading figure, performing far more than pastoral duties for the Catholic inhabitants. Spalding related the unfolding of Archbishop Ireland's plan:

> He chooses a priest, with a special view to his knowledge of farming and farm life, to preside over the new colony. He is on the ground to receive the first settler, who upon his arrival finds a father and a friend. The church is the first building put up, and around this the earliest colonists choose their lands. Town sites are laid out at proper distances along the line of the railroad. In a few weeks after the colony is opened there is a post-office and a country store, but no saloon. The lumber to build the cottages of the settlers is brought by the

---

[101] Ibid., 174.
[102] O'Connell, *John Ireland*, 136–137.

railroad at reduced rates.... The country is a rolling prairie. No trees are to be felled, no roads are to be made, and, as there is a herd law in these Western states, no fences are built.... None are invited to come until they have made themselves thoroughly acquainted with the conditions and all the details of the new mode of life upon which they are about to enter.[103]

The bishop of Peoria was at great pains in his account to note that in each of the Irish settlements there could be found people from all walks of life: bankers and business owners from the cities, miners from the coalfields of Pennsylvania, workers from the textile plants of New England. His point was to refute the argument that those who had worked in factories or mechanical trades, those who had spent years of their lives in large cities, or those accustomed to a more genteel sort of existence were not likely to last long in the Minnesota settlements. While Spalding made his point, the fact remained that the overwhelming majority of Irish coming to this country continued to populate the Eastern cities. There were several reasons the colonization plan never caught on.

First, most urban dwellers were simply more comfortable with the devil they knew than the one they did not. The Colonization Bureau never became more than a "clearing house" where immigrants could discover where cheap land could be obtained; it had no land of its own to be distributed. Further, the great majority of Eastern Irish did not have the funds to make the initial trip to Minnesota, and many were dissuaded by the fact that, once there, they somehow had to make ends meet until the first cash crop came in—nearly sixteen months after arrival. The colonies' houses were small and cheap, though often more comfortable than apartment

[103] Spalding, *Religious Mission of the Irish People*, 174–177.

dwellings in the city, but prospective residents also needed to fund furniture, a yoke of oxen and a plow, fuel and food, a milking cow, and more. This all went far beyond the financial realities of the majority of immigrants.[104]

Other Catholic Immigrants

An entirely different sort of problem beset German Catholic immigrants, who were largely found in the big cities of the Midwest. In 1891, the St. Raphael's Verein, an international German Catholic federation, presented Pope Leo XIII with a number of requests that had come to them from several countries, including United States. The American proposal was first introduced by Father Peter Abbelen, a priest of the Archdiocese of Milwaukee, who feared that, if German Catholic concerns were not answered, many might leave the Church.

The full petition presented appeared in the *New York Herald* on May 28, 1891: It "seems necessary" to unite immigrant groups into their own parishes; it "seems necessary" to have such parishes led by priests of the same nationality as the parishioners; it will be "especially necessary" to establish parochial schools in these parishes, with the history and culture of the fatherland being taught alongside those of their adopted land; it "seems necessary" that the national priests assigned to these parishes be given the same "rights and privileges" as those enjoyed by other priests; it "seems very desirable" that in areas where substantial numbers of Catholics of a certain national background are found, bishops of the same nationality be appointed; it "seems desirable" that charitable organizations, sodalities, and mutual aid societies to help such

---

[104] O'Connell, *John Ireland*, 147.

immigrants be strongly encouraged; and finally, it would be "very desirable" for the Holy See to establish special seminaries and apostolic schools for training missionaries for emigrants, as well as St. Raphael Societies for their protection.[105] The final document was signed by representatives from several countries, and apparently served some useful purpose, as German parishes, schools, religious communities of women, and seminaries proliferated.

Another Catholic immigrant group that expanded substantially in the later years of the nineteenth century was the Italians. Much like the Irish, they seemed to prefer the Eastern seaboard. Perhaps the crowning glory of Italian-American Catholicsm in that period was Mother Frances Xavier Cabrini, the first naturalized citizen of the United States to be canonized. Born in 1850 in Sant'Angelo Lodigiano, in the province of Lodi, Kingdom of Lombardy-Venetia, she and six other women who had taken religious vows founded the Missionary Sisters of the Sacred Heart of Jesus. Her community began by taking in orphans and opening day schools. They had much success, and Mother Cabrini approached Leo XIII about the possibility of opening missions in China. Instead, he requested they go to the United States, where the need to care for Italian emigrants was great. She and her sisters arrived in New York in 1889, where they immediately organized catechism and education classes, and Mother herself opened an orphanage and a hospital; the latter evolved into the Cabrini Medical Center, which continued to function until 2008. In Chicago, she opened Columbus Hospital in the heart of the city's Italian neighborhood, and she went on to found sixty-seven institutions throughout the United States — schools, orphanages, and hospitals. Pope Pius XII canonized this remarkable woman in 1946.

[105] Ellis, *Documents*, 497–498.

Prelude: The Late Nineteenth Century

Catholic Temperance Movement

Alcohol abuse was rampant in this era, especially among the immigrants whose lives had been destabilized by the move to America. One of the great spiritual remedies, known to have helped thousands, was the Catholic Total Abstinence Union, founded in the city of Cork, Ireland, by an Irish Capuchin, Father Theobald Mathew. In 1849, he came to the United States and visited twenty-five of the then-thirty states. This crusade took him to more than three hundred cities, and he personally administered the group's pledge to more than five hundred thousand individuals at large rallies. These Catholic men promised "with the Divine Assistance to abstain from all intoxicating drinks."

The movement quickly won the support of the American hierarchy and those on the political scene; in fact, Father Mathew became only the second foreigner to address a joint session of Congress. He was received by President Franklin Pierce, and his initial efforts resulted in the founding of state chapters of the organization across the country. This was followed by the establishment of diocesan unions, and along with the adult members of the Father Mathew Society, groups of younger boys called Cadets were formed. Each year, Catholic Temperance parades were held in major cities on October 10, Father Mathew's birthday. The national organization, found in at least ten states, won the admiration of President Theodore Roosevelt, who addressed a convention in Wilkes-Barre, Pennsylvania, in 1905.

The Heresy of Americanism?

The nineteenth century ended for the American Church with a very significant crisis, but not necessarily one that affected the average Catholic in the pew. The concept at issue has been referred to as "Americanism," or by some as the "phantom heresy" of Americanism. As with other issues of the day, this controversy seemed to divide the hierarchy into Americanists versus anti-Americanists.

The origins, however, were more European. Catholic leaders there had long had a lively interest in the growth and progress of the Church in the United States. The strength She had achieved in such a short time appeared to them as startling and prompted many to seek the reasons for this success. Germany had only recently lived through Bismarck's anti-Catholic Kulturkampf; an anti-clerical government in Italy was making it difficult for the Church to function; and France was immersed in a serious crisis of church and state. To a younger, more democratically minded generation of European Catholics, the success of the American Church seemed something to be imitated. Admiration for the American approach appeared to be highest among Catholic republicans in France. To the country's royalists, however, the independence the American Church enjoyed from its government only aggravated their fear of the strict separation of church and state in France, which, they thought, would usher in a situation worse than the French Revolution.

As early as 1886, Cardinal Gibbons was already setting the stage for the controversy by praising American-style religious liberty in official documents. The Australian hierarchy held a plenary session that year and sent a letter of greeting to the bishops of the United States. Responding for his colleagues, the archbishop of Baltimore expressed pleasure at the progress the Church in America had made, wished the same for Australia, and noted that

> for this advancement of the cause of religion in both countries we are in no small measure indebted, under God, to the religious freedom which constitutes so noble a feature of our respective governments. They hold over us the aegis of

their protection without intruding into the Sanctuary; and by leaving inviolate our spiritual prerogatives, enable us to fulfill our sublime mission without fettering our apostolic liberty.[106]

What, then, was the "Americanism" that became so constested? One of the leading clerical participants in the dispute, Bishop John J. Keane of the Catholic University of America, a close ally of Gibbons, attempted an answer:

> Americanism is merely the sentiment of Catholics toward their country—a feeling of satisfaction, of gratitude, and of devotion to which Archbishop Carroll first gave expression. It is not a system, not a doctrinal program, not any kind of propaganda.[107]

Possibly. But that was not the view of many conservative French Catholics, or, for that matter, of many American Catholics. The immediate cause of the Americanism crisis was a French translation of a biography of Father Isaac Hecker, founder of the Paulists, by a member of his community, Father Walter Elliot. Adding substantial fuel to the flames was a preface to the French version, written by Abbé Felix Klein, a professor in the Institut Catholique in Paris. The preface seemed to imply the following: The external guidance of the Church was less important than the private inspiration of the Holy Spirit in individual souls; natural virtues were of greater importance than supernatural ones; a distinction should be made between the active and passive virtues, with active ones superior to passive; the life of the vows was not nearly as necessary as a life of social activism; and the older methods of charity and self-sacrifice

---

[106] Ellis, *Life of Gibbons*, 2:5.
[107] Cited in Arline Boucher and John Tehan, *Prince of Democracy: James Cardinal Gibbons* (Garden City, NY: Doubleday, 1962), 230.

were a somewhat antiquated notion at the dawn of the twentieth century.

Regarding this controversy, there were two differing mindsets in the American hierarchy. One group tended to interpret the disputed material broadly and somewhat tolerantly, hoping that by so doing they might more easily facilitate the faithful's assimilation into the mainstream of American life. These prelates included John Ireland, John Lancaster Spalding, John Keane, Monsignor Denis O'Connell, and His Eminence of Baltimore. On the opposite side were those who feared the infiltration of philosophical liberalism into the Church and were thus less inclined to show a spirit of accommodation to American ways. They were led by the Archbishop of New York, Michael A. Corrigan, who was joined by Bishops Bernard McQuaid of Rochester, Ignatius Horstmann of Cleveland, and Frederick X. Katzer of Milwaukee. Of the Americanists, Keane, Ireland, and O'Connell were freer to speak at greater length on the subject; Gibbons, because of the delicacy of his position as *primus inter pares*, spoke less, but when he did it was with great conviction.

Following the French translation of the Hecker biography, Gibbons felt the need to describe the situation in greater detail to Cardinal Rampolla, Pope Leo XIII's secretary of state:

Of course we love our country and are devoted to it; we like its institutions because they allow us our whole liberty for goodness and allow us to spread more and more the action of Religion and the influence of the Church. It is not here a matter of theory, of system, of maxims set up like absolute principles, it is entirely a matter of practice. If that were all they call Americanism, wherein is the harm? But no, they are using the word like a scarecrow; they want to suggest a perverse tendency of a doctrine not only suspicious, but clearly erroneous and even heretical, as people talk of liberalism, Gallicanism, and other qualifications of the kind. Well, I can guarantee to Y.E. that all this is false, unfair, slanderous. No doubt, among us, as everywhere else, there are differences of opinion or appreciation, but I have no hesitation in affirming, you have not in the whole world an episcopate, a clergy, and believers more fundamentally Catholic, firmer in their faith and more wholly devoted to the Holy See.[108]

In the same explanatory vein, Monsignor O'Connell was invited to describe the meaning of Americanism at the Fourth International Scientific Congress in Fribourg, Switzerland, in 1897. He drew a careful distinction between the political meaning of the term, and the sense in which it applied to civic matters, specifically the separation of church and state. Gibbons was quite pleased with the address, and wrote to congratulate O'Connell, telling him "every sentence contains a pregnant idea, and the relations of Church and State are admirably set forth, especially for the eye of Rome.... I have often written and spoken on the subject, but you have gone more profoundly to the root."[109]

The crisis largely abated after 1899, with the publication of an encyclical letter from Leo XIII, *Testem Benevolentiae*. The Holy Father, in a benign way, and with much praise for all that the Church had achieved in America, nonetheless summarized the perceived errors in Americanism and said if these points were indeed true, they could not be reconciled with official Church teaching and were injurious to the health of the Church in the United States. Though Leo had spoken in the most pastoral of terms, his clarity left no one doubting his position. The conservative members of

---

[108] Gibbons to Rampolla, August 27, 1898, cited in Ellis, *Life of Gibbons*, 2:60–61.
[109] Cited in Boucher and Tehan, *Prince of Democracy*, 232.

the American hierarchy were delighted that the heretical concepts that had become associated with Americanism had been exposed and dealt with. No American bishop dissented in the slightest way, and Cardinal Gibbons made an entry in his diary for March 17, 1899, stating that he had sent the pope a reply, "assuring him that the false conceptions of Americanism emanating from Europe have no existence among the prelates, priests or Catholic laity of our country."[110] In fact, Gibbons was very forthright to Leo:

> The doctrine which I deliberately call extravagant and ab-
> surd, this Americanism as it has been called, has nothing in
> common with the views, aspirations, doctrine and conduct of
> Americans. I do not think there can be found in the entire
> country a bishop, priest or even a layman with a knowledge
> of his religion who has ever uttered such enormities. No,
> that is not — it never has been and never will be — our
> Americanism. I am deeply grateful to Your Holiness for hav-
> ing yourself made this distinction in your apostolic letter.[111]

Gibbons's leading biographer, Monsignor John Tracy Ellis, noted that if by "Americanism" is understood the love of one's country and its institutions, "there was never in the history of the Catholic Church of the United States a more conspicuous example than Cardinal Gibbons." Ellis was quick to add that the Baltimore prel- ate "never lost an opportunity of putting before his audiences at home and abroad the values he attached to the American way of life."[112] A study of his mindset bears this out. By the advent of the twentieth century, there were more than fifteen million Catholics in the United States, and Gibbons noted the perfect harmony

---

[110] Cited in Allen Sinclair Will, *Life of Cardinal Gibbons*, 2 vols. (New York: E. P. Dutton, 1922), 1:557–558.

[111] Cited in Ellis, *Life of Gibbons*, 2:71.

[112] Ibid., 4.

existing between their religious beliefs and their duties as American citizens. They prefer the American form of government over all others, he averred, and admire the spirit of its laws:

> The separation of Church and State in this country seems to them the natural, inevitable and best conceivable plan, the one that would work best among us, both for the good of religion and of the State. Any change in their relations they would contemplate with dread. They are well aware, indeed, that the Church here enjoys a larger liberty and a more secure position than in any country today where Church and State are united.[113]

On June 30, 1886, having been elevated to the sacred purple, Gibbons was invested with the robes of his office on the silver jubilee of his priestly ordination in the Baltimore cathedral. Less than a year later, he traveled to Rome to take formal possession of his titular church, Santa Maria in Trastevere. He used his sermon, often quoted to this day, as an occasion to deliver "clear insight" into the greatness of the United States Constitution. Gibbons took note of Leo XIII's teaching that the Church is able to accommodate Herself to all sorts of governmental structures, leaving them all with "the sacred leaven of the Gospel." In the process, She had often been hampered in Her divine mission, but in America, this was never the case:

> For myself as a citizen of the United States, and without closing my eyes to our shortcomings as a nation, I say, with a deep sense of pride and gratitude, that I belong to a country where the civil government holds over us the aegis of its protection, without interfering with us in the legitimate

---

[113] James Cardinal Gibbons, *The Church and the Republic* (Brooklyn: International Catholic Truth Society, 1909), 3-4.

exercise of our sublime mission as ministers of the Gospel of Christ. Our country has liberty without license, and authority without despotism.[114]

Finally, on the occasion of his golden jubilee in 1911, he would address the question again. Underscoring one of his favorite themes, of church and state "moving amicably in parallel lines," the cardinal preached that

> the Constitution of the United States is the palladium of our liberties and our landmark on our march of progress. That instrument has been framed by the anxious cares and enlightened zeal of the Fathers of the Republic. Its wisdom has been tested and successfully proved after a trial of a century and a quarter. It has weathered the storm of the century which it has passed and it should be trusted for the centuries to come. What has been good enough for our fathers ought to be good enough for us. Every change, either in the political or religious world, is not a reformation.[115]

Forceful as the cardinal was in his patriotic expression, and clear as were the Americanizing bishops on the reality of the situation domestically as opposed to perceptions in the European mind, the event did have repercussions for years. One historian has noted that, regarding Catholic intellectual life in the United States, most scholars "now slipped more or less peaceably into a half- century's theological hibernation."[116] This was compounded by a condemnation of modernism by Leo's successor, Pope Saint Pius X. Following

---

[114] Cited in Will, *Life of Cardinal Gibbons*, 2:309.

[115] James Cardinal Gibbons, Sermon preached in the Baltimore Cathedral on the occasion of the public observance of his golden jubilee, October 1, 1911, Catholic University of America Archives.

[116] Hennesey, *American Catholics*, 203.

soon after *Testem Benevolentiae*, Pius's encyclical *Pascendi Dominici Gregis* of 1907 strengthened the condemnation earlier that year of some sixty-five heresies associated with "modernism," some of which were related to the ideas associated with "Americanism." The encyclical was followed three years later by the introduction of an anti-modernist oath to be taken by all Catholic bishops, priests, and academic teachers of theology.

It has been written that, properly speaking, there was no real modernism in the United States.[117] Catholic scholarship in the United States was, after all, in its infancy, while some publications did produce significant work. One such was the *New York Review*, published at Saint Joseph's Seminary in the Dunwoodie section of Yonkers. It had begun in 1905 at the encouragement of Archbishop (later Cardinal) John Farley. The rector of the seminary, Father James Driscoll, was a Sulpician, and as the journal kept producing scholarly articles, the reaction of Driscoll's Sulpician superior became more negative. As a result, Driscoll and some other Sulpicians on the faculty withdrew from the Society of Saint Sulpice and were incardinated into the Archdiocese of New York.

The *Review* did publish articles by European intellectuals, some of whom were thought to be modernists. The last straw came with the publication of four articles by Father Edward J. Hanna, a professor of Scripture at St. Bernard's Seminary in Rochester, New York. These articles dealt with the human knowledge of Christ, the first three of which raised the question of the limitations of Christ's human knowledge. The fourth largely retracted points made in the others and was written under the direction of Cardinal Satolli, apostolic delegate in the United States. A further complication was the request of the archbishop of San

---

[117] Fogarty, *The Vatican and the American Hierarchy*, 191.

Francisco that Hanna be appointed his auxiliary bishop, which never came to fruition.[118]

A further episode occurred in Gibbons's own seminary of St. Mary's in Baltimore, involving a Sulpician, Joseph Bruneau, who had taught at Dunwoodie and had written articles for the *Review*. Gibbons was alerted by Cardinal Rafael Merry del Val, secretary of state, and others, that prominent publications such as *La Civiltà Cattolica* and *L'Osservatore Romano* had criticized several errors in a book the Baltimore Sulpician had written and that he, Gibbons, should make a special investigation of Bruneau's orthodoxy. Gibbons replied to Merry del Val that the priest in question would most gladly submit his writings to the Holy Office and added that the Sulpicians, since their arrival in Baltimore 120 years earlier, "had never been anything other than pious, orthodox, and loyal to the Holy See."[119]

One could say, with little fear of contradiction, that the Catholic Church in America had matured greatly and was well poised to enter the twentieth century. The growth of its physical plant, its educational structures, its care of the immigrant flock, its emergence as the Church of the urban dweller, its forays into the nation's political life, and especially the strength of its episcopal leadership, divided though they may have been on certain topics, all contributed to the making of an institution prepared to grapple with entirely new situations.

[118] Hanna was eventually appointed archbishop of San Francisco in 1915 upon the death of Archbishop Riordan.
[119] Fogarty, *The Vatican and the American Hierarchy*, 193.

2

The Twentieth Century Begins:
Progressively and Internationally

Industrialization

The first two decades of the twentieth century are best remembered domestically for the Progressive Movement and internationally for the first global conflict in which the United States engaged, World War I. The Progressive Movement encompassed economic, political, social, and literary attempts to alleviate what many saw as the gross inequalities in American society. This had roots in the nineteenth century and has often been viewed as a creative response to the problems of industrialization. Industrialization and the problems caused by it can be broken into three areas. First was the increase in the scale of production, and therefore the advance of bureaucratization. The growth of the large corporation had been considered a creative innovation by some, while others felt it was a natural outcome of the growth of the railroads. Andrew Carnegie, the Pittsburgh steel magnate, summed up the prevailing wisdom among the industrialists well:

> Civilization depends upon the triple law of the sacredness of private property, free competition, and free accumulation of wealth. This triple law, which allows free play to economic forces is indispensable to all progress, and nothing should

be permitted to interfere with its operation. Its indispensability is one of the facts of life which cannot be changed. One can only make the best of it.[120]

Small businesses increasingly did not fit into the new dispensation and were swept away by larger corporations. Workers were, for the most part, forced to resort to factory jobs, while the ranks of independent artisans and craftsmen diminished. Economic growth appeared to be destroying skills in the name of efficiency. Traditional retailers and wholesalers were being seriously threatened. At the same time, however, real wages rose over the period 1890 to 1917 by some 40 percent—and even more as 1920 approached. There seemed to be much room for advancement in the workforce, especially if one was a WASP.[121]

Meanwhile, efforts to seek new forms of organization for workers expanded; the Knights of Labor, as mentioned, wanted to bring about a cooperative capitalism by creating a major political organization. From its ashes rose the American Federation of Labor, an association of trade unions in which skills meant something. Some of their affiliates, though, took in less than the aristocracy of labor.

The nationalizing of the economy—not in terms of the expansion of the public sector, but in terms of the de-emphasis on local and regional economies in favor of national networks and interdependence—was a second facet of industrialization. This drew farmers into the industrial system, forcing them to become specialists and making them dependent on distant, unpredictable markets. Mechanization meant, for many farmers, more land *and* more debt. Many found themselves in a squeeze, often leading to overproduction that crashed the price of staple foods.

[120] Hudson, *Religion in America*, 304.
[121] The acronym WASP stands for "White Anglo-Saxon Protestant."

Finally, industrialization gave rise to WASP America's traditional fears of being overwhelmed by Catholics in the workforce. They worried that the unwashed Catholic masses would bring about alien attitudes and anti-American thinking. There was a revival of the Know-Nothingism of decades earlier, and it would not be long before newer forms of anti-Catholicism would manifest themselves. Closely aligned with this was the rapid growth of cities, spurred by the growth of the (majority-Catholic) immigrant population from both Western and Eastern Europe. This all placed strains on city governments and gave rise to many of the urban problems that progressives would begin to address. The Progressive Movement has to be viewed against this background, as an attempt to resolve these existing problems and to establish a viable system given new realities. For some, progressivism meant nothing less then a total overhaul of the capitalist structure.

The Progressives

Politically, prior to 1896, neither major political party could achieve dominance. Since the Civil War, the presidents had mostly been Republicans, but their margins of victory were small and Congress was never decisively controlled by Republicans for lengthy periods of time. The Gilded Age, as the late nineteenth century became known, was seen by many historians as an age of evasion of growing and grave issues that neither party grappled with.

Some years ago, a newer school of historical interpretation emerged, pitting "pietists" against "ritualists." Pietism was equated with militant Protestantism, which was seen to have taken hold of the Republican Party. The godly had to stamp out wickedness in whatever form it took. The ritualists, on the other hand, were more associated with a Catholic point of view. The world is a valley of tears, they said, and sin is very much present in our midst.

Members of the hierarchy and priests serve as direct intermediaries between God and man and should be listened to more than all others. They wanted to perpetuate their views through the parochial school system, and many priests felt that the laity, especially the Irish, should become more Americanized.

The Democrats saw themselves as the party of personal liberty, whereas the GOP[122] felt it was charged with putting God's will into effect, being the instrument for carrying out the divine will. Practically, the GOP stood as the party of protection for manufacturing, along with stability and progress. This rhetoric was frequently used, but practical solutions to growing industrial-era problems appeared to be scant. Under Republican William McKinley, elected president in 1896, few concrete alternatives were proposed; it was not until the advent of the new century, and the accession of Theodore Roosevelt to the presidency following McKinley's assassination, that a concrete plan of action was put into operation, and Republican progressivism may be said to have begun. This process continued during the administration of William Howard Taft and, to a much greater extent, under the Democrats and Woodrow Wilson. Though both major parties seemed to have embraced progressive reform, the philosophies underlying each varied greatly.

What began after 1900 was a shift from a laissez-faire ideology to a greater stress on the general welfare, from social Darwinism to state intervention. The perfectibility of man came to be seen as coming not from individuals but from collective action. The traditional view of economic progress emerging from an unfettered marketplace was now taking a back seat to governmental initiatives to address the many social ills that had become a deep reality of American life. Given the judicial conservatism of the Supreme

---

[122] GOP stands for "Grand Old Party," the traditional name given to the Republican Party.

Court from 1880 until the New Deal era, reformers knew they could count little on the judicial process; legislative and executive action would have to be the norm.

The new thinking was popularized by academics, and even more so by a literary group called muckrakers, who proposed their ideas in such publications as *McClure's*, *Colliers*, and the *Saturday Evening Post*. They elaborated the thoughts of the social scientists of the day, all of whom disdained the previously faddish social Darwinism. This thinking even found its way into American Protestant theology in the writings of ministers such as Washington Gladden and Walter Rauschenbusch, both of whom represented the shift in emphasis from the Gospel of Wealth to the Social Gospel.[123] Most Protestants, being on the right side of the fence in a traditionally WASP country, were far removed from the scenes of industrial conflict; to remedy this, socially minded ministers organized study groups to discuss these problems and to allow the average church member to become acquainted with the plight of the worker.

Washington Gladden represented a rather mild progressivism that recognized the rights of labor, advocated municipal ownership of public utilities, and placed strong emphasis on the Golden Rule

---

[123] Winthrop Hudson, in his study *Religion in America*, stresses what the Social Gospel preachers wanted to move away from: "Carnegie's gospel of wealth was closely intertwined with the doctrine of stewardship of time, money and talent that had been staple fare in Protestant moral teaching. Consequently it was but a small step for current principles of economics to be translated into laws of God's providential ordering of society. Phillips Brooks, Henry Ward Beecher, and a host of lesser luminaries of the Protestant pulpit embraced the gospel of wealth with fervent devotion, but Russell Conwell—with his lecture on *Acres of Diamonds* (they are in one's own backyard) and his exhortation that everyone has a 'duty to get rich'—was its most eloquent clerical spokesman." *Religion in America*, 305.

as the royal law of brotherhood. The latter theme was picked up and romanticized by Charles M. Sheldon (1857–1946), pastor of the Central Congregational Church in Topeka, Kansas, in a parable novel that was destined to win a place beside *Uncle Tom's Cabin* and *Ten Nights in a Bar Room* as one of the great American tracts. *In His Steps*, or *What Would Jesus Do?*, as previously mentioned, was the story of the revolution that occurred in a small city when members of a single congregation resolved to live for a year in accordance with the teachings of Jesus.[124]

Walter Rauschenbusch has been described as an outstanding prophet of the Social Gospel. He was converted to this way of thinking while serving as pastor of a small Baptist church of German immigrants in a tenement section of New York City. Some years later, while serving on the faculty of Rochester Theological Seminary, he came to national attention. Some of his fellow Baptists considered him more "rhetorical … than scientific," perhaps because of his self-identification as a "Christian socialist." He lacked much of the optimism found in the writings of other Social Gospel advocates but nonetheless was instrumental in having courses on social concerns taught in any number of Protestant seminaries.[125]

These writers and thinkers mounted a frontal attack on laissez-faire, competitive society. They felt the world should be a Christian commonwealth, that self-sacrifice should replace self-interest, and that individuals should act according to the terms of stewardship in God's service. One could not, in their view, separate economic actions from the rest of the moral life. Many churches sponsored settlement houses to help the poor help themselves — not merely flophouses, but places where immigrants could be taught skills. Rather than being welfare houses, they were facilities that tried to

[124] Hudson, *Religion in America*, 312.
[125] Ibid., 313–314.

integrate the immigrant into American society and the economy, making him or her self-sustaining. One of the finest examples of this was found in the work of Jane Addams at Hull House, on Chicago's South Side.

There also developed a new school of American political economics, associated with economists such as Richard Ely of Johns Hopkins University and Henry Carter Adams,[126] that included a new emphasis rejecting classical thought. Most of these economists were young and educated in Germany, and they argued that America should be far more open to economic planning, which produced concrete action. Laissez-faire, they said, was wrong because competition was not universal. There were, for instance, natural monopolies that were not regulated by competition, and as a result, entire classes of business were unaccounted for in free-market theory. Competition between unequals was basically unfair and led to monopolies. Following self-interest was not always good: Many people are ignorant and wasteful.

Finally, a neoclassical school of economics emerged, of which John Bates Clark was the best representative. This was an attempt to reconcile classic laissez-faire theory with present-day realities. The neoclassical approach argued that the competition mechanism could be used to regulate the economy: Remove the frictions and blockages from the economy, and competition will be able to carry out its tenets. It was an attempt to maintain the adequacy of competition with a positive role for the state — accentuating a positive role for government without disregarding traditional economics.

Those who labeled themselves progressives, whether Republicans, Democrats, or socialists, seemed to favor the same objectives:

---

[126] Years later, Ely would direct the doctoral dissertation of Monsignor John A. Ryan, which, Ely noted, was the first serious attempt to construct a Roman Catholic system of political economy.

They felt the national government was too centralized, and there should be a greater role for the states, especially in the field of reform. The model state was Wisconsin, and under Governor Robert La Follette, the Wisconsin Plan became the blueprint for progressive reform across the country. They believed, too, in greater regulation over industries and transportation, especially the railroads. Another area of concern was the underprivileged, especially Blacks, Native Americans, and immigrants; in later years, this came to include, in a particular way, the Polish, Russian, and Italian immigrant groups who would take any menial job for low wages and who usually had less interest in unionizing.

They proposed simply a better moral code for politicians, which they thought more enlightened procedures could bring about. They preferred the commission and city manager type of government at the municipal level, discouraging the strong mayoral offices that seemed to be hotbeds of corruption. Finally, progressives were also wedded to the newspapers; they were intellectuals who wrote and felt that access to new ideas, especially their ideas, would turn the world in their favor.

Their concrete objectives included: women's suffrage by constitutional amendment; the introduction of the Australian ballot, or secret ballot, in voting (oral voting still existed in parts of the United States); direct primaries; direct election of U.S. Senators by the people; the introduction of the initiatives and referendums on the local level; civil service reform at all levels; tax reform; and the city manager form of government.[127]

Aside from presidential leadership, the Progressive Movement attracted well-known members of both political parties. The

[127] Both initiatives and referendums allow citizens to place new legislation on a popular ballot, or to place legislation that has recently been passed by a legislature on a ballot for a popular vote.

Democrats produced William Jennings Bryan of Nebraska, a great orator who could speak at tremendous length and had an enormous following in rural America, especially in the Midwest. His senate career came to the forefront when his party nominated him to run against William McKinley in 1896. On the Republican side, in addition to La Follette of Wisconsin, New York governor Charles Evans Hughes, presidential nominee against Woodrow Wilson in 1916, became famous for his investigation of insurance fraud in his state.[128] Somewhat later, Governor Alfred E. Smith was responsible for much constructive legislation in the Empire State, along with his earlier work rewriting the state's constitution. In their respective states, Governors Gifford Pinchot of Pennsylvania and Hiram Johnson of California stood out among the reformers as well.

Judicially, though the Supreme Court remained a bastion of conservativism until the 1930s, Wilson had appointed Louis Brandeis as an associate justice. He was known for speaking on progressive issues and helped Wilson in drafting much progressive legislation.

Literature also continued to stir the consciences of many Americans. Henry Demarest Lloyd, a reporter for the *Chicago Tribune*, wrote *Wealth against Commonwealth*, an indictment of Standard Oil as well as the Rockefellers. Thomas Lawson followed with *Frenzied Finance*, a strong attack on the copper trusts and interests. Lincoln Steffens, a professional newsman and freelance writer, visited several major U.S. cities, and in his work, *The Shame of the Cities*, he uncovered countless abuses while severely criticizing mayors and local politicians. Jane Addams was joined by Lillian Wald, whose book *The House on Henry Street* spoke of life in a tenement district on New York City's Lower East Side, exposing the terrible living conditions. Well known to newspaper readers throughout

---

[128] Hughes went on to become the eleventh chief justice of the Supreme Court.

the country was Jacob Riis, a police reporter whose articles on tenement-house reform produced much responsive action by local politicians eager to rid their cities of any embarrassing abuses that might be uncovered.

Catholics and the Progressive Movement

Progressivism, unsurprisingly, was largely the concern of WASP America, and not a movement in which Catholics were found in vast numbers. This is understandable, as the main preoccupation of the lion's share of Catholics was becoming assimilated to their new land and hoping to better themselves through work—under conditions that progressives were working to improve. Nonetheless, there was a significant Catholic contribution to the Progressive Movement, largely emanating from the Church's more intellectual classes. Bishops such as William Stang of Fall River, Massachusetts, and Peter Muldoon of Rockford, Illinois, personally sought to better the lot of the Catholic workingman by using Church agencies to aid in whatever way possible. In journalism, Father Peter Yorke was the editor of two publications on the West Coast, the *Monitor* and the *Leader*. Both championed the cause of American Labor, strongly decried the American Protective Association, and did much to advance the cause of Irish nationalism.

There was also the work of Monsignor John J. Curran of Wilkes-Barre, Pennsylvania. Growing up in the coalfields of Northeastern Pennsylvania, Curran had worked as a breaker boy and a mule driver in the mines. From the time he left this work as a teenager, he became convinced of the cause of the laborer, and as years passed, he became a close friend of John Mitchell, who had risen to become president of the United Mine Workers of America. Curran was ordained in 1887 and openly advocated the formation of local unions. He came to national attention for his arbitration work during the Anthracite Coal Strike of 1902. From the pulpit, Curran had, for years, attacked what he felt were the evils of the industrial age; he gave countless interviews to the press and corresponded with leaders of industry in order to defend the rights of coal miners:

> Though the vast majority of America wrote off his intervention as the work of a radical, President Theodore Roosevelt was not among them. Impressed by the case made for the anthracite miners, the Chief Executive summoned the owners to the White House ... and asked them to give serious consideration to the demands of their employees. The group adamantly refused to do so. Justifiably angered by their obstinacy, President Roosevelt turned to Father Curran. Between them, they devised a plan to break the impasse.... Binding arbitration was proposed and a blue ribbon presidential commission was named. With public sentiment in favor of the solution and with John Mitchell's acceptance of the panel, the mine owners capitulated. Thereupon, the strike ended.[129]

Catholic sociologist Monsignor William J. Kerby, for many years a faculty member at the Catholic University of America, was a pioneer in the development of the School of Social Work, as well as the architect of the National Conference of Catholic Charities, an organized effort to bring about Catholic contributions to social service. In addition, layman Warren Mosher from Youngstown, Ohio, started the Catholic Summer School of America, consisting of clergy and laity, and aiming to foster intellectual culture in harmony with Christian faith by means of lectures and special

---

[129] John P. Gallagher, *A Century of History: The Diocese of Scranton: 1868–1968* (Scranton: Diocese of Scranton, Pennsylvania, 1968), 307.

classes resembling university extension courses. Originally begun in New London, Connecticut, it moved to Cliff Haven, New York, on Lake Champlain, and the Delaware and Hudson railroad donated a permanent building, adjacent to the Hotel Champlain, to house the lectures. Estimates place attendance at ten thousand annually, with 75 percent being women. Lectures focused on the sciences and humanities and topics of current interest and, according to one historian, resembled the Protestant Chautauqua Movement of the same period.[130]

Yet another Catholic progressive voice was that of Humphrey Desmond, owner of a chain of Catholic newspapers throughout the Midwest. He challenged the priorities of his Church, calling for cutbacks on expenditures on parochial schools and institutions of "pathological charity," such as hospitals and foundling homes, and more emphasis on preventative charity, such as "half-way houses, temperance societies, young peoples clubs and homes, employment bureaus, and settlement houses." Mary Theresa Elder, sister of Archbishop William Henry Elder of Cincinnati, was of much the same mindset. She could not understand why priests "would risk their lives to administer the last rites to the dying while so little attention was paid to opportunities to 'govern and guide' the living."[131]

American Catholicism's foremost social thinker of the day was Monsignor John A. Ryan, also of the Catholic University of America. A native of Minnesota who was ordained by Archbishop John Ireland in 1898, he was raised by his Irish parents in the populist tradition so prevalent in his state. Early on, he was exposed to the problems faced by farmers, was deeply influenced by Henry George's *Progress and Poverty,* and, after years of study — especially

---

[130] Hennesey, *American Catholics,* 211.
[131] Ibid.

of Leo XIII's *Rerum Novarum* — saw the social reform debate of the
early twentieth century as essentially between individualists of a
libertarian bent and collectivists concerned with economic equality. From this vantage, he concluded that an emphasis on human
welfare based on natural law theory might well be the beginnings of
a solution, or at least a way to bring together conflicting concerns
in some form of commonality.

His doctoral dissertation under Richard T. Ely at Johns Hopkins,
A Living Wage: Its Ethical and Economic Aspects, later published
in book form, had significant influence within and outside the
Church and served as the basis, many thought, for the program of
governmental reform enacted years later by Franklin D. Roosevelt.
Ryan insisted that

> employers had an obligation in justice to pay wages sufficient
> to maintain the worker and his family in decent comfort
> and argued for a minimum wage of $600 per year (the urban
> average in 1906 was $571), the eight-hour day, restrictions
> on child labor and work by women; legalization of picketing,
> compulsory arbitration of labor disputes, accident and old
> age insurance, housing programs, public ownership of mines
> and forests, government control of monopolies, progressive
> income and inheritance taxes, and government regulation
> of stock exchanges. Ryan opposed socialism on philosophical
> grounds, but bluntly declared that "the spirit and traditions of
> the church" were less favorable to the contemporary preten-
> sions of industrial capitalism than was commonly believed.[132]

One final progressive objective the Church concerned Herself
with was the question of women's suffrage, which passed both
Houses of Congress and was ultimately ratified by the states as the

---

[132] Ibid., 213.

Nineteenth Amendment to the Constitution in 1919. It was an issue that Cardinal Gibbons addressed on many occasions—not, in the beginning, very favorably.

> Equal rights, said the Cardinal, did not imply that both sexes should engage promiscuously in the same pursuits, but rather that each sex should discharge those duties which were adapted to its physical constitution and were sanctioned by the canons of society. To debar woman from certain pursuits was not to degrade her. To restrict her field of action to the gentler avocations of life was not to fetter her aspirations after higher things. On the contrary, to secure to woman not so-called equal rights, but those superabundant rights which could not fail to endow her with a sacred influence in her own proper sphere was to enhance her dignity, for as soon as woman trenched on the domain of man she must not be surprised to find that the reverence once accorded to her would be in part withdrawn, and she would be destined to be soiled by the dust of the political arena.[133]

The cardinal was surely a product of his time, though even then the tide was strongly running against this kind of thinking. In fact, when the Nineteenth Amendment was finally ratified, Gibbons gave his unqualified support and reminded Catholic women that it was not only their right but their serious obligation to exercise their constitutional prerogative.

Teddy

During the long course of his episcopacy, Cardinal Gibbons could claim the friendship of several American presidents, including

---

[133] Ellis, *Life of Gibbons*, 2:539–540.

Grover Cleveland and especially Benjamin Harrison. As the years passed, these friendships continued. Shortly after William McKinley was inaugurated in 1897, he indicated that he would be delighted to meet with the cardinal on any day when the latter felt it convenient to call. Gibbons quickly became friends with the president, and one year into his presidency, McKinley sought the cardinal's opinion on whether the United States should retain the Philippine Islands after the Spanish-American War had concluded. The prelate had several other occasions to confer with the chief executive and to participate with him at various civic occasions, particularly in October 1899, when the president presented Admiral George Dewey[134] with a sword awarded to him by Congress; the cardinal gave the benediction at the impressive ceremony.

After McKinley's assassination in 1901, his vice president, Theodore Roosevelt, succeeded to the office. After Roosevelt's 1904 election, his vice president, Charles Fairbanks, also became a friend of the cardinal. The cardinal wrote to congratulate him on being selected for the nation's number-two position, and Fairbanks replied that "no word has come to me which is more gratifying than yours."[135] Later, Mrs. Fairbanks, as president general of the Daughters of the American Revolution, asked the cardinal to give the invocation at the dedication of Continental Hall in Washington.

Very few presidents have had as much Catholic contact, or Catholic friends, before, during, or after their presidencies than Theodore Roosevelt did. What follows is only a sampling. Mr. and Mrs. Bellamy Storer, both devout Catholics, were close friends of Mr. and Mrs. Theodore Roosevelt in Theodore's days as a New York assemblyman. In 1894, Mrs. Storer showed Roosevelt a letter in

---

[134] George Dewey (1837–1917) was best known for his victory at the Battle of Manila Bay during the Spanish-American War.
[135] Ellis, *Life of Gibbons*, 2:509.

which Bishop Keane of the Catholic University of America stated that the secretary of the Democratic National Committee asserted that the Republican Committee was circulating publications of the American Protective Association highly critical of Catholicism. The following day, Roosevelt went to GOP headquarters and was informed there was no truth in the rumor. The same day, T.R.[136] wrote Bishop Keane telling him he was as "opposed to the A.P.A., or to anybody who seeks to attack a man politically because of his creed, or to bring the question of religion into American politics, as any one could be." He felt very strongly "the same indignation at any discrimination political or otherwise against a Catholic because of his religion," that he felt "if a Protestant is discriminated against for similar reasons," and he would pay no heed "to party considerations in denouncing any man or body of men who thus, in a political contest, discriminated against Catholics or Protestants."[137]

One year later, as police commissioner of the City of New York, Roosevelt again wrote to Mrs. Storer when she informed him of anti-Catholic activities from the APA. While she did not think he could provide direct aid to the city of Cincinnati, he nonetheless had opportunity to express his view:

> My own personal appointees in this office, my private Secretary and my Special Roundsman, are both Catholics. I rather think two-thirds of the appointees to this force, since I have been in office, have been of your faith; ... but the gratifying feature of the work ... has been that the question of creed has not entered into it any way. As you know, I am a rather stiff-necked heretic and ultra believer in a non

---

[136] T.R. has traditionally been a form of familiarity to describe President Theodore Roosevelt.

[137] Frederick J. Zwierlein, *Theodore Roosevelt and Catholics: 1882–1919* (Saint Louis: Central Bureau of the Central Verein, 1956), 7–8.

sectarian system of State-aided education. If I thought, on any given issue, any member of the Catholic Church or all its members, no matter how high they were, were wrong, I would attack them just as freely as I attacked those A.P.A. Ministers, but so long as a man does his duty and is a good American citizen, I don't give a rap for his creed.[138]

A very interesting episode in the career of Archbishop John Ireland of Saint Paul was also brought to Roosevelt's attention while he was Governor of New York. The occurrence was once again a letter Mrs. Storer had received from William Howard Taft, a jurist and future president. Many in the Church felt that Ireland should be made a cardinal. Roosevelt replied that it would delight him to do anything he could for Ireland, who represented "that type of Catholicism which in my opinion must prevail in the United States if the Catholic Church is to attain its full measure of power and usefulness with our people and under our form of government."

I may add that the bigoted opponents of Catholicism are those who are most anxious to see the triumph, within the ranks of Catholicism, of this reactionary spirit and the throwing out of men who have shown a broad liberalism and Americanism. Of course I feel that I was not justified in intervening in any way, directly or indirectly, with [a] matter of the Vatican, but it is only fair in response to your letter that I should write you fully and frankly of my great appreciation of Archbishop Ireland and of my firm conviction that the real future of the Catholic Church in America rests with those who in the main work along his lines.[139]

[138] Cited in ibid., 11–12.
[139] Ibid., 25.

Toil and Transcendence

Obviously Roosevelt deemed an intervention on his part to be inappropriate; nonetheless, his thoughts do indicate his strong preference for the Americanizing element in the Catholic hierarchy. Early in 1911, as a former president, he wrote to Maurice Francis Egan, a devout Catholic and U.S. minister to Denmark, about an article he had read in *Outlook* magazine that had pleased Catholics and offended some non-Catholics. It dealt with the work of Father John J. Curran in Wilkes-Barre, especially how he "worked hard to improve the condition of labor by his efforts in behalf of Total Abstinence, his neighborhood centers for boys and girls of all faiths, his insistence on beauty in church architecture." Curran, in T. R.'s mind, had demonstrated "those qualities of the American Catholic Church which made it a great and growing source for social good in the United States."

> As you know, I am not myself an orthodox person although I try to avoid that species of intensively offensive spiritual pride which takes the form of sniggering conceit in being heterodox. I am a great believer in the doctrine of works, and I know that many good men can believe doctrines which in theory are absolutely incompatible and which makes these good men unable to get on together, and yet they can really work together in absolute harmony. For instance, I spent a night with Father Curran at Wilkes Barre coal fields and met some thirty priests in his home at lunch, besides dining with Robert Hoban at Scranton. I really cannot say that I was very much concerned one way or another with their theology.... Their work was what appealed to me in practical fashion, the "zeal," the energy, the sincerity and self- devo- tion ... as the disciples of a church of the "democracy" and any help I could give them I wanted to give. On the other hand, I most strongly condemned any attitude like that of

Archbishop O'Connell of Boston who frowns on the wider freedom in the search for scientific truth and who seeks to deny, whether overtly or covertly, the work of the scientific man to investigate such doctrines as that of evolution.[140]

Roosevelt was also a good friend of Father John A. Zahm, a Holy Cross priest from Notre Dame University who taught science for many years and served as vice president of the school. He became well known for his work in easing tensions between Catholicism and Darwinian biology, and became a popular speaker at Catholic Summer School lectures in upstate New York. Zahm argued, in the 1890s, that Catholicism could fully accept an evolutionary view of biological systems that excluded Darwin's theory of natural selection. He developed these views in a work titled *Evolution and Dogma,* but after the Vatican censured the book in 1898, Zahm fully withdrew from writing on the relation between religion and science. Zahm, whose friendship with Roosevelt first centered on similar literary interests, persuaded the former president to participate in what became known as the Roosevelt-Rondon Scientific Expedition to South America, which included T. R.'s son Kermit. The expedition was little short of disastrous: One man drowned, another was murdered, and Roosevelt himself contracted malaria

---

[140] Ibid., 350–351. The reference to Robert Hoban in all likelihood is a reference to a layman. Scranton's Catholic bishop at the time was Michael J. Hoban, who also knew the former president rather well. It seems unlikely, however, that T. R. would not have indicated the bishop by his proper designation. When Roosevelt died in 1919, his widow personally requested Monsignor Curran to participate in the final obsequies at Oyster Bay, New York. T. R. also wrote to a William R. Thayer, author of an article in *Outlook,* telling him he was delighted with his historical essays, "that the lead of men like Bishop O'Connell in the Church is a real menace to American life." Ibid., 352.

and other infections that, in the opinion of some medical experts, shortened his life by as much as a decade.

Another occasion to deal with Catholics came to Roosevelt from a wealthy pioneer lumberman from Flagstaff, Arizona, named Riordan. He informed T.R. of a generous endowment from another Catholic layman to the YMCA and of the fact that the YMCA did not permit Catholics to hold directorships in its organization. The former president wrote to Cleveland Hoadley Dodge, a member of the international YMCA committee, telling him of his great admiration for the work the organization was carrying out in the country, but also adding:

> It seems to me both unwise and ungenerous to bar Catholics from admission to the directorships on the Y.M.C.A. boards. I did not know that such was the custom, but am now informed that it is. I feel that it is of the utmost importance to this country that our people, who are straight and decent, shall associate together as much as possible without regard to theological differences, and from my own knowledge of the Y.M.C.A.'s, I know that no Catholic is denied any privileges therein accorded to any Protestant, and that no man has any species of religion thrust upon him, but is simply given the opportunity to get it if he wishes. Therefore I cannot see why such a discrimination as that mentioned should be continued. It cannot solve any useful purpose and it does cause irritation. Wherefore a Catholic priest or layman, who is in hearty sympathy, as I know many Catholic priests and laymen are, with the purposes and work of the Y.M.C.A., I believe that they should be admitted to directorships and to every other position of influence just as freely as Protestants.[141]

[141] Ibid., 352.

In June 1911, Roosevelt enthusiastically attended the celebration of the golden jubilee of Cardinal Gibbons's ordination in Baltimore. To a priest friend of his in Brooklyn, he wrote, "The Cardinal is a trump; and I earnestly desire to do him honor."[142]

Later that same year, an editorial appeared in *Outlook* on the appointment of three new cardinals: Diomede Falconio, who up to then had been apostolic delegate to the United States; John Murphy Farley, archbishop of New York; and William H. O'Connell, archbishop of Boston. The *Outlook* editorial described the delegate as "a man of tact and ability," Farley as "an admirable administrator, a man of kindly nature and benignant spirit, but not a leader," and O'Connell as a "representative of the reactionary spirit in the Church, the most prominent American representative of the Spanish influence in the Vatican, an aggressive leader of the narrow school within his own church." If Americans had been sufficiently consulted, the editorial went on to speculate, they would have chosen Archbishop Ireland of Saint Paul, Archbishop Keane of Dubuque, and Bishop Spalding of Peoria. Benedictine Charles Mohr, abbot of Saint Leo's Abbey in Florida and a longtime friend of Roosevelt and his family, thought the former president had written the article. T. R. responded that he had not and, in his response to the abbot, confided thoughts he wished to be kept private. He sincerely wished the Catholic Church well and confessed that there were "few Protestant clergymen with whom I have been able to work as I have been able to work with a number of parish priests, because they seem to me to possess the union of high purpose and of practical power to do good which is essential if we are to get achievement." He expressed great admiration for the abbot as well as for Archbishop Keane and Bishop Spalding, all of whom possessed "the same combination of serene and lofty spirituality,

[142] Ellis, *Life of Gibbons*, 2:548.

the broad-minded charity and sincere desire to do good." At the same time,

> Archbishop O'Connell represents just the opposite that you three men represent. He is intensely worldly; he is very narrow; he is anti-American and anti-democratic; and as to his attitude toward scientific and philosophical investigation among laymen, his position is really that of a medieval reactionary. Now you would be astonished if you knew how many of my Protestant friends and of my friends who are neither orthodox Protestants nor orthodox Catholics, triumphantly bring up Archbishop O'Connell as an illustration of my folly in taking the attitude I do toward the Catholic Church as a whole, toward Catholic clergymen and Catholic laymen.[143]

Years after he had left the presidency, and had been defeated as the Progressive Republican candidate for president in 1912, Roosevelt reflected on the increase of anti-Catholic feeling in the country during Woodrow Wilson's presidency. Looking back on his administration, he reflected:

> In my Cabinet Catholic and Protestant and Jew sat side by side. Some of the men in my administration, in whom I most trusted and on whom I most relied, were Catholics. I would have broken the neck of any one of them if I had found that he was acting toward any American citizen in an un-American manner, having in view that citizen's creed, whether in discriminating for or against him. But I would have stood by him to the last if he himself had been attacked because of his creed or because of his national origin: and this I would have done as regards every man in the Republic

---

[143] Zwierlein, *Theodore Roosevelt and Catholics*, 353–354.

whether he was of English, or Irish, or French or German origin. I have always tried to act so as to feel that I had a right to the support of the right thinking Catholic just as much as of the right thinking Protestant and that in my public deeds and words I represented one just as much as the other.[144]

Roman Adventures

On June 7, 1911, the *Washington Post* reported that "the business of the United States government, superficially at least, was at a standstill for four hours yesterday owing to the exodus of public men to attend the anniversary ceremonies."[145] The reference, of course, was to the golden sacerdotal anniversary of Cardinal James Gibbons. Both President Taft and former president Roosevelt were in attendance, as well current vice president James S. Sherman, speaker of the house Champ Clark, chief justice Edward Douglass White (himself a devout Catholic), secretary of state Elihu Root, ambassador James Bryce of Great Britain, former speaker Joseph P. Cannon, the mayor of Baltimore, and the governor of Maryland. Each man spoke words of tribute to Baltimore's venerable prelate, but perhaps the president, a good friend of the cardinal, summed it up best:

> The President lauded the services which Gibbons had given to the nation by his inculcation of respect for constituted authority, for religious tolerance, and for the wholehearted interest which he had always shown toward the moral and material welfare of all elements of the population. "But what we are especially delighted to see confirmed in him and his life," said Taft, "is the entire consistency which he has

[144] Ibid., 361–362.
[145] Cited in Ellis, *Life of Gibbons*, 2:549.

demonstrated between earnest and single-minded patriotism and love of country on the one hand, and sincere devotion to his church and God on the other." That the Cardinal might long continue to occupy the high position he has always had in the secular movements of the Republic was, said the President in conclusion, "the fervent prayer of Catholic and Protestant, of Jew and Christian."[146]

Summarizing the remarks offered by all the participants that day, the *Washington Post* concluded its coverage by observing that "such a demonstration was never before seen on this hemisphere. Probably the world never witnessed a more generous outburst of enthusiasm for one with whose theological principles many of the participants are at variance."[147]

Such moments of praise are, as in the case of all public figures, only part of the story. One year prior to the cardinal's priestly milestone, his friends former Vice President and Mrs. Fairbanks were visiting Rome. They had been encouraged by Catholic friends to seek an audience with Pope Pius X. On the day prior to the scheduled audience, Fairbanks was committed to a talk before Rome's Methodist Association. There had been growing displeasure at the Vatican over increasing Methodist proselytizing, and news reached the former vice president through the rector of the North American College that the papal audience would have to be canceled if the talk to the Methodists went on. Since it was impossible to cancel the talk, he had to forgo the papal audience, though he did attend a reception and luncheon in his honor at the North American College. Later, he gave Cardinal Gibbons a detailed report of the event:

---

[146] Ibid., 549–550.
[147] *Washington Post*, June 7, 1911, cited in ibid., 552.

I replied that it would be absolutely impossible for me to break my engagement to speak; I had made a rule never to do so; that I had always held myself free to address Catholics and Protestants of all denominations whenever they desired and whenever it was possible; that I had treated all absolutely alike in this regard; that I had traveled many miles and delivered many addresses to Catholic bodies, and that one of the two occasions when I was absent from the Senate I went to Chicago to aid in the dedication of a great Parochial School and I said that some of the best friends I had, amongst whom I mentioned your good self, understood all of this perfectly. I said that while I regretted that the question had arisen the alternative left me no course but to forgo the pleasure of the audience and keep my engagement in the afternoon.[148]

The next day, Archbishop Ireland gave a Chicago newspaper an interview that was carried in the *New York Times* on February 9, 1910, in which he said the Vatican's position was based on the actions of Methodists in the city of Rome, and not on the Methodist Church in general. Cardinal Gibbons, who was in New Orleans when this story became public, quickly contacted his Archbishop friend, to praise his interview. Shortly thereafter, Gibbons sent a copy of Fairbanks's letter to Cardinal Merry del Val, Vatican Secretary of State, assuring him that he, Gibbons, had always been friendly with Fairbanks, and that during his tenure in office, the vice president had always shown courtesy to Catholics and had been extremely helpful to the Church on numerous occasions.

No sooner had the Fairbanks episode closed than a similar occurrence arose, this time involving Theodore Roosevelt himself. T. R.

[148] Cited in ibid., 510.

arrived in Rome the first week of April 1910, after a hunting trip in Africa. Similar to the episode with his vice president, Roosevelt grew angry when the Vatican asked him to cancel a proposed talk to the Methodists in Rome; at the same time, he grew equally angry when he heard of one of the leading members of the Methodist Committee making insulting comments about Pius X. In the end, he left Rome without a papal audience or addressing the Methodists. Soon after the story became public, Cardinal Gibbons visited President Taft in the White House, and, when leaving, commented that "the President and I both regret this incident."[149]

A story began circulating the same day that President Taft had expressed regret over Roosevelt's action in the Eternal City. The president's personal secretary, Frederick W. Carpenter, got in touch with Gibbons immediately and encouraged him, in view of the possible implications a story of this sort might carry, to state simply that the White House visit had been scheduled prior to events in Rome, that the visit had no bearing on the Roosevelt episode, and that Taft had taken no part in it, nor expressed any opinion on it. The fact remained, though, that Gibbons had said what he said on leaving the White House, and, as a final agreed-upon solution, the story went out that the president and the cardinal had both expressed regret that any unpleasantness had occurred—not that either had been upset about Roosevelt's actions in Rome. As for his part, T. R. felt

> I made no mistake. I acted precisely and exactly as I ought to have acted, and as I would act again. Any American, whatever his creed, who does not believe that I acted well, is lacking in the elementary knowledge of what good American citizenship means. To talk of my having insulted Catholics

[149] Cited in ibid., 513.

by what I did in Rome, is utter nonsense as it would be to talk of my having insulted the Methodists by what I did in Rome.[150]

Chilly Wilson

Cardinal Gibbons's relations with Presidents Roosevelt and Taft were close and very friendly. This was never the case, however, with Taft's successor, Woodrow Wilson. Born in Staunton, Virginia, the son of a Presbyterian minister, Wilson rose to become president of Princeton University,[151] then governor of New Jersey. His eight years in the White House produced significant progressive legislation, which was the Democrat Party's response to the Republican progressivism of the previous two administrations. His administration is also synonymous with American involvement in the First World War. In both domestic matters and foreign affairs, Wilson's Calvinistic background manifested itself. It has become apparent to most historians that the twenty-sixth president harbored deeply

---

[150] Zwierlein, *Theodore Roosevelt and Catholics*, 356. After the event, Robert J. Collier, editor of *Collier's Weekly* and a Catholic and a staunch Republican, wrote to Cardinal Gibbons suggesting that the latter should use his good offices to restore any lost harmony between the former president and Catholics. Gibbons should give a private dinner, he proposed, to which he would invite T. R. and some other prominent men. The cardinal replied to Collier that he and Roosevelt shared a close friendship, one which he cherished greatly. Also, Catholics felt a deep sense of gratitude for the former chief executive for his staunch support of the Church and his many favors to Catholics, personally and collectively. However, he was not certain that his presence at such a dinner would be correctly interpreted in all circles and must politely decline the proposal. Ellis, *Life of Gibbons*, 2:513–514.

[151] Wilson was the first president of Princeton not to be an ordained Presbyterian minister.

anti-Catholic views; stories began circulating early on, particularly regarding Cardinal Gibbons's first visit to the new president.

It was said that at their first meeting, Wilson had neglected to give the cardinal his proper title, referring to him merely as "Mr. Gibbons," and also that Wilson never invited the cardinal to be seated, but kept him standing throughout the visit. The first response to this episode came some years later from Monsignor William T. Russell, pastor of St. Patrick's Church in Washington, and the cardinal's representative in the capital.

> We called at the White House because the Cardinal desired to pay his respects to the President. I was present at the whole interview. I can say if the President addressed the Cardinal as Mr., I did not hear him; and furthermore, I am convinced that he did not do so, as I was not more than two feet from the President during the whole interview, and I heard all the conversation that took place. I do not believe the President would consciously do anything that might be considered as a lack of courtesy or consideration for any Catholic priest or prelate.[152]

In the fall of 1916, Wilson sent the cardinal an autographed photo of himself, to which the cardinal responded with his thanks,

---

[152] Cited in Ellis, *Life of Gibbons*, 2:516. Ellis also includes a footnote citing a letter from Father Eugene J. Connelly, the cardinal's secretary, to a woman who was seeking to use Gibbons's influence to have her husband appointed to a federal office. Connelly quoted Gibbons as saying that the cordial relations that had existed with the former five occupants of the White House no longer prevailed, nor had there been any indication it would. Connelly went on to say that the cardinal and the president were "at variance over the great national questions, which has not helped any in making for friendlier feelings." Connelly to Mrs. John J. Boylan, Baltimore, February 17, 1916, cited in ibid., 516.

while wishing the president all happiness in his future life with Mrs. Edith Bolling Galt, to whom he had recently become engaged. For his part, Wilson replied: "May I not express to your Eminence my very deep and sincere appreciation of your generous message of October 9th? It gave me the deepest pleasure and gratification."[153]

When Wilson was running for reelection in 1916, the story of disrespect to Gibbons surfaced again. Members of the Democratic National Committee contacted Wilson's personal secretary, Joseph P. Tumulty, an Irish Catholic and former mayor of Jersey City. They were looking for material that might refute the charges, and Tumulty sent a copy of Monsignor Russell's statement, a statement from Gibbons, and the dates of the cardinal's calls at the White House in 1913. This contented some, but others within Wilson's party remained unconvinced. Redmond F. Kernan, a prominent Catholic Democrat, went to Baltimore to see the cardinal, and he received a further denial from Gibbons that Wilson had ever displayed any discourtesy toward him.

Kernan went on to New York City, where he spoke with Frank I. Cobb, editor of the *New York World*, who told him he had spoken to Wilson about the alleged incident, and the latter had called it preposterous.

> Wilson was quoted as saying that at the interview he had not offered the Cardinal a chair since diplomatic usage decreed that an ambassador be received by the President standing to imply their equality, and Wilson had treated Gibbons as one having that rank.[154]

Shortly after, a reporter from the *New York World* called on the cardinal in Baltimore to inform him of growing opposition to

[153] Cited in ibid., 517.
[154] Ibid., 518.

Wilson's reelection from Catholics, especially in Indiana. Gibbons replied that he was not aware of this, was not himself in politics, never authorized anyone to quote him as favoring one presidential candidate over the other, and reiterated the position that "every Catholic voter has an inherent right to vote according to his own individual conscience, and that I am sure that the Roman Catholic hierarchy of the United States would never interfere with that right."[155]

The Great War

Woodrow Wilson's administration is largely remembered for American involvement in what Wilson called, quite erroneously, the war to end all wars. The First World War began with the assassination of Archduke Franz Ferdinand of Austria-Hungary in 1914 and lasted until 1918. During these years, the Central Powers of Germany, Austria-Hungary, Bulgaria, and the Ottoman Empire fought against the Allied Powers of Great Britain, France, Russia, Italy, Romania, Japan, and the United States.

Europe had experienced regional conflict for years, especially the Balkan region of Southeast Europe. Several alliances involving European powers, the Ottoman Empire, and Russia had been tried, but political instability in the Balkans threatened to destroy these agreements.[156] The spark igniting the international conflict was the archduke's murder in Bosnia by a Serbian nationalist whose goal was to end the Austro-Hungarian dominance over his

---

[155] Ibid. Decades later, Monsignor Ellis, in an interview with Monsignor Louis R. Stickney, was told that he, Stickney, often accompanied Gibbons to the polls, "but in all the years he lived with him he could not recall a suggestion of any kind from the Cardinal which might have indicated his party affiliation." Ibid., 523.

[156] In particular, the Balkan regions of Bosnia, Serbia, and Herzegovina.

ethnic homeland. Russia had supported Bosnia, and as soon as the German kaiser Wilhelm II told Austria-Hungary his government would support them, the monarchy sent Serbia an ultimatum with terms so harsh as to be almost impossible to accept. The Serbian government, sure that Austria-Hungary meant war, ordered their army to mobilize and asked Russia for assistance.

Within days, Russia, Belgium, France, Great Britain, and Serbia had lined up against Austria-Hungary and Germany, and the First World War had begun. In the course of the European conflict, internal events in Russia, led by poverty-stricken workers and peasants, led to the overthrow of Czar Nicholas II. Led by Vladimir Lenin and the Bolsheviks, the Communist Revolution brought Russian participation to a halt. Russia reached a peace agreement with the Central Powers in December 1917, forcing German troops to face the remaining allies.

Up to this time, the United States had remained neutral, with its chief executive rather unrealistically urging his countrymen to remain neutral in both thought and speech. By 1915, Germany had declared the waters surrounding the British Isles to be a war zone, and German U-boats sunk several commercial and passenger vessels, including some American ships. Tremendous protest against the sinking of the British ocean liner *Lusitania*, traveling from New York to Liverpool with hundreds of American passengers on board, significantly turned the tide of American public opinion against Germany. After four more U.S. merchant ships were sunk, Wilson asked Congress for a declaration of war. The war's remainder, told so often in textbooks and in hundreds of specialized studies, was the story of the unmaking of Germany and her eventual capitulation.

The Paris Peace Conference at Versailles in 1919 was the war's official ending, as the Allied Powers stated their desire to build a postwar world that would be safeguarded against future international conflicts. What was different about this conference, though, was the American president's announcement that he would personally lead the American peace delegation and put forth his own plan for postwar reconstruction. Germany felt forced and tricked into signing a humiliating treaty. The Treaty of Versailles was signed on June 28, 1919, and would never achieve the lofty goals Wilson had laid out. As the years passed, German hatred of the treaty continued to smolder, resentment that twenty years later would be counted, in the minds of most historical observers, as one of the causes of the Second World War.

The reign of Pope Benedict XV coincided with the war years, and the Holy Father, for a variety of reasons, was eager to play an active role in the peace process. He had a specific proposal for the restoration of peace on the continent that closely resembled Wilson's famous Fourteen Points.[157] The official American response, influenced by Wilson's drive to crush German militarism, expressed a desire for a just peace but was quite clear that the German government could not be trusted.

> By the Spring of 1917, Wilson had already emerged as the dominant figure on the Allied side, and therefore as the future leader of the world, and this was confirmed by his reply to the papal Peace Note of August [1917]. As such he would brook no rivals. This Calvinist idealist who was convinced of his own moral and intellectual superiority, was also notoriously anti-Catholic (though not at election time), and tended to see all Europeans as parochial and

---

[157] The particulars of Pope Benedict's plan included: renunciation of indemnities; disarmament; the substitution of arbitration for war; the evacuation of Belgium and a guarantee of its complete independence; the evacuation of occupied territories; freedom of the seas; and the examination of territorial claims in a spirit of equity and justice. Richard B. Morris, *Encyclopedia of American History* (New York: Harper & Row, 1965), 311.

unenlightened, including Benedict.... Wilson's "Peace without Victory" speech of January 1922 swept Benedict and his peace efforts aside. The only "victory" which the Pope could claim over the President was a moral one: the famous "Fourteen Points" speech made by Wilson in January 1918 was so close in content and formulation to Benedict's note that the only conclusion to be drawn is that it was heavily inspired by it.[158]

If Wilson was not eager to have Benedict's participation in the peace process, he was equally uninterested in Vatican participation in the League of Nations, Wilson's signature postwar proposal for international order. There is no evidence to suggest that the Vatican was ever asked to join the League, even after the establishment of the independent sovereign State of Vatican City in 1929. If European attitude is anything to go by,

> Britain and France would have opposed its admission [as early as] 1920. The USA would surely not have supported the idea either: a certain Senator Sherman made a speech claiming that "twenty-four of the forty Christian nations are spiritually dominated by the Vatican, thus the Pope wishes to rule the world through the League": the speech was dismissed by other senators, but President Wilson would have been too wary of the strong Protestant lobby in the United States to have ever countenanced Vatican involvement in the League.[159]

---

[158] John F. Pollard, *The Unknown Pope: Benedict XV (1914–1922) and the Pursuit of Peace* (London: Geoffrey Chapman, 1999), 127–128.

[159] Ibid., 146. The senator referred to was Lawrence Yates Sherman (1858–1939), Republican Senator from Illinois, known as one of the "irreconcilables" who opposed both the Treaty of Versailles and the League of Nations. From the tone of his rhetoric, and the

Toil and Transcendence

Cardinal Gibbons was well aware of the pope's peace initiatives and strongly supported them, but knew very well the sort of reception they would receive in Washington. When criticism of Benedict began to surface, Gibbons penned a defense, *The War Policy of the Pope*. The cardinal made no attempt to persuade the president about the pope's plan — all the more prudent, in the mind of one historian, in light of French Ambassador Jules Jusserand's comment to Gibbons about Wilson's "ill humor at Benedict's wanting to 'butt in' (his own words)."[160] The observation is, then, quite correct that "while Woodrow Wilson sat in the White House, American Catholic forays into international diplomacy largely ended in blind alleys."[161]

Although the friendship between the White House and the cardinal's residence on Charles Street in Baltimore was not nearly as friendly as in the days of the Republican administrations, Gibbons did support the Treaty of Versailles and the League, as he had strongly backed the Preparedness Movement prior to American entry into the global conflict. In the fall of 1917, he had accepted the chairmanship of the League of National Unity, a patriotic movement appealing to Americans across the board to unite fully behind the war effort and to support the war to its conclusion. Gibbons's support for Wilson's postwar world, according to Tumulty, the president's private secretary, were not shared by Boston's Cardinal William O'Connell nor New York's Archbishop Patrick Hayes.

One of the great accomplishments in the American Church in these years was the establishment of the National Catholic War Council, which ultimately developed into the National Council

---

dismissal of his speech by other senators, one could easily discern his anti-Catholicism.

[160] Hennesey, *American Catholics*, 227.

[161] Ibid., 228.

of Catholic Bishops (NCCB). Prior to 1917, the Church had no national organization other than the annual meeting of the nation's bishops, and leading figures thought that the efforts of Catholic agencies should be more effectively coordinated. Cardinals Gibbons, O'Connell, and Farley gave their approval, and the first gathering, in August 1917, included delegates from sixty-eight dioceses and twenty-seven Catholic societies. Paulist Father John J. Gillis, editor of the *Catholic World,* was elected first president; he was to be assisted by an executive council made up of representatives from all over the country, as well as the Knights of Columbus. Its formation was considered "a major organizational step for the Catholic Church in the United States." For the first time in its history, an institutional commitment was being made to social and political action.[162]

The Irish Question

During these years, an event of great interest to many Catholics in the United States, especially those of Irish ancestry, was the Easter Rising of 1916, which led ultimately to the independence of Ireland. The rebellion was launched by Irish republicans to end British rule on the island and to establish an independent Irish state. Sixteen of the rising's leaders were executed in May 1916, but the brutal

---

[162] Ibid., 227. The Knights of Columbus was founded by Father Michael J. McGivney in New Haven, Connecticut, in 1882 and has become the world's largest Catholic fraternal service organization. It originally served as a mutual benefit society for working-class and immigrant Catholics, and it developed into a fraternal benefit society dedicated to providing charitable services, including war and disaster relief, promoting Catholic education, defending Catholicism in various ways, and supporting and defending Church positions in the public arena.

nature of these executions and subsequent political developments only accelerated the cause of independence.

The Irish Volunteers were led by schoolmaster Padraic Pearse, and were joined by the smaller Irish Citizen Army of James Connolly. The British Army brought in thousands of reinforcements, fierce fighting ensued in the streets of Dublin, and the uprising was eventually suppressed. Pearse agreed to an unconditional surrender, and the country remained under martial law. More than four hundred persons were killed in the Easter Rising: 54 percent were civilians, 30 percent were British military and police, and 16 percent were Irish rebels. A couple of years later, the Anglo-Irish War, or the Irish War of Independence, commenced, leading to a December 1918 election in which the republican party, Sinn Féin, won a landslide victory and formed a breakaway government. A yet more bloody conflict ensued, often called the Black and Tan War, named for recruits from Britain who had been brought in to aid the Royal Irish Constabulary. The war ended in July 1921 with a truce; from the British perspective, it appeared as if the Irish Republican Army's military campaign would last indefinitely, with spiraling costs in British manpower and resources.

The British government was facing criticism at home and abroad for the intensity and cruelty of their operations in Ireland. What finally became known as the Anglo-Irish Treaty was ratified in January 1922, allowing Northern Ireland to opt out of the Irish Republic: Six of Ulster's nine counties would remain under direct British rule, and the remaining twenty-six counties of the island became the independent Republic of Ireland.

These events had direct repercussions in the United States, where so many thousands of Irish had migrated, culminating during Woodrow Wilson's second presidential campaign in 1916. The first episode involved a message Wilson received from the president of the American Truth Society, Jeremiah O'Leary, a New York City lawyer. The society had been incorporated to circulate what it believed to be truthful accounts of international events. It largely comprised Irish and Germans, and both groups harbored serious concerns about Wilson's foreign policy: The former objected to his unwillingness to aid the cause of Irish independence, and the latter suspected that the president desired to enter the war against the Central Powers. O'Leary sent the president a lengthy communique sharply critical of him on these issues. Charles Evans Hughes was Wilson's Republican opponent, and he had received significant support from German Americans. Hughes was therefore in a difficult position: On the one hand, he advocated "straight Americanism," and on the other, he conferred with the most extreme pro-German spokesmen in the country, promising them that, if elected, he would take strong action against the British. When Wilson received O'Leary's message, he quickly responded:

> I would feel deeply mortified to have you or anybody like you vote for me. Since you have access to many disloyal Americans and I have not, I will ask you to convey this message to them.[163]

If the story is true that Charles Evans Hughes went to bed on election night confident he had won the presidency, it is equally true that Wilson went to bed feeling he could soon turn affairs of state over to someone else and be free to devote himself to other concerns. Neither proved to be true. Traditional Democratic support went, as expected, to the incumbent, while the German vote was more divided. As for the Irish:

> A part of the Catholic hierarchy and many priests and Catholic journals entered the campaign against Wilson.... The

---

[163] Cited in Arthur S. Link, *Woodrow Wilson and the Progressive Era: 1910–1917* (New York: Harper & Row, 1963), 247.

opposition of the Catholic Church had its most profound impact upon the Irish-Americans, who were really angry because Wilson had refused to intervene on behalf of the Irish during the Rebellion of the preceding April and May. They left the Democratic party in droves, and Wilson did not carry a single state in which they were an important factor.[164]

The story of Wilson's Irish trouble really begins with his initial run for the presidency in 1912. Across the Hudson from his home state of New Jersey, Tammany Hall was strongly opposed to his nomination. Among its leaders was Judge Daniel F. Cohalan, a New York State Supreme Court judge active in the Clan na Gael and other Irish organizations.[165] He was a close friend of John Devoy, an Irish revolutionary leader and newspaper editor. Cohalan was involved with financing and planning the Easter Rising in Dublin, and for years Wilson remained convinced that Cohalan had plotted with the German government to start a rebellion in Ireland while England was too preoccupied on the continent to respond adequately. Wilson was a committed Anglophile, and it was well known that Irishmen who dreamed of the day their country would be free of British domination were anathema to the would-be president. Wilson never forgot their move to block his nomination at Baltimore's Democratic Convention in 1912, unsuccessful though it was. Four years later, the mood of Irish-Americans was even more hostile to the administration, and John Devoy, in his paper, the *Gaelic American*, did not mince his words:

That President Wilson hates the Irish with the implacable hatred of the Ulster Orangeman — the stock he comes

[164] Ibid., 251.

[165] The Clan na Gael, or Clan For Ireland, was an Irish republican organization in the United States in the late-nineteenth and twentieth centuries. It still exists, though on a smaller scale.

of—has been shown so many times since he became President that there can be no successful denial.... Mr. Wilson's mean and despicable attack on the Irish at the unveiling of the Barry monument in Washington on May 16, 1914, was deliberate and premeditated. And it was as cowardly as it was mean and untruthful, for he was protected by the character of the occasion from the possibility of reply or rebuke.... Since then Mr. Wilson has never missed an opportunity of repeating his false accusations of disloyalty against a race that proved its loyalty on the bloody battlefields of the Civil War fighting for the Union, while his relatives were fighting to destroy it and his father was desecrating a Christian pulpit by ranting in favor of human slavery.[166]

By the summer of 1918, following the Easter Rebellion, the British had instituted strong repressive measures in Ireland. When word of their severity reached Washington, California Senator James D. Phelan requested that Wilson make some brief statement

[166] Cited in Charles Callan Tansill, *America and the Fight for Irish Freedom: 1866–1922* (New York: Devin-Adair, 1957), 213. The Wilson speech Devoy refers to is one in which the president was sharply critical of hyphenated Americans. When one became truly American, he said, the hyphen would drop of its own accord. Barry, said Wilson, was not an Irish-American, but an Irishman who became an American. Those who need hyphens need them because only part of them has come over. Sincere affection for our countries of origin are valid, but America must live her separate and independent life. *Address of President Wilson at the Unveiling of the Statue to the Memory of Commodore John Barry at Washington, D.C., Saturday, May 16, 1914* (Washington: Government Printing Office, 1914), 3–5. Commodore John Barry, a native of County Wexford, because of his numerous naval successes, has been referred to as the Father of the American Navy. During the Eisenhower administration, a statue of the commodore was placed in Wexford Harbor by the U.S. government.

supporting Ireland's right to autonomous government. The president's reply was not uncharacteristic:

> I realize, of course, the critical importance of the whole Irish question, but I do not think that it would be wise for me in any public utterance to attempt to outline a policy for the British Government with regard to Ireland. It is a matter ... of the utmost delicacy, and I must frankly say that I would not know how to handle it without risking very uncomfortable confusions of counsel.[167]

In May 1918, Wilson received a letter from a young girl named Marguerite Maginnis, who addressed him as "the greatest man in the world today." She told him how much his speeches thrilled her—but added the request, "Please, won't you do something for my people, the Irish?" She told the president that the newspapers say that to be anti-British is to be un-American, and therefore pro-German, adding, "You are bigger than the newspapers, so I write to you." She did not believe there was a German plot to support Irish rebels, reminded Wilson that events in Ireland in 1916 preceded America's entry into the war, and stated her belief that "my America demands an open and hasty trial for the Sinn Fein prisoners." She firmly believed that the president could do something and that England would not dare refuse any request he made of them. As soon as Wilson read the letter, he felt it would be dangerous for him to answer personally, and he referred it to his Irish Catholic secretary, Joseph P. Tumulty. The Irish would believe Tumulty to be more interested in his position with respect to Wilson than in helping the land of his ancestors when his reply to the president eventually became public:

[167] Tansill, *America and the Fight for Irish Freedom*, 268.

At the Sinn Fein meeting held in New York this week at which speeches of the most seditious character were made, one of the orators of the evening was a man named Maginnis. I would not be surprised if this girl were in some way related to this individual. I suspect that the hand of some able Sinn Feiner is back of this letter and that an attempt is being made to draw you out. I do not think you ought to recognize it in any way or that you should personally acknowledge it and to say that it will be brought to your attention at the earliest possible moment.[168]

So the story came to a close, with Wilson not lifting a hand for those who, in the majority, he considered hyphenated Americans.

Another episode in Wilson's fraught relationship with the Irish question came about in 1919, when Irish republican statesman Éamon de Valera arrived in the United States. He had recently escaped from an English jail in a somewhat sensational way: After a duplicate key was smuggled into the jail in a cake, he exited dressed as a woman. His plan in America was to secure recognition for the emerging Irish nation, tap into the huge Irish American community for funds, and try to pressure Washington to take a position on Irish independence. Judge Cohalan attempted to secure the privilege for de Valera of addressing Congress, and Idaho's Senator William Borah, a strong opponent of the Treaty of Versailles and the League of Nations, and a leading isolationist, was very much in favor of letting the Irish leader speak. De Valera, however, did not want to proceed without the support of the Democrats in the Senate:

Judge Cohalan, knowing the loyalty of most Democrats in the Senate to President Wilson and realizing that the President himself would be strongly opposed to the appearance

[168] Ibid., 272–273.

of De Valera before either branch of Congress, expressed the opinion that Borah alone should handle the matter. De Valera was adamant in his refusal to work through Borah, so Cohalan, De Valera and Harry Boland, one of De Valera's aids who had recently arrived in America, had a conference with both Borah and Senator Phelan. Phelan said he would have to discuss everything with his Democratic colleagues in the Senate, with the result that a prompt negative was soon announced. It was difficult for De Valera to realize that Democrats in the Senate like Phelan and Thomas J. Walsh were not disposed to advance the cause of Ireland in the face of strong Presidential opposition.[169]

So rested the Irish and Catholic questions in the Wilson administration. After two decades of progressivism, international conflict, and what many considered unnecessary concern for affairs in the rest of the world, an inward-looking return to normalcy sounded very appealing to many Americans. It would be these sentiments that would propel U.S. Senator Warren Harding from Ohio to the presidency in 1920. It would be a very different sort of administration in Washington, and the decade of the twenties would present an entirely new perspective to Americans. And it would also be a decade in which the Church would face a new set of challenges.

---

[169] Ibid., 344. James D. Phelan was a U.S. Senator from California, Thomas J. Walsh from Montana.

3

∞

The Church of the Twenties

Themes of the Twenties

The era following America's involvement in the First World War was unique in many ways. For the Church, it was a period of substantial growth and unusually strong leaders; for the nation, it was one of substantial growth and largely forgettable leaders. After the war, it seemed that the nation was looking for a cause to throw itself into; the unity that coalesced around the defeat of the Axis Powers needed a new direction, and a more domestic focus provided the answer to this need.

The Russian Revolution of 1917 had unleashed on the world a new political enterprise that was to last until the later decades of the twentieth century. The growing fear in the American people of what this might mean for the United States became focused on the radical fringes in the labor movement. Given events of previous decades, it was easy to see why leftists felt that the best means to circulate the propaganda of the new communist philosophy was within organizations that had been home to radical thinking for years. And so, fairly or not, the unionism and strikes of previous years quickly became associated with the new threat of communist world revolution. The Industrial Workers of the World (IWW), influential in western mining unions, had long advanced the theory of violence and the abolition of the wage system; though they had made little impression in most industries, it appeared to be guilt by association in many American minds.

This was compounded by the fact that so many workers who affiliated with labor unions were immigrants, few of them American citizens. The wartime fear of alien saboteurs became a fear of foreign radicals controlling the labor movement. Many historians have felt that wartime patriotism gave way to the overwhelming Americanism of the twenties. A very real Red Scare had emerged in the United States, and the administration of President Wilson, still in office as the decade opened, knew a response had to be made. It came in the form of the Palmer Raids, named for A. Mitchell Palmer, Wilson's attorney general. Palmer had been a typical progressive: a strong supporter of the League of Nations and of several domestic reforms. For a long time, Palmer tried to resist the prevailing mood, insisting that in the United States the oppressed of any and every foreign regime would find a true refuge. As time moved on, however, Palmer felt his position more and more idealistic and untenable. As a result, he established a General Intelligence Division in the Department of Justice, headed by a young man just coming into his own, J. Edgar Hoover. As a result of the Palmer Raids

> about 6,000 persons were taken into custody, many of them citizens and not subject to the deportation laws, many others totally unconnected with any radical cause. Some were held incommunicado for weeks while the authorities made futile efforts to find evidence against them. In a number of cases, individuals who came to visit prisoners were themselves thrown behind bars, on the theory that they, too, must be Communists.... Out of 6,000 seized in the Palmer Raids, only 556 proved liable to deportation. The widespread ransacking of communists' homes and meeting places

produced mountains of inflammatory literature, but only three pistols.[170]

The raids were unsuccessful in the aggregate, and xenophobia did not quickly cease in the American mind. A widespread prejudice, especially against Eastern and Southern Europeans resulted, in 1920, in the establishment of a quota system limiting annual immigration to 3 percent of the number of foreign-born residents from each nation in 1910. Under this system, approximately 350,000 could come in annually, but since each country's quota was based on the number of its immigrants in 1910, the newer additions from southern and eastern Europe would be severely limited, since a decade prior most foreign-born Americans were from Northern and Western Europe.

Religious fundamentalism was another issue as America entered the new decade. Baptists and Presbyterians had especially strong fundamentalist factions who asserted the complete, *literal* truth of the Bible. In the 1920s, the theory of evolution provided the most significant challenge to date to this tradition of interpretation among Protestants, and many fundamentalists strongly campaigned for laws outlawing any mention of Charles Darwin's theory in textbooks or public school classrooms. The leading proponent of the cause was Nebraska's William Jennings Bryan, a former member of Woodrow Wilson's cabinet, who, upon leaving government service, devoted much of his time to religious and moral causes. Bryan traveled the country, lecturing against the evolutionary theory, in some speeches offering any member of the audience $100 if they could prove they were descended from an ape. Such rhetoric won a victory in 1925 when the Tennessee State Legislature passed a law forbidding instructors in state schools

---

[170] Garraty, *The American Nation*, 2:285.

and colleges to teach any theory contradicting the narrative of divine Creation in the Bible.

The American Civil Liberties Union immediately went on the offense, offering to finance a test case if some teacher was willing to defy state law and teach evolutionary theory. John Scopes, a biology teacher in Dayton, Tennessee, took them up on their offer and was arrested. The judge read the state law completely during the trial, along with the opening chapters of the book of Genesis, in which Creation is elucidated. This was followed by the testimony of several high school students from Scopes's class that he had indeed advanced the theory of evolution. No sooner was the teacher indicted by the grand jury than a number of nationally known lawyers came forward to defend him, while William Jennings Bryan gladly advanced the state's case. This quickly became famous as the "Monkey Trial."

The judge in the trial, John Raulston, was very strongly prejudiced against the defendant and forbade any testimony on the validity of evolutionary theory. Scopes's conviction was a foregone conclusion—the point wasn't to win in Dayton but to appeal to higher courts—but a major highlight of the trial was when Bryan agreed to testify as an expert witness on the Bible. He was cross-examined by Clarence Darrow, one of the country's best-known trial lawyers,[171] who "mercilessly expos[ed] his childlike faith and his abysmal ignorance."[172] For his part, Judge Raulston

---

[171] Clarence Darrow (1857–1938) was a leading member of the American Civil Liberties Union and defended many high-profile clients before Scopes. An agnostic, he seriously questioned the doctrines of Christianity. He disputed the saying that the fear of God is the beginning of wisdom; rather, he felt that such fear is the death of wisdom, whereas skepticism and doubt lead to study and investigation.

[172] Garraty, *The American Nation*, 2:288.

was defeated in his bid for reelection, Scopes quickly moved from Dayton, and William Jennings Bryan died in his sleep just a few days later.

The Eighteenth Amendment to the United States Constitution—that is, Prohibition—also occupied the minds of Americans in the twenties. What was specifically prohibited was the manufacture, transporting, and sale of intoxicating beverages. It was another limited victory for WASP America that set off a division between the rural and urban cultures of the United States that would last until the amendment's repeal in 1933. Even with the application of the Volstead Act, the amendment's enforcement statute, alcohol was easily attainable through smuggling, speakeasies, and so on. Enforcement was never more than sporadic; and, since alcohol was almost always associated in the American mind with foreigners, usually Catholics, Protestant America was only too happy to adopt the language of a moral crusade. This would become an issue of some significance, as we will see, in the presidential election of 1928, when a national party for the first time nominated a Catholic for the White House.

Turbulent Times

Around the Western world, though especially in Europe, the era after the traumatic Great War was intellectually turbulent. The United States experienced what has been called the "revolt of the intellectuals"—which included a number of fallen-away Catholics. Authors and literary types such as F. Scott Fitzgerald, Ernest Hemingway, Theodore Dreiser, James T. Farrell, and Eugene O'Neill, baptized Catholics all, fell prey to the times and apostasized. Much as they may have attempted to leave their faith tradition behind, Catholic allusions are to be found with regularity in their writings.

Toil and Transcendence

Fitzgerald rose to fame in 1920 with his first book, *This Side of Paradise*. He tried to describe the mores and attitudes of contemporary youth, whom he described as the lost generation. The gaiety of the age, at least as far as the young were concerned, concealed fear and confusion. Some years later, when he wrote *The Great Gatsby*, he continued his commentary on the confusion of the times, the immorality of the youth, and their relentless pursuit of sex and money. He was, in some ways, describing himself; he squandered the fortune he accumulated from his books and became a serious alcoholic.[173]

Ernest Hemingway was born in Illinois in 1898 and worked as a reporter for the *Kansas City Star*. His service in the Abraham Lincoln Brigade in the Spanish Civil War has been well documented, but he also served in the Italian army during World War I. He completed his first novel, *The Sun Also Rises*, some years before his Spanish military service. In this book, he portrayed the lot of expatriots, the meaninglessness of life, amorality, and the desperation of rootlessness. This was followed seven years later (1929) by *A Farewell to Arms*, which drew upon his military experience to describe the confusion and horror of war. Hemingway's books became national best sellers in his lifetime, mostly for their unique style rather than for any intellectual novelty.

H. L. Mencken and Sinclair Lewis both represented a distaste for the climate of their times. Mencken, Baltimore born, served many years as a reporter before founding the *American Mercury*, one of the great magazines of the era, in which he had free rein to express his boundless cynicism. Lewis, probably the most popular novelist of the twenties, became an overnight success with his book *Main Street*, published in 1920. In it, he portrayed the "smug

---

[173] In the end, Fitzgerald was buried in Saint Mary's Cemetery, Rockville, Maryland.

ignorance and bigotry of the American small town" so accurately that even Lewis's victims recognized themselves. His next book, two years later, *Babbitt*, was an image of the businessman of the twenties, a "hustler, a booster, blindly orthodox in his political and social opinions, slave to every cliché, gregarious, full of loud self-confidence, yet underneath a bumbling, rather timid, decent fellow who would like to be better than he was but dared not." From here, Lewis dissected a number of American attitudes, with his most critical indictment of religion being found in his 1927 work, *Elmer Gantry*.[174]

"Normalcy"

Politically, America was ready for a return to normalcy, a phrase coined to describe the 1920 political campaign of Warren G. Harding. The Republican Senator from Ohio campaigned against his own state's governor, Democrat James M. Cox. The country was increasingly isolationist, fatigued of Wilson's idealism, suspicious of the League of Nations, and intent on developing national prosperity and true Americanism. In short, the times were ripe for a Republican victory.

Harding chose as his running mate Calvin Coolidge, a native of Vermont who had worked his way up the ladder of Massachusetts politics to become governor and had come to national attention during the Boston Police Strike of 1919, with his statement that there is no right to strike against the public safety by anyone, anywhere, at any time. The ticket won easily, though Harding was to serve as president only until August 1923, when he died suddenly in the Palace Hotel in San Francisco.

[174] Garraty, *The American Nation*, 2:295.

Toil and Transcendence

His administration has been associated generally with dysfunction and malfeasance, especially in the Teapot Dome Scandal. During William Howard Taft's presidency, the federal government had purchased three valuable oil deposits — two in California, at Elk Hill and at Buena Vista, and the third at Teapot Dome, Wyoming. These three reserves were controlled by the federal government for national emergencies, to provide for available fuel in wartime. In June 1920, it was decided that the secretary of the Navy should hold these reserves specifcially for the future use of the U.S. Navy. When Harding's administration came in, Albert B. Fall, secretary of the interior, requested that the president transfer these reserves to the Department of the Interior. A large protest came from the Navy, claiming the Interior Department had no such right, but, in the end, the president approved the transfer.

In 1921, Fall had many debts, and he had not paid taxes on his ranch in New Mexico for nine years. In April 1922, he leased the Teapot Dome reserve to Harry Sinclair, president of Sinclair Refining Company. The lease was so secret that Fall denied it had ever occurred, and his denial was published. Very quickly, Sinclair stock rose tremendously, and the primary stock holder was Harry Daugherty, the administration's attorney general. The lease was brought to the United States Senate, and Secretary Fall was called in to testify. Meanwhile, Sinclair stock had increased by $50 million, and those who were in on it made a fabulous fortune.

Then, in November 1921, Edward Doheny, president of Pan American Petroleum Company, wrote to Secretary Fall to inquire about leasing the first oil reserve in Elk Hill, California. Fall was hesitant about a second transfer and told Doheny that before it could be done, he would need a small contribution. Doheny's son gave the secretary $100,000, and Fall gave him a promissory note. This transaction was never recorded in Pan American's books, and when the Senate heard what had happened, Fall's signature was quickly torn off the note; only Doheny's word prevailed.[175] Many oil companies in the United States began protesting to Harding. The chief geologist of the United States was queried as to whether these reserves had been tapped, and he replied they had. In January 1923, Fall resigned as secretary of the interior, and Harding offered him an associate judgeship on the Supreme Court.

In June 1923, Harding and his family left for Alaska. He looked tired and drawn, and he knew that within a short time fantastic disclosures would be made public that would embarrass him and the Republican Party. His sudden death raised many questions: His wife would not permit an autopsy, and his doctor was dead within a year. Immediately, Coolidge assumed the presidency, his father administering the oath of office to him in the same cabin in Plymouth, Vermont, in which he had been born. Coolidge was to preside over an era of tremendous prosperity. While his and his predecessor's ideologies were similar, their personalities were not:

> Harding was genial and friendly; Coolidge was aloof and austere. Harding could understand and tolerate the low ethical standards of the ordinary politician; Coolidge made a fetish

---

[175] Edward Doheny (1856–1935) was born to Irish immigrant parents from County Tipperary, in Fond du Lac, Wisconsin. Though implicated in the Teapot Dome Scandal, he and his second wife, Carrie Estelle, were noted philanthropists in the Los Angeles area, especially to Catholic schools. They donated the funds for the construction of St. Vincent's and St. Edward the Confessor Churches in the Los Angeles Archdiocese, as well as giving money from the family estate to Loyola Marymount University and much land for one of the campuses of Mount St. Mary's University, south of downtown Los Angeles. Upon Mrs. Doheny's death in 1944, she left antiquities and funds to St. John's Seminary in Camarillo, California, and ten years later, in 1954, her estate provided funds and a certain amount of her possessions to the library building of St. Mary's of the Barrens Seminary in Perryville, Missouri.

of honesty and propriety. Harding liked people and people liked him; Coolidge held himself aloof from the crowd, and made friends with difficulty. Harding was big and handsome; Coolidge was wizened and unimpressive. Nevertheless for the Republican party, with a nauseating set of scandals about to break, the succession to the presidency of such a man as Coolidge was a matter of the greatest good fortune. What the country needed was a "Puritan in Babylon."[176]

End of an Era

Catholic life in the twenties must surely begin with the death of Baltimore's Cardinal Gibbons on Holy Thursday, March 24, 1921. Ailing for months, the cardinal said his last Mass on December 9, 1920, in the Oratory of the Shriver family in Union Mills, Maryland—a family with whom he had maintained very close ties for years. Gibbons knew well his final days were approaching, and he asked to be brought back to his residence in Baltimore, just behind the Cathedral of the Assumption. The obsequies occurred following Easter, and it was estimated some two hundred thousand mourners filed past his casket during the three days of public viewing. The crowd assembled one block away on Mulberry Street, and the governor of Maryland requested every working person in the state, regardless of where or what occupation, to pause for one minute of silence while the funeral was taking place.

Archbishop (later Cardinal) Glennon of Saint Louis preached the funeral Mass and made the oft-quoted remark that in death,

---

[176] John D. Hicks, *Republican Ascendancy: 1921–1933* (New York: Harper & Row, 1960), 81. The reference to a Puritan in Babylon comes from the book by William Allen White, *A Puritan in Babylon: The Story of Calvin Coolidge*, published in New York in 1938.

the cardinal left his body to Baltimore, his heart to the Catholic University of America, and his soul to God. As might be imagined, tributes poured in from around the country and the world. Among the first was the president of the United States, Warren G. Harding:

> In common with all our people I mourn the death of Cardinal Gibbons. His long and most notable service to country and to church makes us all his debtors. He was ever ready to lend his encouragement to any movement for the betterment of his fellowmen. He was the very finest type of citizen and churchman. It was my good fortune to know him personally and I held him in the highest esteem and veneration. His death is a distinct loss to the country, but it brings to fuller appreciation a great and admirable life.[177]

Practically all newspapers from coast to coast wrote appreciative editorials and gave generous space to the cardinal's life and accomplishments, as well as the details of his final farewell. The *New York Herald* made a particularly poignant statement when it observed that

> the death of Cardinal Gibbons is more than the passing of an old man and an honored churchman. It is the ending of the life of a great American, a fine figure in the national scene. In the sense that Francis of Assisi is everybody's saint, James Gibbons was everybody's Cardinal. No matter what their religious beliefs, Americans who knew him held him in the highest respect and esteem.[178]

There was no one of consequence in the national government who did not extend an expression of sympathy. At the funeral,

[177] Cited in Ellis, *Life of Gibbons*, 2:628.
[178] *New York Herald*, March 25, 1921, cited in ibid., 630.

Toil and Transcendence

President Harding was represented by Will Hays, his postmaster general. The Catholic chief justice of the Supreme Court, Edward Douglas White, was in attendance, along with "the Governors of Maryland and Ohio, members from the two Houses of Congress, the envoys of a dozen foreign nations, and a score of Protestant and Jewish clergymen, together with a vast throng of minor prelates from Baltimore and other cities, who filled the cathedral to its capacity."[179]

There are many facets of this remarkable life that have been analyzed in the century since Gibbons's death. A significant number of those who had reason to be disappointed or even angered by decisions the cardinal made nonetheless held him in great esteem. One historian feels this was due "partly to an exceptional ability to coat unpalatable judgments with soothing words and to couch harsh dicta in disarming rhetoric."

> If he was ... aristocratic in his views, he could be, when occasion demanded, democratic in his manner. He could spend a Fourth of July ... with the miners of Mount Savage and the next day leave in a private railroad car with a Republican Governor of Maryland to visit another Republican high in the national organization.[180]

It appeared that not even John Carroll, the nation's first Catholic bishop, had been so warmly embraced by his country. The *Baltimore Sun* had opined five years before the cardinal's death that there were other Catholics in the continent, but only one Cardinal Gibbons. Of all the Catholic prelates who had governed their flocks in the United States, none had commanded the "same

[179] Ibid., 631.
[180] Thomas W. Spalding, *The Premier See: A History of the Archdiocese of Baltimore, 1789–1989.* (Baltimore: Johns Hopkins University Press, 1989), 289.

general confidence and the same earnest esteem." The *Sun* tried to explain why: "To all he seems to speak in their own tongues by some Pentecostal power, or by some subtle affinity that makes nothing human foreign to him."[181]

The cardinal's principal biographer, Monsignor John Tracy Ellis, who studied his subject far more thoroughly than anyone, delivers a balanced account of Gibbons's lengthy ecclesial career. Interestingly, he points out that, unlike John Henry Newman or Henry Edward Manning, Gibbons left no intimate journals or diaries that would give insight into his spiritual life. There was little of the mystic or ascetic about him; rather, he was a "man of action with an intensely practical turn of mind." Yet the faithfulness with which he observed all the exercises and devotions so common in priestly life "gave a tone to his daily living and established him in the minds of others as a true man of God."[182]

> He was ... quite unoriginal. There was no great project which owed its origins to his personal initiative and which he brought to completion. The Third Plenary Council of 1884 arose as a result of the suggestion of bishops of the Middle West, the university was largely the idea of Bishop Spalding, and the defense of the Knights of Labor probably owed as much in origin to Keane and Ireland as it did to

[181] Cited in ibid., 318.
[182] Ellis, *Life of Gibbons*, 2:640. John Henry Newman (1801–1890) was the most famous convert to Catholicism in the nineteenth century. A writer of enormous intellect, he converted from Anglicanism in 1845 and remained a leading Catholic intellectual light until his death. Henry Edward Manning (1808–1892) was an Anglican minister who converted to Catholicism following the death of his wife. He was ordained a Catholic priest and rose to become cardinal archbishop of Westminster. He was also known for extensive spiritual writings.

Gibbons. But once these movements had been launched, there was no single factor that contributed more to their ultimate success than the manner in which the Cardinal stepped forward with the great prestige of his office and name to lead them, and here his management was well-nigh perfect. The same lack of originality showed itself in his sermons and writings, for one could look in vain in what he preached and wrote for evidence of the gifted researcher, orator and prose writer. Yet there has never been a more effective exponent before the American public of the truths of the Catholic faith. If one turned to the field of administration there, too, there was little of striking accomplishment to record for Gibbons' long tenure in the See of Baltimore.[183]

Ellis concluded that this "failure to find brilliance of mind, depth of learning, mastery of administrative detail, resourceful and fighting qualities of leadership, powerful oratory and majestic diction" should not lead one to think that Gibbons was not a uniquely gifted man—quite the contrary:

> His gifts of prudence, discretion, and delicacy of perception were of an altogether uncommon order, and they were employed to the utmost advantage in his dealings with others. These gifts, resting upon a noble character and implemented by a quick and agile mind, did more than many others could have done who were far more richly endowed than James Gibbons. Men are not easily led unless leadership is strengthened by love and high respect, and the love which the Cardinal engendered for his person was so profound and

---

[183] Ellis, *Life of Gibbons*, 2:645.

genuine that it enabled him to accomplish wonders where more gifted men would have failed.[184]

Filling the Vacuum

Strong leadership was not absent in the Church following the death of Cardinal Gibbons, though it is difficult to see among the episcopal personalities any who could be described as the *primus inter pares* the way Gibbons was. Of the four leading candidates in 1921, one would have to begin with William Henry O'Connell, cardinal archbishop of Boston, described by one historian as "most fabulous of all,"[185] though not necessarily meant in the most favorable way. This historian, Ellis reminisced, was once walking along Michigan Avenue in Washington when he was asked by an undergraduate at Catholic University of America who the prelate was walking on the opposite side. When the professor replied that it was O'Connell, the student replied, "He looks like a battleship in full sail to me."[186] The instructor concluded that the student's observation had not been far off the mark.

William O'Connell was born in Lowell, Massachusetts, on December 8, 1859, the son of Irish immigrant parents from County Cavan.[187] Educated in Rome, he obtained his doctorate in the Eternal City, rose rather quickly in the ecclesial ranks, and was named Bishop of Portland, Maine, and eventually coadjutor to

[184] Ibid., 646.
[185] John Tracy Ellis, *Catholic Bishops: A Memoir* (Wilmington, DE: Michael Glazier, 1983), 67. These were personal recollections of prelates Monsignor Ellis had personally known through his career.
[186] Ibid.
[187] Coincidentally, the day of O'Connell's birth was the day the Pontifical North American College opened in Rome, where he would eventually serve as rector.

Toil and Transcendence

Archbishop Williams of Boston, succeeding to the office on Williams' death. In 1911, he became the first archbishop of Boston to be named a cardinal. In contrast to that of his contemporaries, O'Connell's literary output was significant: His multivolume *Sermons and Addresses*, along with his memoirs, *Recollections of Seventy Years*, though far from scholarly masterpieces, did contribute a fair volume of historical insight. O'Connell became a close friend of Rafael Merry del Val, who became the secretary of state to Pope St. Pius X and was likely the cause of his Boston appointment. As the years progressed, O'Connell's aristocratic bearing "had a tendency to put others off, including his fellow Bishops, and his occasional outbursts of temper alienated some who might have otherwise been won to his leadership."[188]

Nevertheless, O'Connell was revered by many in his archdiocese. In 1932, he led many of the faithful to the International Eucharistic Congress in Dublin—the largest individual pilgrimage, numbering over fifteen hundred, from his archdiocese.

---

[188] Ellis, *Catholic Bishops*, 74. Ellis relates a story from a Catholic University colleague who was a good friend of Archbishop Filippo Bernardini, first dean of the School of Canon Law at Catholic University, and nephew of Benedict XV's secretary of state, Cardinal Pietro Gasparri. The story is of Benedict XV confronting O'Connell during a private audience about the latter's nephew, Father James O'Connell, a priest of the Archdiocese of Boston, who left the priesthood, married, and took a substantial sum of archdiocesan funds when he left. O'Connell is said to have denied it, only to have Benedict XV open his desk drawer and produce a copy of James O'Connell's marriage license from Crown Point, Indiana. O'Connell is said to have dropped to his knees and asked the pope for mercy. It was further related that the pope was so indignant at O'Connell that he gave some thought to removing him from Boston. For the next twenty-five years, any influence O'Connell may have had at Rome was reduced to a minimum. Ibid., 73.

On the voyage over on the Cunarder *Samaria*, forty Masses were celebrated each morning; the rosary was recited in common every afternoon, and lectures on Ireland and her history in the evenings re-animated love of the old country in each heart. "Here in Ireland, where our forefathers lived and suffered for the faith," said the Cardinal in his broadcast to America, June twenty-seventh, "our pilgrims have made a renewal of that loyalty and fidelity to the Faith of Christ, given to His Holy Church and which the children of Erin have kept, knowing it to be God's gift and therefore their most precious possession in life."[189]

The Boston cardinal was consistent in his view that the Church should not meddle in politics, and never in his career did he endorse a political candidate. He appears not to have been close with politicians, as Gibbons was, though, before nominating the Catholic Pierce Butler to the Supreme Court, President Harding held up the decision for two weeks until he received a favorable reply from O'Connell. One biographer described him as "emphatically not a flag waver," one who "did not proclaim his love for America from the housetops; rather he was content to let his works bespeak his affection for his native land."[190] Perhaps this was the reason Theodore Roosevelt, in several letters previously cited, appeared to take such a dim view of O'Connell.

His administrative capabilities were well recognized. Under O'Connell, the archdiocese purchased the *Pilot* newspaper from its previous owners, and it became the official organ of the archdiocese. The Catholic Truth Guild, begun under his leadership in

---

[189] Dorothy G. Wayman, *Cardinal O'Connell of Boston* (New York: Farrar, Straus and Young, 1954), 234.

[190] Brendan A. Finn, *Twenty-Four American Cardinals* (Boston: Bruce Humphries, 1947), 117.

1907 and composed solely of Catholic laity, was the forerunner of the Catholic Evidence Guild in England, both dedicated to Catholic apologetics.

O'Connell was known for his love of music, literature, and art. Indeed, he had great musical talent and wrote lyrics and music for several hymns that appeared in Catholic hymnals of the period. A recognized orator, he was also remembered as having "possessed a power of expression which was unique. He was by nature a scholar and a thinker, and he was accustomed to thinking on his feet."[191] He was a presence larger than life, to be sure, a presence to be reckoned with, and definitely a presence not to be crossed.

A far gentler personality was the archbishop of New York, usually referred to as the "Cardinal of Charities," Patrick Hayes. Born on the Lower East Side of Manhattan in 1867, in the shadow of today's City Hall and St. Andrew's Church, he was, up to that point, the only cardinal and one of the very few archbishops in the country to receive his entire education in the United States. Ordained a priest of New York in 1892, he was, twenty-two years later, consecrated an auxiliary bishop of the archdiocese by the prelate he would ultimately succeed, Cardinal John Murphy Farley. Three years later, Pope Benedict XV named him bishop ordinary of the Army and Navy, with full ecclesiastical authority over Catholic chaplains and all Catholic members of the armed forces. This position of military vicar would be associated with the archbishop of New York for more than sixty-five years. Within one year of his appointment, Hayes secured nine hundred priests to serve as commissioned and noncommissioned chaplains in the United States and Europe.

Hayes raised enormous sums of money for Catholic Charities of the archdiocese and coordinated departmental efforts so that,

[191] Ibid., 118.

when the severe economic depression of 1929 hit the nation, "no agency in the entire nation was better prepared to meet the challenge than Catholic Charities of New York."[192] Closely tied to this was the formation, in 1920, of the Parish Visitors of Mary Immaculate, by Mother Mary Teresa Tallon in Manhattan. All the Sisters were trained social workers; in a letter written in 1922, Cardinal Hayes explains that

> the Parish Visitors of Mary Immaculate, organized two years ago in New York, have proved, within this very short period of time, a veritable benediction to our big city, and a most efficient help to many an anxious pastor of souls. Men, women, children and entire families, knowing neither sheepfold nor shepherd, and apparently lost to the faith, have been searched out by the Parish Visitors in a remarkable spirit of charity, kindness, sympathy and intelligence. Dark and hidden places, which the zealous priest neither reaches nor even knows of, are uncovered and flooded with the light and grace of Christian hope and happiness. Distress of soul and body is healed or relieved by the ardent faith, persevering zeal, spiritual touch, and human ministry of consecrated women who work as handmaidens of Christ's own love and compassion for the poor, the afflicted, the outcast, the neglected, and the wayward. The method employed by the Parish Visitors may seem somewhat novel and modern for women; but substantially it is the way, ever ancient and ever new, of the changeless Church, which has ministered untiringly to the ills and sorrows of human nature throughout the centuries. There can be no more excellent way than following the example of the Good Shepherd by

[192] Ibid., 180.

going after, seeking, and searching for the lost and wandering sheep. This the Parish Visitors strive to do and are doing very successfully under the supervision of the head of the diocese and in conjunction with the clergy.[193]

It is telling that Cardinal Hayes, and the Church in America generally at this time, were deeply concerned with the country's declining birth rate, Hayes condemned artificial birth control many times from the pulpit of St. Patrick's Cathedral. He explained to his congregation that

the Catholic Church's condemnation of birth control, except it be self-control, is based on the natural law, which is the eternal law of God applied to man, commanding the preservation of moral order, and forbidding its disturbance.[194]

Dennis Dougherty of Philadelphia is yet another example of strong episcopal leadership in these years. The cardinal was born some four months after the Civil War ended, in Honesville, Schuylkill County, Pennsylvania, to County Mayo immigrant parents. He was Rome-educated and ordained to the priesthood in 1890. Dougherty was at that time the only American prelate to govern four dioceses: two in the Philippines, the Diocese of Buffalo, and finally his native archdiocese. In the first twenty-five years of his episcopacy in Philadelphia, he established 106 new parishes, built 75 new churches, opened 146 new schools and academies, and established seven hospitals, seven homes for the aged, seven orphanages, and three retreat houses for women and one for men. It seems parochial schools, though, were among his highest priorities.

[193] Cited in Ibid., 181. As this book is written, the Parish Visitors of Mary Immaculate are preparing to celebrate their centenary of foundation.
[194] Ibid., 187.

Archbishop Dougherty was so insistent upon the establishment of parish schools that some of the older conservative pastors felt that he had become obsessed with the idea. He quoted frequently from the Third Plenary Council of Baltimore which ordered that in every Catholic parish in the United States, a school should be provided for the education of Catholic children. He also frequently reminded the pastors that the Baltimore Council stated that every pastor must see to the erection of a parish school in his own parish; and if through neglect he failed he was liable to removal.[195]

Dougherty would become a powerful player in the American hierarchy and would remain one until his death in 1951. His manner has been described as authoritarian, in keeping with the prevailing way of governing in that era, and quite difficult for the post–Vatican II mind to comprehend. The fact is that these men's words were taken very seriously by clergy and laity alike, and the ecclesial ship of state was steered on a firm course. When, for example, Cardinal Dougherty spoke on the topic of decency in motion pictures, Catholics were very well advised and largely refrained from attending any production the Church deemed unacceptable.

The cause of Irish Independence is one area where Dougherty moved with much caution. Until the establishment of the Irish Free State in 1922, the post–World War I world was sharply divided on the subject. There were several native Irish priests in Philadelphia who were actively engaged in the cause, including one who took a large collection of money and personally gave it (albeit secretly) to

---

[195] Hugh J. Nolan, *"The Native Son,"* in James F. Connelly, *The History of the Archdiocese of Philadelphia.* (Philadelphia: Archdiocese of Philadelphia, 1976), 354.

the Irish leader Éamon de Valera. Dougherty, who always wanted his priests far removed from political matters, became so disturbed that he transferred the priest from the city of Philadelphia to a town way off in the countryside.

The fact remained that many native Irish in Philadelphia were very concerned with their family members in the old country, and a collection of nearly $100,000 was taken up in the archdiocese and forwarded to Cardinal Logue, primate of all Ireland. The Irish primate profusely thanked his Philadelphia colleague, describing the collection as "phenomenal from one Archdiocese."

> There is pressing need owing to wholesale wreck and burn-
> ings in the south and west of Ireland. We can never repay
> our debt to Philadelphia, but we can pray, as I do earnestly
> that God may shower special blessings on Your Eminence
> and your generous people.[196]

Finally, the fourth of the power players, and the only cardi-nal not of Irish descent, was George Mundelein of Chicago. He was, like Patrick Hayes, born on Manhattan's Lower East Side, but to parents of German extraction. The family had been in America for generations: His grandfather fought in the Civil War and was the first casualty at the bombardment of Fort Sumter in Charleston Harbor in April 1861. Mundelein was educated and ordained in Rome and won his doctorate from the Urban College of the Propaganda in 1908. He became auxiliary bishop of Brooklyn at a young age and was installed as archbishop of Chicago in 1916. Describing Chicago as a "typical American city," the archbishop set out to "awaken [it] to a sense of its re-sponsibilities to the nation and the world." In doing so, he made

---

[196] Ibid., 353.

Chicago "one of the greatest centers of Catholic influence and activity in the entire world."[197]

As the Archdiocese was preparing for its 175th anniversary, the cardinal announced his plans for the construction of a major seminary, Saint Mary of the Lake, about forty miles from the center of the city. That seminary today proudly bears his name. Raised to the sacred purple in 1924, the cardinal presided two years later over the International Eucharistic Congress in Chicago, the first such gathering held in the United States. Cardinal Bonzano, a former apostolic delegate to the United States, was the pope's legate, and the congress attracted more than a million of the faithful from all over the world. No fewer than eleven other Princes of the Church were his guests during the ceremonies. Three hundred seventy-three archbishops and bishops attended, together with some five hundred Monsignori and eight thousand priests. The grounds of the Seminary of Saint Mary of the Lake provided the liveliest imaginable background for the majestic final procession of the Eucharist and solemn pontifical Benediction.[198]

Though men like Cardinals O'Connell and Dougherty were conspicuous for their absence from politics, the same was not true for Mundelein. The Chicago cardinal was a close personal friend of Franklin D. Roosevelt, and he hosted the president at his residence when he came to dedicate a bridge connecting the North and South sides of the city. Mundelein seemed a staunch supporter of Roosevelt's New Deal and was completely sympathetic with those portions that were in harmony with principles put forth by Leo XIII in *Rerum Novarum* and by Pius XI in *Quadragesimo Anno*.[199]

---

[197] Finn, *Twenty-Four American Cardinals*, 153.

[198] Ibid., 161–162.

[199] Leo's was the first great labor encyclical; Pius wrote his, as the title suggests, on the fortieth anniversary of Leo's.

Toil and Transcendence

Catholic Generosity

The twenties were also a period of great Catholic philanthropy and enormous Catholic wealth. A case in point is the papal marquis Martin Maloney. Born in County Tipperary, Ireland, he was brought to the United States by his parents at the age of six. He worked in the coal mines of Pennsylvania, opened a plumbing shop in Scranton, and eventually moved to Philadelphia, where he invented a gasline burner for streetlamps that made him a tremendous fortune. He eventually became president of the Pennsylvania Heat, Light, and Power Company, and organized the United Gas Improvement Company. His benefactions included a gift to help repair the Basilica of Saint John Lateran in Rome, as well as gifts to Saint Peter's Basilica, the Maloney Home for the Aged in Scranton, the chemical laboratory at Catholic University of America, and a medical clinic at the University of Pennsylvania. Pope Leo XIII made him a papal marquis, and Pius X conferred the title papal chamberlain on him. Maloney's summer home at Spring Lake, New Jersey — called Ballingeary after his native town in Ireland — was patterned on Leinster House, the Irish Parliament in Dublin. His guests were a veritable who's who of hierarchy, clergy, politicians, and influential Catholic laity. Maloney also built St. Catharine's Church at Spring Lake, where he and several family members are interred.[200]

Nicholas Brady, a financier and philanthropist, was born in Albany, New York, in 1878. He was the son of an Irish father who had lapsed from the Faith and raised his children in the Episcopal Church, of which his wife was a devout member. The elder Brady was a self-made businessman who left an estate of seventy million dollars. Nicholas graduated from Yale and followed his father into

---

[200] For more on Maloney see John J. Delaney, ed. *Dictionary of American Catholic Biography* (Garden City, NY: Doubleday, 1984), 342.

a Wall Street career. By the time he was thirty-four, he was president of the New York Edison Company and the Brooklyn Edison Company, and by the time of his death in 1930 he was chairman of both companies, as well as a director of more than one hundred corporations.

In 1906, he married Genevieve Garvan, a devout Catholic from Hartford, Connecticut. Before his marriage, he was received into the Catholic Church and became very serious about his Faith. The Bradys' estate on Long Island was called Inisfada, and they maintained there a private chapel in which Nicholas often served daily Mass. On journeys to their winter home in Florida, they often received permission from the apostolic delegate to have Mass offered in their private railroad car. The Bradys also owned a villa in Rome, where they hosted and became friends with many of the rising officials in the Vatican Secretariat of State. Francis J. Spellman, a future archbishop of New York, became friendly with them during his years in Rome, and through this friendship, Eugenio Pacelli, the future Pius XII and a close friend of Spellman, was their house guest at Inisfada when he visited the United States in 1936. The Bradys' benefactions to the Church amounted to more than twelve million dollars, including the construction of the Jesuit Novitiate in Wernersville, Pennsylvania, where they are both buried.[201]

Not at all conspicuous for the practice of Catholicism, and of dubious reputation, was Thomas Fortune Ryan. Born in Virginia in 1851, he was orphaned at an early age and went to Baltimore to find work. Along with "several well-known financial manipulators," he became involved in consolidating utility companies, and

---

[201] Michael Glazier and Thomas J. Shelley, eds., *The Encyclopedia of American Catholic History* (Collegeville, MN: Liturgical Press, 1983), 163.

in 1892, he formed the Metropolitan Street Railway Company in New York, the first American holding company. Some years later it merged with August Belmont's Interborough Rapid Transit Company, which financed the New York City subway system. Ryan's business deals were almost entirely secretive, which added to the dubiousness of his character, whether it be in banking, the American Tobacco Company, or the Seaboard Air Line Railroad.

He aroused protests from policyholders when he purchased a controlling interest in the Equitable Life Assurance Company — so much so that the firm was later turned over to a board of trustees headed by former president Grover Cleveland. Despite all of this and his owning one of the finest art collections in the world, his benefactions to Catholic charities amounted to more than twenty million dollars. One of the finest pieces of church architecture in New York City, St. Jean-Baptiste, was built through his generosity on Lexington Avenue for French-speaking Catholics, where a conspicuous plaque in the vestibule encourages the faithful to pray for the happy repose of Ryan's soul.[202]

Catholic Letters

Catholic literary figures abounded in America from the twenties onward. One of the most distinguished of the period was Agnes Repplier. Born in Philadelphia in 1855, she began publishing short stories at age thirteen. She contributed to both the *Catholic World* and *Young Catholic*, and by the mid-1880s, she was writing for the *Atlantic Monthly*, among the most prestigious journals in the nation. Few of her essays dealt directly with religion, but her faith does permeate her works. Repplier advanced the idea of spiritual commitment regardless of one's background, was strongly critical

---

[202] Ibid., 1231.

of materialism and individualism in American culture, and, though she continually emphasized the equality of the sexes, she did not support women's suffrage. Miss Repplier had a fifty-five-year writing career before her death in 1950 and compiled seventeen volumes of essays. In later years, she also wrote historical biography. She received any number of honorary degrees from universities, and the University of Notre Dame bestowed on her its prestigious Laetare Medal.[203]

Joyce Kilmer was born in New Brunswick, New Jersey, in 1886, attended Rutgers, and graduated from Columbia University. He and his wife, the former Aline Murray, had five children. After a brief career of teaching, Kilmer worked for three years on the staff of the *Standard Dictionary*. He began contributing poems and essays to various publications and served as literary editor of the Episcopalian magazine *Churchman*. In 1913, he and his wife converted to Catholicism. The same year, he joined the staff of the *New York Times Sunday Magazine and Book Review*, and his poems and essays were collected and published in multiple volumes: *Summer of Love* (1911); *Trees* (1914); and *Main Street* (1917). Kilmer enlisted in the army during the First World War and was killed in the Battle of the Marne in 1918. Though his literary output slightly preceded the 1920s, his work reached its greatest popularity during this decade. He was both a poet and an idealist, and "became a symbol of the soldiery bravery of American youth in World War I."[204]

Educational Freedom

A significant milestone for the Church in the United States occurred in 1925 in the Supreme Court case *Pierce v. Society of Sisters*.

---

[203] Ibid., 1204.
[204] Ibid., 764.

Toil and Transcendence

In 1922, the voters of Oregon adopted an initiative requiring children between the ages of eight and sixteen to attend public school. The law was unique, and the initiative campaign was "organized primarily by the Ku Klux Klan and the Oregon Scottish Rite Masons. It was the product of post–World War I fears about Bolshevism and the influx of aliens." Supporters of the legislation firmly believed that "the separation of children of different religions in private schools would cause dissention and discord."[205] A federal district court declared that the Oregon initiative violated the due process clause of the Fourteenth Amendment and issued an interlocutory injunction restraining the defendants from enforcing the law.

Several options were open to the Supreme Court after they had agreed to hear the case, but the one they chose was to affirm that "states may compel attendance at some school, but the parents have a constitutional right to choose between public and private schools."[206] Associate Justice James McReynolds, a Democrat and a Protestant, wrote the decision for a unanimous court.

> [McReynolds] declared that a child is not a creature of the state and that parents have both the right and the duty to recognize and prepare their children for other obligations. States may regulate private schools (e.g., regulate the number of days in the school year and require secular subjects like arithmetic and reading), but they may not prohibit the school's existence. The decision directly concerned the property right of private schools to operate in Oregon, but it clearly rested on the primary right of parents in the education of their children, a personal right. Also, insofar as

---

[205] Kermit L. Hall, ed., *The Oxford Companion to the Supreme Court of the United States* (New York: Oxford University Press, 1992), 634.
[206] Ibid., 635.

one of the schools was religious, the decision was in favor of religious liberty.[207]

The court went on to observe that private schools were "a kind of undertaking not inherently harmful, but long regarded as useful and meritorious." *Pierce* has been hailed as a Magna Carta for Catholic education in the United States. The case attracted wide interest and support, with *amicus curiae* briefs attacking the law's constitutionality filed by the Episcopal Church, the Seventh-day Adventists, and the American Jewish Committee.[208]

The Church and the Klan

As has been the case in all periods of the history of the Church in the United States, anti-Catholicism raised its head in the twenties in the form of the Ku Klux Klan. This was the second time in our nation's history that the Klan emerged. Its first appearance was in the South during Reconstruction, but it more or less died out in the 1870s. It had sought to overthrow the Republican state

---

[207] Richard J. Regan, *A Constitutional History of the U.S. Supreme Court* (Washington, D.C.: Catholic University of America Press, 2015), 97. One scholar contends that the *Pierce* decision profoundly affected the evolution of civil liberties in the United States for three-quarters of a century. It emphasized fundamental rights not expressly articulated in the Constitution and also family autonomy. It was a forerunner to later privacy decisions, such as affirming the right to abortion in *Roe v. Wade* (1973) and access to contraceptives in *Griswold v. Connecticut* (1965). Hall, *Oxford Companion*, 635.

[208] Hennesey, *American Catholics*, 248. *Amicus curiae* (friends of the court) filings are statements of support for the defendants or plaintiffs and their cause. In the case of *Pierce v. Society of Sisters*, Pierce was the governor of Oregon, and the law's constitutionality was challenged by the Sisters of the Holy Names of Jesus and Mary and by a nonsectarian school, the Hill Military Academy.

governments in the South, especially by violence toward African Americans. Many of the individual chapters of the Klan were suppressed in the South by federal law enforcement. The Klan had developed a highly structured organization, along with its own unique costumes, consisting of robes, masks, and conical hats designed both to frighten and to conceal their identities.

The second Klan began in Georgia in 1915 and grew substantially after 1920. They took inspiration from a silent film produced by D. W.Griffith, *The Birth of a Nation*, which was a legendary account of the founding of the first Klan. The second Klan was rooted in local Protestant communities and sought to maintain white supremacy, opposed Catholics and Jews, and also stressed its opposition to the political power of the pope and the Catholic Church.

An Alabamian, William J. Simmons, is credited as the founder of the second Klan and supposedly had a view of the renewed organization as primarily fraternal. By 1924, the Klan claimed that thirty thousand Protestant ministers had "taken the hood as members of the Invisible Empire."[209] A Klan lecturer in the early twenties claimed that 75 percent of Klan members were taken from the Masons, and findings indicate that the group drew much support from the Methodist, Baptist, United Brethren, and Disciples of Christ churches. One of its compelling arguments was that the Invisible Empire attracted a far broader spectrum of Protestantism than any one individual denomination could, and the organization might serve as a very effective rallying point for Protestant interests (and hostilities) and a fine means of socialization among kindred spirits.

[209] Thomas R. Pegram, *One Hundred Percent American: The Rebirth and Decline of the Ku Klux Klan in the 1920s* (Chicago: Ivan R. Dee, 2011), 8.

The Klan insisted on 100 percent Americanism and naturally joined in the chorus of opposition to American entry into the League of Nations. Simmons went even further in his chauvinism when he declared that "the Roman Church ... is fundamentally and irredeemably, in its leadership, in politics, in thought, and largely in membership, actually and actively alien, un-American and usually anti-American."[210] Many accepted this as gospel truth; estimates of Klan membership in the twenties — the peak of its influence — vary from two to five million. The largest concentrations appeared in Indiana, Ohio, Texas, and Pennsylvania. Illinois, Oklahoma, and New York were close behind, and even less populous states such as Oregon and Colorado had significant Klan activity.

Hiram W. Evans was Imperial Wizard of this somewhat bizarre structure of resistance and had even more strident views than Simmons:

> Pluralism, [Evans] declared, was antithetical to American institutions and should be excluded from public influence. American democracy, in his view, took the form of "Protestantism translated into government," a mixture of individualism, equality within a select community of believers, and a militant posture toward outside hierarchies and rival systems of law and belief. Antithetical religious traditions, especially Roman Catholicism, ethnic customs and loyalties derived from foreign cultures, and nonwhite racial identity, which Evans collectively characterized as "alienism" could not be made compatible with this vision of governance and culture. From the Klan's perspective, the "melting pot" model of assimilation had failed to produce real Americans.[211]

[210] Ibid., 12.
[211] Ibid., 47–48.

Toil and Transcendence

The Klan's targets were not only Africans and Catholics, but also Jews:

> The Protestant and Nordic qualities of white racial identification were paramount in shaping the anti-Semitism of the Klan. On the one hand, the Invisible Empire shared in and drew upon the intensified hostility toward Jews evident both in Europe and the United States in the aftermath of World War I and the Bolshevik Revolution. In the bigoted imaginations of Henry Ford, Tom Watson, and other influential twentieth-century American anti-Semites, the traditional caricatures of the stateless wandering Jew and the materialistic Shylock fused with the more recent radical image of Leon Trotsky to produce a unique threat to Americanism.... Klansmen boycotted local Jewish merchants or protested the works of Jewish film producers, often repeating these common tropes of the 1920s.[212]

Most students of the Klan, however, see anti-Catholicism as an even deeper motivating prejudice, because of the threatening numbers of Catholics in the United States. By 1922, estimates place the Catholic population over eighteen million. Catholics had been elected governors, senators, state legislators, and mayors of large cities: They were helping determine public policy at the local, state and national levels. One area of concern in the Klan mind was that Catholics, for the most part, refused to support Prohibition, and the Church, though always encouraging personal temperance, did not feel government intrusion into one's drinking habits a proper exercise of civil authority. Such positions, many Klansmen said, gave clear evidence of "patriotic shortcomings and

[212] Ibid., 53.

criminal inclinations" among this very foreign cast of intruders. The Imperial Wizard spoke forthrightly:

> "The Roman Church seems to take pains to prevent the assimilation" of Catholic immigrants.... Its parochial schools, its foreign born priests, the obstacles it places in the way of marriage with Protestants unless the children are bound in advance to Romanism, its persistent use of the foreign languages in church and school, its habit of grouping aliens together and thus creating insoluble alien masses—all these things strongly impede Americanization.[213]

Most Klansmen believed that the Church, by Her very presence in America, was undermining true American identity. This message was advanced in many ways, but especially through a publication called the *Fellowship Forum,* based in Washington, D.C. It was a nationally circulated twelve-page weekly founded by a high-ranking Southern Mason George Fleming Moore. The paper was singled out during the 1928 presidential campaign by Catholic governor Alfred E. Smith of New York, the Democratic candidate, as "notorious," offering "senseless, stupid, foolish attacks."[214] The publication later expanded into radio, further carrying its anti-Catholic propaganda to the listening public.

The paper and radio diatribes were countered by *Tolerance,* a publication based in Chicago and operated by a Catholic lawyer, Patrick Henry O'Donnell, in the name of the Catholic-dominated American Unity League. In one issue in July 1923, a depiction of a Klansman appears on the front page with the inscription "The Midnight Lure of a Poison Flame." It is supported by small images

[213] Ibid., 72.
[214] Felix Harcourt, *Ku Klux Kulture: America and the Klan in the 1920s* (Chicago: University of Chicago Press, 2017), 51.

of smiling people with wings, each displaying some title they wished to apply to the Klan: petty, bigot, grafter, and so on. In addition to the public work of the Knights of Columbus in refuting the claims of the Klan, and underscoring the true patriotism of American Catholics, such magazines as *Tolerance* proved effective counterbalances to Klan propaganda.[215]

Perhaps surprisingly, some Americans saw humor in all of this. Others used the vehicle of humor to communicate their hope that a brighter day would come. American evangelist Harry Emerson Fosdick, minister of New York's First Presbyterian Church, predicted that "the millennium will come when the Ku Klux Klan and the Knights of Columbus play a basketball game with a Negro umpire for the benefit of the Jewish employees of Henry Ford at Zion City."[216] One particular satirical advertisement came right to the point:

BASKETBALL GAME
Ku Klux Klan vs. Knights of Columbus
Benefit
Jewish Relief Fund
In The Masonic Auditorium

Sponsored by the Advancement of Colored People

St. Patrick's Day, March 17th
Beer Served by the Baptist Church[217]

While humor may have served to take the edge off some of these tensions, sometimes they flared up violently. In 1924, for instance, trains of Klansmen from Chicago and elsewhere converged on South Bend, Indiana, home of the University of Notre Dame, the

---

[215] Ibid., 18.
[216] Ibid., 168.
[217] Ibid., 169.

nation's most prominent Catholic university. Their attempt was to demonstrate, forcefully, the strength they had in American society.

The Grand Dragon of the branch of the Klan in Indiana was David Curtis (D. C.) Stephenson. A convicted murderer and rapist and four times married, he was also head of recruiting for the Klan in seven other states. (He later led those groups to independence from the national organization.) He had close relationships with several Indiana politicians, including the governor, Edward L. Jackson, another avowed Klansman. Stephenson was denied a pardon by the governor for his crimes, but years later was paroled.[218] With Jackson's election as governor in November 1924, generating euphoria among the Indiana Klan, a tristate rally was planned for South Bend in May of that year.

The president of Notre Dame, Father Matthew Walsh, C.S.C., was worried for the campus and the students. He directed Father J. Hugh O'Donnell, C.S.C., his prefect of discipline, and Father George Holderith, C.S.C., director of off-campus students, to have a meeting with the South Bend chief of police, Laurence Lane. The chief assured them there would be no Klan parade through the streets of South Bend, and surely no cause for worry.

Some of the early Klansmen were rolling into South Bend. They were shocked at the reception they received on the train platform from the locals, menacing bands of jeering young men who encouraged them to go back home. Many of the Klansmen were veterans of the rallies at Kokomo and Valparaiso; they were accustomed to being welcomed with open arms, as if they were visiting rotarians or fairgoers. In

---

[218] For a complete treatment of Stephenson's sordid career, see M. William Lutholtz, *Grand Dragon: DC Stephenson and the Ku Klux Klan in Indiana* (West Lafayette, IN: Purdue University Press, 1991).

the South Bend Klan headquarters at the corner of Michigan and Wayne Streets, the local Klansmen erected a "fiery" cross made of red lightbulbs in their third floor windows.[219]

That cross would become the focal point of backlash within hours. Notre Dame's young students, like Catholics in general, had grown up hearing slurs, lies, and innuendos about their Faith. Time and again they had heard their patriotism challenged. Now, one of the greatest tangible forces of anti-Catholicism was coming to South Bend for a public display. It had been anticipated for weeks, and the students were ready.

Klansmen kept arriving at the train station, all looking for Island Park along the St. Joseph River, where a public rally was to take place. Threats of violence abounded, and when the first squads of Notre Dame men began running through the streets, Governor Emmett Branch was asked to mobilize the Indiana National Guard; fearing the political consequences of intervening on either side, though, he simply refused. The *South Bend Mirror* reported students rushing to the scene of the rally to "help Larry out,"[220] while the *South Bend Tribune* reported that by 11:30 a.m. on the morning of the event, "not a Klansman could be seen in the business district."[221] Klansmen found themselves retreating for safety:

Fortunately for the students, the first floor of the Klan's building housed a grocery, and barrels of potatoes sat outside the store. The first potato shattered the third floor window that shielded the cross, showering a few pedestrians with glass as they ran for shelter. A fusillade of potatoes followed. Each time one hit its target, a red bulb would burst with a

[219] Todd Tucker, *Notre Dame vs. the Klan: How the Fighting Irish defeated the Ku Klux Klan* (Chicago: Loyola Press, 2004), 148.
[220] A reference to Laurence Lane, chief of police.
[221] Tucker, *Notre Dame vs. the Klan*, 153.

pop and a shower of golden sparks. Occasionally an angry looking Klansman would peek out through a window, but a barrage would quickly drive him back into the shadows. Soon, only the top bulb of the cross remained glowing.[222]

D. C. Stephenson was infuriated that the rally and parade in South Bend was canceled. He arrived to hear the news and drove quickly out of town "half expect[ing] to see Evans and his cronies behind barricades on the outskirts of South Bend, guns drawn, waiting for the papal army to march southward."[223] South Bend residents, many Catholics among them, were devastated and angry with the destruction of property and claimed that Lane had done nothing to stop it; the *South Bend Mirror* editorialized that he should resign. Lane, for his part, was furious; he had gone easy on the Notre Dame students and had been humiliated. On the following Monday evening, he received a tip that students would again attack Klan headquarters. About nine o'clock, all appeared quiet, but as the Klansmen raised their repaired fiery cross in the third-floor window, about five hundred students emerged out of the darkness. But this time, the result was different. As the Klansmen stood rather passively in front of their headquarters,

> the police charged in on the Notre Dame men from behind. The Notre Dame men were surprised; they didn't expect resistance from the Klan after Saturday's rout, and they certainly didn't expect it from the previously lax police department. Lane jabbed the butt of his club into the ribs of a Notre Dame man and threw him to the ground. He watched one of his men bring his club down hard across the top of a young man's head. The student fell to his knees with a

---

[222] Ibid., 154.
[223] Ibid., 163. The reference here is to Hiram Evans.

stunned look on his face. The charging policemen stood in the student's path of retreat while the Klansmen blocked them on each side. As the students were absorbing the fact that the police were attacking them, the Klansmen on the sidelines began to participate in the fray. They hurled bottles and rocks indiscriminantly into the crowd.[224]

It was the far more reasoned voice of Father Walsh who climbed atop a Gettysburg monument to address the crowd and ultimately bring order out of chaos. The irony of it all was not lost on the college president; it was at Gettysburg that another Holy Cross priest, Father William Corby, had climbed a rock to grant general absolution to soldiers about to go into battle; it was the same Corby who had welcomed Walsh into the Congregation of Holy Cross.[225]

Political Breakthrough

The presidential election of 1928 has been of vital interest to historians of the Catholic Church in the United States practically since the event itself. It was the first time in the nation's history that a Roman Catholic was nominated by one of the major political parties: Alfred E. Smith, the Democratic governor of New York.[226] On the Republican side, Calvin Coolidge, the incumbent, could have had the nomination for the asking, and would likely have

---

[224] Ibid., 168.

[225] Corby's giving general absolution must always be understood in the proper Catholic context: Surviving the battle, the soldier who previously may have been in the state of serious mortal sin, must, like all penitents, make a good confession and seek particular absolution for his sins.

[226] Charles O'Conor, a New York City lawyer, was nominated by a third party in the race of 1872; he polled several hundred thousand votes, but no electoral votes.

been reelected, as he was presiding over one of the greatest periods of economic prosperity in the nation's history. For whatever reason, while on vacation in the Black Hills of South Dakota, he made his famous statement that he would not seek reelection:

> Perhaps he really meant to take himself out of the race; perhaps he only meant that he would not personally do anything to obtain the Republican nomination. He never clarified his enigmatic statement. But other aspirants, including his Secretary of Commerce, Herbert Hoover, interpreted his words to mean complete withdrawl, and promptly became candidates.[227]

Despite some opposition, the Republican nomination was Hoover's on the first ballot. He possessed "most of the qualifications for the Presidency that tradition-bound Americans had come to expect."[228] He was born in West Branch, Iowa, in 1874, into a family of devout Quakers. After the early deaths of his parents, he was raised by various family members. Many in his family expected him to attend the Quaker college, Earlham, in Richmond, Indiana; instead, in 1891, he enrolled at Stanford and was hired for summer work with the United States Geological Survey, which paid his tuition. Soon after graduating, he began working with a prominent San Francisco engineer, and his talent for organizing took him the rest of the way. During the First World War, Wilson appointed him chairman of the Commission for Relief in Belgium, then called him back to the United States to head the Food Administration. He became secretary of commerce under Presidents Harding and Coolidge and "outshone them both."[229]

---

[227] Hicks, *Republican Ascendancy*, 201.
[228] Ibid., 208.
[229] Ibid.

Toil and Transcendence

Smith, on the other hand, was born in the shadow of the Brooklyn Bridge in 1873. After his father's death when he was thirteen, he dropped out of St. James Grammar School on the Lower East Side of Manhattan to go to work to support his family. One of his jobs was at the Fulton Fish Market, and for years thereafter he listed his most coveted academic degree as "F.F.M." As a young man he came to the attention of Tom Foley, a political boss at Tammany Hall, and through that connection, Smith quickly climbed the political ladder: municipal court clerk, state representative, speaker of the state assembly, Manhattan sherriff, president of New York City's Board of Aldermen, and, beginning in 1918, four terms as New York's governor. Devoutly Catholic throughout his life, and very much molded by the parish priests and sisters of St. James parish, Smith never for a moment hid his Catholicism. Rather, he took lifelong pride in his faith heritage.

Smith was certainly one of the most colorful politicians during the roaring twenties. He was easily spotted on the streets of New York in his brown derby hats, striped suits, and with an ever present cigar. On the "radio" his gravelly voiced New York accent was unmistakable. But he was also widely recognized for his firm grip on human and public affairs and for his integrity and independence.[230]

Growing up on the "sidewalks of New York," Al Smith was no stranger to religious bigotry. He was raised in an atmosphere dominated by those who were appalled at the continuing influx of immigrants from Ireland, Italy, and Eastern Europe. He surely read the words of a prominent New York City Presbyterian minister: "The vast hordes flocking to this land strike at our national life,

---

[230] George J. Marlin, *The American Catholic Voter: 200 Years of Political Impact.* (South Bend, IN: Saint Augustine's Press, 2004), 174–175.

which we count most precious, while the ballot gives them power which they know too well how to use."[231] In fact, one delegate to New York City's Democratic Convention in 1924 prided himself on his membership in the Klan and said, "We want the country ruled by the sort of people who settled it—this is our Country!" To a large number of the delegates, a man like Al Smith was "the captive of Tammany Hall, and Tammany Hall was a brothel whose allegiance was pledged to the 'Whore of Babylon'—the Pope of Rome."[232]

> Klansmen don't doubt the loyalty, integrity and bravery of Catholics, Jews, Negroes and foreign born persons. We realize that these classes proved themselves good and brave Americans during the recent war and we are not against them. Catholics bar themselves [from the Klan] by their allegiance to the Pope; the Jews because they do not believe in the birth of Christ and Negroes because of their color. We want only Caucasians, who, so far as their allegiance is concerned, have it all confined within the boundaries of the United States. That does not mean we are opposed to them. We are organized to maintain American principles and are opposed only to lawlessness and lack of Americanism.[233]

In many ways the candidates in 1928 were close in their views and proposals. Smith, for example, had principles most would associate with Republicans: He believed in "stable, close-knit family life, loyalty to community, discipline, sexual restraint, hard work, frugality, individual responsibility, and respect for private property."

[231] Ibid.,178.
[232] Ibid.
[233] Ibid., 178.

Toil and Transcendence

Although Al Smith opposed prohibition, Sunday closing laws, and other sumptuary legislation he believed to be aimed at his fellow Catholics, he neither disputed Victorian notions of vice nor automatically rejected government regulation of immoral behavior. He supported state laws to close lewd theatricals and to ban obscene literature irrespective of its literary merits.[234]

Smith had a distinctly urban style, and strongly desired to repeal Prohibition. Aside from this, and his Catholicism, he had generally conservative views, and a mostly laissez-faire view of business.

Indeed, some of the Democrat's positions were distinctly traditionalist; he dislikes women's suffrage, the expansion of government, and extensive regulation of business. As Martin Fausold points out, "In many respects, Hoover was the more liberal and progressive candidate in 1928". On a whole, however, the men were not far apart ideologically; neither roamed far from the political mainstream of their time, and each might be considered counter-left. Their chief differences were in style and personality. The glad handing, ebullient New Yorker who chose as his theme song "The Sidewalks of New York" may have given the impression that his philosophy lay to the left of Hoover's, but these differences were largely superficial. Hoover was much better known nationally and internationally than Smith, and both candidates were men of integrity who never deliberately said a false or unkind word about each other.... Smith's

---

[234] Allan J. Lichtman, *Prejudice and the Old Politics: The Presidential Election of 1928* (Chapel Hill: University of North Carolina Press, 1979), 234.

chief enemy ... [was] the deceiving glow of Coolidge era prosperity.[235]

The ever present "Protestant myth" came to the forefront in the 1928 election far more than in any previous time in American political history. According to its line of thought, America "always had been and must forever remain a dominantly Protestant country."

Never before Smith's time had a Roman Catholic seriously sought a presidential nomination. Anti-Catholic prejudice was an old American heritage that dated back to colonial times and had flared up strongly again with each major accretion of Catholic immigrants. To most Americans religious prejudice was principally a matter of feeling rather than reason.[236]

In truth, though, the election raised genuine questions that went beyond mere Protestant bigotry. Would a Catholic president owe a dual allegiance to the pope and to the U.S. Constitution he had sworn to uphold? What would he think about the concept of all religions equal before the law? What would he think about the "separation of church and state," or the venerable position of America's free public schools? Formally, these questions were raised in a detailed article in the *Atlantic Monthly* by Charles C. Marshall, a New York City lawyer and prominent member of the Episcopalian church. In his essay, Marshall quoted numerous papal encyclicals dating back centuries that stressed the Church's temporal and spiritual authority over Her members. Marshall asked Smith to

---

[235] Glen Jeansonne, *Herbert Hoover: A Life* (New York: New American Library, 2016), 195–196. The historian referenced in this citation is Martin Fausold, *The Presidency of Herbert C. Hoover* (Lawrence: University Press of Kansas, 1985).
[236] Hicks, *Republican Ascendancy*, 206.

contrast his candidacy with these pronouncements as well as to explain how they would affect his public-policy decisions. He also inquired about Smith's views on parochial schools, how he would look upon non-Church marriages, and how he would lead the United States in dealing with conflicts with Catholic countries.

For his part, Governor Smith initially sought to ignore the article, claiming that, despite his lifelong and fervent Catholicism, he had no familiarity with the documents Marshall quoted. Upon the strong recommendation of his advisers, however, Smith soon concluded that Marshall's queries could not go unanswered. For assistance, he turned to a friend, Father Francis P. Duffy, of the faculty of Saint Joseph's Seminary in Yonkers. Father Duffy was a well-respected theologian and psychologist, perhaps best remembered as "Fighting Father Duffy," the famed Chaplain of New York's "Fighting 69th" during the First World War.[237] And so, in the May 1927 issue of *Atlantic Monthly*, Smith responded by asking Marshall about the conflict he suggested between Smith's faith and high office: "It may exist in some lands which do not guarantee religious

[237] Father Francis P. Duffy (1871–1932) was born in Canada and was ordained a priest of the Archdiocese of New York in 1896. He obtained his doctorate from Catholic University of America in 1905, became editor of the *New York Review*, a very well-respected theological journal, and was quite active with the Catholic Summer School movement prior to enlisting for military service. Duffy was decorated for his military service and, according to General Douglas MacArthur, was considered for the post of regimental commander. Following the war, he wrote *Father Duffy's Story*, based on a manuscript begun by Joyce Kilmer before his death. It was Father Duffy's intention to continue the manuscript as his friend Kilmer had planned, but the chaplain was convinced to write more of his personal reminiscences. At the time he aided Governor Smith, he was serving as pastor of Holy Cross Parish in Hell's Kitchen, just a few blocks from Times Square, where a famous monument to him was erected.

freedom, but in the wildest dreams of your imagination you cannot conjure up a possible conflict between religious principle and political duty in the United States." And in any event, he continued, wouldn't a Protestant experience similar tensions? And wouldn't he resolve those tensions, just like a Catholic, through the "dictates of conscience"? Regarding specifics, he went on:

> My personal attitude, wholly consistent with that of my church, is that I believe in peace on earth, good will to men, and that no other country has the right to interfere in the internal affairs of any other country. I recognize the right of no church to ask armed intervention ... merely for the defence of the rights of a church.... I believe in the worship of God according to the faith and practice of the Roman Catholic Church. I recognize no power in ... my church to interfere with the operations of the Constitution of the United States for the enforcement of the law of the land. I believe in absolute freedom of conscience and freedom of all churches, all sects, all beliefs before the law.... I believe in the absolute separation of church and state.... I believe that no tribunal of any church has any power to make any decree of any force in the law of the land, other than to establish the status of its own communicants within its own church. I believe in the support of the public school as one of the cornerstones of American liberty ... [and] in the right of every parent to choose whether his child shall be educated in the public school or in a religious school supported by those of his own faith ... and I believe in the common brotherhood of man under the common fatherhood of God. In this spirit I join with fellow Americans in a fervent prayer that never again will any public servant be challenged because of his faith.[238]

[238] Marlin, *American Catholic Voter*, 182–183.

Toil and Transcendence

Al Smith chose Senator Joseph Robinson of Arkansas as his running mate. Robinson, a "dry," balanced the "wet" Smith on the Prohibition issue. The party held their convention in Oklahoma City, and before a crowd of thirty thousand, Smith decried intolerance, not simply because he was a good Christian but also because he was a good American, a product of American institutions: "Everything I am, everything I hope to be, I owe to these institutions."

> The world knows no greater mockery than the use of the blazing cross, the cross upon which Christ died—as a symbol to instill in the hearts of men a hatred for their brethren, while Christ preached and died for the love and brotherhood of man.[239]

Protestant Backlash

Despite Smith's best efforts, there is little doubt that among the reasons for the distinctive political alignments in the 1928 campaign, religion was the dominant factor. As one historian who has concentrated on this particular race put it:

> A bitter conflict between Catholics and Protestants emerged ... [and] religious considerations preoccupied the public, commanded the attention of political leaders, and sharply skewed the behavior of voters. Regardless of their ethnic background, their stand on prohibition, their economic status, and other politically salient attributes, Catholics and Protestants split far more decisively in 1928 than in either previous or subsequent elections. No other division of the electorate stands out so distinctively in that presidential year. This cleft between Catholics and Protestants was not

[239] Ibid., 184.

confined to particular regions of the nation, to either city or country, to either church members or nominal Protestants. Both Protestants and Catholics responded to the religious tensions of 1928. Smith benefited from a pro-Catholic vote and Hoover from an anti-Catholic vote.[240]

There were some who, because of the rhetoric of the campaign, became convinced that religious bigotry was wrong and that each person had an obligation to clear his or her mind of such prejudice and objectively vote on the issues. On the other hand, those who were not about to be convinced under any circumstances remained intransigent. New York's *Methodist Christian Advocate*, while trying not to voice too strident opposition, did observe that even though faith should be a matter between a man and his God, "unfortunately [it] cannot be wholly isolated from the arrogant political theory of the Roman Church." A New York monthly, the *American Lutheran*, admitted that the mere mention of a Catholic president has aroused concern among Lutherans around the country, and it should be emphasized "before our people those cardinal principles which came forth as a fruit of the Reformation, on which our government is founded and which have made Lutheranism possible." One of the most piquant attacks was found in the *Christian Leader*, which reminded its readers:

A Roman Catholic assassinated President Lincoln.
A Roman Catholic assassinated President Garfield.
A Roman Catholic assassinated President McKinley.[241]

Statistical surveys, show that out of 8,500 Southern Methodist preachers, only four supported Al Smith, and the moderator of the Presbyterian church stated that it was "the plain duty of every

---

[240] Lichtman, *Prejudice and the Old Politics*, 231–232.
[241] Marlin, *American Catholic Voter*, 184–185.

churchman to work and pray for the election of Herbert Hoover."[242]
In a work titled *What Price Tolerance?*, a Protestant publisher on
Long Island was only too happy to include a photograph of Al
Smith with Cardinal Hayes, with another priest standing behind
the governor looking as though he was propping him up—the
implication being the candidate was too intoxicated to stand on
his own.

John Roach Straton of New York City's Calvary Baptist
Church declared that Smith represented "card playing, cocktail
drinking, poodle dogs, divorces, novels, stuffy rooms, dancing,
evolution, Clarence Darrow, overeating, nude art, prize fighting,
actors, greyhound racing and modernism." The popular fundamentalist preacher and self-proclaimed "Ambassador of God"
Billy Sunday referred in his sermons to Smith's male supporters
as "the damnable whiskey politicians, the bootleggers, crooks,
pimps and businessmen who deal with them," and to his female
supporters as "street walkers."[243]

There was never much of a chance Smith would win the election. A Hoover victory was predicted from the outset, but the
magnitude of that victory was a surprise to many of the pundits:

[Hoover] carried forty-two states, with 444 electoral votes
to Smith's 87 votes and eight states. Hoover overwhelmed
the Democrat with 58.1 percent of the popular vote in one
of the most decisive victories in American history up to
that time. Incredibly, Hoover won five former Confederate states, usually Democratic bastions. Smith won only
Massachusetts, Rhode Island and a tier of resolutely Southern Democratic states in the "black belt": South Carolina,
Georgia, Alabama, Mississippi, Arkansas and Louisiana.

[242] Ibid., 185.
[243] Ibid., 186.

Though he had appeared a strong candidate and an energetic campaigner, Smith proved weak in every region, even
where Democrats had won easily in previous contests. The
defeat was nationwide and conclusive. Hoover, a more sedate, restrained campaigner, had won wet states, corn belt
states, Southern states and states that sympathized with
Smith because of his religion, most by large margins. The
only genuine national issue was prosperity and the desire to
maintain the status quo. "Mr. Hoover, after all, was better
qualified for the Presidency", the *Washington Post* wrote. The
magnitude of Hoover's victory made a political comeback
for Smith unlikely. [244]

Hoover's triumph in carrying more than half the states of the
old Confederacy won headlines, but "Smith's success in diverting
122 northern counties from the Republican to the Democratic
column was the more important and the more permanent."[245] These
counties were found throughout New England, where French Canadians and Italian Americans had both settled. They and their
descendants became and remained members of the Democratic
household. In the view of many historians, the election of 1928 did
not indicate any major realignments nationwide, nor did it serve
as a forerunner to the electoral victory of Franklin D. Rosevelt in
1932. On the contrary:

> Attention both to the empirical evidence and to theory in
> social psychology suggests that the ebbing of overt hostility
> toward Catholics primarily meant that, with Smith's sound
> defeat, anti-Catholicism became temporarily less salient for
> most of the public. But Americans who objected to Smith's

[244] Jeansonne, *Herbert Hoover*, 204.
[245] Hicks, *Republican Ascendancy*, 212.

religion had not necessarily changed their views of the consequences of voting for a Catholic candidate. Later evidence from surveys and from the presidential election of 1960 indicates that Protestant ideas about Catholic presidents were not transformed in 1928. These results underscore the importance of distinguishing changes in salience from changes in attitudes toward members of out-groups. They also point to the tenacity of prejudice and to the possible reappearance of intolerance toward particular groups long after tranquility seemed to have been restored.[246]

For his part, Herbert Hoover was exemplary in his handling of the religious issue. In his acceptance speech at the Republican National Convention in Kansas City, Missouri, in August 1928, Hoover reminded his audience that while Al Smith was the first Catholic nominated for president, he was himself the first Quaker.

> I come of Quaker stock. My ancestors were persecuted for their beliefs. Here they sought and found religious freedom. By blood and conviction I stand for religious tolerance both in act and in spirit. The glory of our American ideals is the right of every man to worship God according to the dictates of his own conscience.[247]

Hoover felt Smith was right that a man's religion should not disqualify him from the presidency—but up to then it had been, in Hoover's view, an "underground issue." By raising it, Smith had inflamed bigoted Protestants, especially in the South. In response to a "violent" letter sent out from a Protestant organization in Virginia, Hoover issued a reply:

---

[246] Lichtman, *Prejudice and the Old Politics*, 232.

[247] *The Memoirs of Herbert Hoover: The Cabinet and the Presidency: 1929–1933* (New York: Macmillan Company, 1952), 207.

Whether this letter is authentic or a forgery, it does violence to every instinct that I possess. I resent and repudiate it. Such an attitude is entirely opposed to every principle of the Republican party. I made my position clear in my acceptance speech. I meant that then and I mean it now.[248]

In responding to scurrilous anti-Catholic circulars, Hoover expressed his indignation, stating that religious questions had no part in the campaign and repeated his position that "neither I nor the Republican party want support on that basis." Hoover contended that there were substantial reasons for returning a Republican administration, "but this is not one of them." In the end, Hoover felt the religious issue had "no weight in the final result." Rather, what had defeated Governor Smith were "general prosperity, prohibition, the farm tarrifs, Tammany, and the 'snuggling' up of the Socialists."[249]

A gentleman from Tennessee, Colonel Horace Mann, who was very active in Hoover's campaign, was believed by many to have played a large role in stirring up the religious issue. There were several ways this could have been orchestrated without Hoover's knowledge or approval. Al Smith, though, was convinced that Mann was behind these smears, and he contacted a certain Monsignor Fulton J. Sheen, professor of philosophy at the Catholic University of America, with whom he was friendly. Sheen was rapidly gaining prestige in the Church nationally, and sometime after the election, he contacted Colonel Mann to see if a conversation might be possible.

Much to Sheen's surprise, the colonel informed him that he had not been responsible for the bigotry directed at the Catholic candidate, but others in the Hoover campaign had. The colonel

[248] Ibid., 208.
[249] Ibid., 208–209.

was obviously an approachable and receptive person, so Sheen lost no time asking if he would be interested in taking instructions in the Catholic Faith. Mann replied that the whole question of authority was a stumbling block to him: He could accept the authority of Scripture but not that of the Church. Sheen reminded him that someone had to compile the many books of Scripture and authenticate their inspired authorship. Sheen then made a comparison using the American government: "As the Supreme Court safeguards the Constitution, so it could be said the Church safeguards the Scriptures." Sheen went on to remind Mann that this same Church had existed throughout much of the Roman Empire before any of the books of the New Testament came to be written. His arguments were effective: Colonel Mann and his wife were received into the Church, and on the day of their First Holy Communion they received a congratulatory telegram from Al Smith.[250]

Thus was the colorful story of the Church in America in the 1920s. All seemed well and prosperous in the country as the decade was drawing to a close, but it was not to last. A depression, the likes of which America had not witnessed, was just around the corner, and an international conflict followed in the Depression's footsteps. All of this presented the Church with significant new challenges that called for a strong response—and for this, many new personalities were to come on the scene.

---

[250] Charles P. Connor, *Classic Catholic Converts* (San Francisco: Ignatius Press, 2001), 171.

4

∞

Depression and War:
The Era of Franklin Delano Roosevelt

Crash

The end of the Roaring Twenties was indeed roaring, but hardly
in a positive way. The trauma of the period has been well captured
by historian Paul Johnson:

> Out of an American population of 120 million, about 29–30
> million families had an active association with the market.
> The economy ceased to expand in June 1929. The bull
> market in stocks really came to an end on September 3. The
> later "rises" were merely hiccups in a steady downward trend.
> On Monday, October 21, for the first time, the ticker-tape
> could not keep pace with the news of falls and never caught
> up. In the confusion the panic intensified ... and speculators
> began to realize they might lose their savings and even their
> homes. On Thursday, October 24 shares dropped vertically
> with no one buying, speculators were sold out as they failed
> to respond to margin calls, crowds gathered on Broad Street
> outside the New York Stock Exchange, and by the end of the
> day eleven men well known in Wall Street had committed
> suicide. Next week came Black Tuesday, the 29th, and the

first selling of sound stocks in order to provide desperately needed liquidity.[251]

The conventional interpretation of older historians was that the Depression, setting in during the administration of Herbert Hoover, a "laissez-faire ideologue" who refused to involve government in any tangible way in economic recovery, triggered interest in a more planned economy, one in which government took an active role to alleviate the nation's plight. To achieve this, Franklin D. Roosevelt, a New York patrician with a winning smile, was elected and started immediately to apply state planning. Quickly, the old story goes, the clouds started to lift. Such thinking has been significantly challenged in recent decades. Hoover has been described recently as a "social engineer," while his successor was a "social psychologist," but in truth neither possessed knowledge sufficient to understand the nature of the Depression, let alone the cure for it. In fact, the policies of both may well have prolonged it.[252]

Historical revision on Herbert Hoover has been slow in coming, but gradually newer writers are coming around to see that his war on the Depression was far more ambitious than he has been credited with. The core of his recovery program was the Reconstruction Finance Corporation, or RFC. It was

> a government corporation for loaning money to banks, businesses, and railroads to prevent failures and stimulate trade and commerce, especially construction ... [and] it remained an integral fixture in the American economy throughout the subsequent New Deal era.... Second on the president's agenda was the Glass-Steagall Act. Its chief purposes were

[251] Paul Johnson, *A History of the American People* (London: Weidenfeld & Nicolson, 1997), 613.

[252] Ibid., 614.

to save the gold standard, stabilize exchange rates, maintain wages, and increase the money supply, because only gold-backed dollars could circulate.... The chief executive asked for a system of home loan discount banks to save homes from foreclosure and for additional capital to fund federal land banks to make low interest loans available to farmers. He called for reorganization of failing railroads, legislation to re-organize the executive branch, and authority to lease Muscle Shoals for private development to revitalize the region. The Chief wanted to be frugal and called for a moderate tax increase to bring soaring deficit under control ... [and] he requested legislation to make assets of closed banks available to depositors and for the legalization of branch banking. The Chief requested a widespread program of public works to be spread throughout the country, strategically placed where unemployment was greatest.... He also called for increased restrictions on immigration to save jobs for Americans and for labor legislation that would prohibit the use of injunc-tions to outlaw strikes.... President Hoover spent more time seeking a solution to farm poverty than to any other issue during his tenure. A Jeffersonian in his view of the yeoman farmer, Hoover—like historian Frederick Jackson Turner, one of his contemporaries who shared many of the president's beliefs—considered the family farm the crucible of democracy. If democracy were to survive, farming would have to change, but farming was so ingrained in the roots of American traditions that the family farm as an institution must endure.[253]

[253] Jeansonne, *Herbert Hoover*, 253–254, 265. Muscle Shoals was a government oil reserve in Alabama. Frederick Jackson Turner (1861–1932) was an American historian best remembered for his "Frontier Thesis." Based at the University of Wisconsin and then

Toil and Transcendence

A Patrician Populist

In the American mind in 1932, however, the "most welcome thing about Franklin D. Roosevelt ... was that he was not Hoover."[254] Born in 1882 into the landed gentry of New York's Hudson Valley, Roosevelt could trace some ancestors to the *Mayflower* and others to colonial French Huguenot settlers. His parents, James and Sarah Delano Roosevelt, were extremely class-conscious, giving their son an excellent education, which included annual summer travel to Europe. He attended Groton School in Connecticut and came under the tutelage of Dr. Endicott Peabody, the Episcopal minister who founded the prestigious institute, patterned after a similar type of education he had received in England. The young FDR then matriculated at Harvard, where he majored in American history, then at Columbia Law School in 1904. His early political career included stints as state senator from Dutchess County, New York, and assistant secretary of the Navy under his cousin President Theodore Roosevelt, followed by two terms as New York's governor. In 1906, he married his fifth cousin, Anna Eleanor Roosevelt, with whom he had six children. In August 1921, while swimming in the Bay of Fundy, he suffered an attack of Polio, which afflicted him for the remainder of his life.

---

at Harvard, he argued that the moving Western frontier shaped American democracy and the American character from the colonial era until the late nineteenth century. Regarding Hoover's plan to alleviate the depression, Rexford Tugwell (1891–1979), an economist who served on FDR's brain trust during the New Deal, wrote twenty books covering the politics of the New Deal, and was instrumental in creating the Agricultural Adjustment Administration, or AAA, observed: "We didn't admit it at the time, but practically the whole New Deal was extrapolated from programs that Hoover started." Johnson, *A History of the American People*, 618.

[254] Ibid., 623–624.

Few politicians in American history have been more shrewd in seeing the importance of the Catholic vote and in using Catholics and the Catholic Church for political advantage. The proof of this shrewdness is that he opposed the Irish Catholic leaders of New York's Democratic Party at nearly every turn in his career yet managed to retain Catholic support throughout his presidency.

> He was not just a Democrat but a New York Democrat, a member of a state party whose leaders and whose most faithful voters were overwhelmingly Catholic, especially Irish Catholic. There was a tension, always, between this Protestant patrician and his Catholic political party, a tension that this congenial country squire and shrewd politician sought to resolve, with much success, but never with finality. For there remained a tension between the Democratic party he created in his own image and the Catholics who were such a large part of its constitutency, until the tie between them snapped sometime in the late 1960's.[255]

By the time Roosevelt had completed one term of office, he had formed a political coalition which was to remain intact until well into the 1960s:

> Ethnicity, race, and religion also importantly shaped the division of the vote and the Roosevelt coalition. Irish, Italian and Polish voters, most of them Catholic, voted overwhelmingly for Roosevelt, in many areas up to 80 percent and more. Within these groups, there was some class differential, particularly among Irish voters, with those toward the upper end

---

[255] Michael Barone, "Franklin D. Roosevelt: A Protestant Patrician in a Catholic Party," in David B. Woolner and Richard G. Kurial, eds., *FDR, the Vatican, and the Roman Catholic Church in America, 1933–1945* (New York: Macmillan, 2003), 3.

of the socioeconomic ladder generally more Republican (but still decisively Democratic) than those toward the lower end. Catholics overall were significantly more Democratic than Protestants outside the Solid Democratic South, where the white Protestant voters returned top-heavy Democratic margins. Jews also voted overwhelmingly Democratic by 1936, with relatively little variation by socioeconomic class.... In a major change, African Americans who could vote largely left the party of Lincoln for the party of Roosevelt. Despite discrimination in New Deal programs and the administration's lack of support for civil rights legislation, African Americans rallied to the president and the party that had also included them in the New Deal, had given them attention, and had brought significant help.... Italian, Polish, Irish, African American, and many Jewish voters as well, tended to be working class and lower income, as did such smaller Catholic ethnic groups as French Canadians and Czechs.[256]

That coalition had its origins in 1932, FDR's first victory. Four years earlier, as Al Smith was running for the presidency, Roosevelt was elected governor of New York. His career up to that point had been one of strong opposition to Tammany Hall, headed for most of FDR's years by political boss Charles F. Murphy. As soon as he was elected, he was faced with major political scandals in the administration of New York City's mayor, Jimmy Walker, which, when discovered, led to the mayor's quick resignation. The Seabury Committee, charged with the investigation, forced Roosevelt to hold hearings, in which he seems to have effectively walked a political tightrope: He did not hand the Republicans an issue for the next election and, at the same time, managed to keep Tammany

---

[256] John W. Jeffries, *A Third Term for FDR: The Election of 1940* (Lawrence, KS: University Press of Kansas, 2017), 21–22.

support, despite the fact that there was much division within its ranks over the Walker issue.

As Roosevelt entered the White House in 1932, he seemed to be, and was, well positioned to take control of the Democratic Party and form it as he desired. The old party coalition of the South and the big cities had been expanded, largely because of economic conditions, to include the industrial belt, the progressive belt of the Upper Midwest, and the West itself. In addition, the party itself had drastically changed:

> The traditional Democratic Party, the party of the first Democratic President Franklin Roosevelt had ever met, Grover Cleveland, was a laissez faire party, a party that believed in a minimalist federal government that pretty much left all kinds of Americans alone. The domestic programs of Woodrow Wilson and, even more, the wartime policies of the Wilson administration, were more interventionist, but they did not at all prove to be popular.... Then Roosevelt's New Deal suddenly inserted the federal government into every local community. NRA set all prices and wages. AAA controlled agricultural production. The Wagner Act established huge industrial unions, which became major institutions in the industrial belt from Pennsylvania to Illinois. WPA employed workers in almost every city and county. [257]

Roosevelt did not overlook Catholics in his administrative appointments. James A. Farley, for instance, became postmaster general. From Rockland County in Upstate New York, he had been FDR's chief political organizer, far removed from the city politics of

---

[257] Barone, "Franklin D. Roosevelt," 7. NRA was the National Recovery Act; AAA, the Agricultural Adjustment Act; WPA, the Works Progress Administration.

Gotham. Joseph P. Kennedy, father of a future American president, was one of two individuals who contributed $50,000 to the campaign. The son of a ward politician from east Boston, Kennedy was shunned by Boston's WASP establishment and relocated his family in the very posh community of Bronxville, New York. He would become chairman of the Securities and Exchange Commission and later U.S. ambassador to England. Edward Flynn from the Bronx became secretary of state of New York while FDR was governor and later chairman of the Democratic National Committee. U.S. Senator Thomas Walsh of Montana died before assuming the position of attorney general, to which Roosevelt had appointed him, while Frank P. Murphy, a former mayor of Detroit, was tapped for an associate judgeship on the United States Supreme Court, after serving as governor of Michigan and U.S. attorney general.

Helpers in the Hierarchy

Roosevelt was particularly adept at cultivating the friendship of, and working with, members of the Catholic hierarchy. Domestically, the one prelate most closely associated with social concern and most attracted to FDR's proposals was Cardinal George Mundelein of Chicago. Just one month after his inauguration, the president wrote to the cardinal on his patronal feast of Saint George. He had learned that Mundelein collected presidential autographs and saw this as a good opportunity. The cardinal replied with delight that "the busiest man in the land, one who now carries the weight of the world on his shoulders [took the time] to write me on my feast day."[258] Mundelein took the opportunity to request a meeting

[258] Gerald P. Fogarty, S.J., "Roosevelt and the American Catholic Hierarchy," in Woolner and Kurial, *FDR, the Vatican, and the Roman Catholic Church*, 16.

with the new chief executive to congratulate him personally on his convincing victory. The request was quickly granted, and the meeting between the two became the first of many, leading to a strong friendship.

In the Archdiocese of Chicago, Mundelein gave the administration of his own social programs to his auxiliary bishop, Bernard J. Sheil. The bishop was an outspoken advocate for social justice. He lent his open support to a number of controversial labor strikes through the years, and in the 1950s, he was a particularly vocal critic of Wisconsin's Senator Joseph R. McCarthy's tactics in rooting out domestic communists and sympathizers. With this social and political orientation, it was not surprising that Sheil became one of the favorites of the Roosevelt administration and of the president himself.

If FDR especially cultivated Mundelein on social matters, the same sort of outreach and eventual friendship would develop in the area of foreign affairs with a rising young prelate who in 1939 was appointed archbishop of New York: Francis J. Spellman. Born in Whitman, Massachusetts, in 1889 to William and Honora Hayes Spellman, from Counties Tipperary and Limerick respectively, he attended Whitman High School and Fordham College, then studied for the priesthood at the North American College in Rome. Ordained in 1916 for the Archdiocese of Boston, he received early parochial assignments and eventually became an assistant chancellor, then archivist for the archdiocese. Spellman became the first American attaché of the Vatican Secretariat of State in 1925, and during a trip to Germany two years later, he struck up a lifelong friendship with Archbishop Eugenio Pacelli, who would become Pope Pius XII. The by-now Monsignor Spellman translated Pius XI's first broadcast over Vatican Radio in 1931, would proceed to serve as an English announcer for Vatican Radio, and was chosen secretary to Cardinal Lorenzo Lauri when the cardinal was selected to be papal legate at the International Eucharistic Congress in Dublin, Ireland, in 1932.

The same year, he became auxiliary bishop of Boston, and in 1936 he was the official escort to then-Cardinal Pacelli when he made an unofficial visit to the United States. Ostensibly, the cardinal was to visit and be the houseguest of the papal duchess Genevieve Garvan Brady and her husband, Nicholas, at Inisfada, their Long Island estate. The greater purpose, however, was for Pacelli to meet with Roosevelt to discuss diplomatic recognition of the sovereignty of Vatican City. Pacelli later told the Apostolic Delegate in the United States, Archbishop Amelto Cicognani, that Spellman had arranged the meeting through Joseph P. Kennedy.

> On November 5 [1936], Roosevelt hosted both Pacelli and Spellman at Hyde Park. Newspapers speculated that the president and cardinal discussed establishing diplomatic relations between the United States and the Holy See, an issue on which Spellman had been working since at least November 1935, through Kennedy and [James] Farley, but without any consultation of Cicognani. Even as he was agreeing to the Hyde Park meeting, Roosevelt asked his Chicago friend (Mundelein) to meet him at the White House on November 9. What transpired between the two is unknown, but, a few weeks after the meeting, Spellman heard rumors that Roosevelt would like him to be the papal representative in Washington, a position he recognized was impossible.[259]

In September 1938, Cardinal Patrick Hayes died; he had been archbishop of New York since 1919. The following March, Pacelli was elected to the papacy. And on April 15, 1939, his friend Spellman

[259] Ibid., 19. Cardinal Pacelli was, at this time, serving as Vatican secretary of state.

was appointed archbishop of New York. From then until his death on December 2, 1967, he would become one of the most powerful prelates of the Catholic Church in the United States, if not the most powerful. At his appointment, most perceived the obvious: that he was the personal choice of Pius XII, "and he dreaded the thought … of letting him down."[260] The sees of Chicago and New York, prominent as they already were, would begin to carry even more influence with their respective occupants' friendship with the president. The Church in these years already had a significantly developed social doctrine, beginning with Pope Leo XIII's *Rerum Novarum* in 1891 and, four decades later, Pius XI's *Quadragesimo Anno*. In addition, in 1919, the bishops of the United States had offered a twelve-point program for social reconstruction: Almost all of their thinking was incorporated into Roosevelt's New Deal legislation.

Monsignor John A. Ryan, the Catholic University economist, wrote in *Commonweal* in October 1934 that "never before in our history have the policies of the federal government embodied so much legislation that is of a highly ethical order. Never before have government policies been so deliberately, formally and consciously based upon conceptions and convictions of moral right and social justice." Bishop Karl Alter of Toledo, Ohio, felt that FDR's inaugural address "breathed the spirit of *Quadragesimo Anno*," while Cardinal Mundelein believed Roosevelt had "more friendly sympathy to the Church and its institutions than any occupant of the White House in half a century." Yet another Chicago auxiliary, William D. O'Brien, long a veteran of work with the Catholic Church Extension Society, noted that "Almighty God raised up FDR — the Apostle of the new Deal."[261] Surely, at the outset, Roosevelt could

---

[260] Robert I. Gannon, S.J., *The Cardinal Spellman Story* (Garden City, NY: Doubleday, 1962), 133.

[261] Hennesey, *American Catholics*, 259–260.

claim enormous Catholic political support; he could also claim the strong admiration of at least some in the American hierarchy.

Catholic Criticism

One of the major topics often overlooked by mainstream historians is the very real conservative opposition to Roosevelt springing up among both Catholics and non-Catholics. It seemed to have affected his electoral victories very little, but the opposition was substantial, cogent, and, as far as FDR was concerned, a viable political threat. Within the Church:

> Constitutional issues bothered Frederick C. Kenkel, veteran editor of *Central-Blatt and Social Justice*, who saw Roosevelt's planned economy as the imposition of state socialism. Patrick Scanlan, lay editor of the *Brooklyn Tablet*, and James M. Gillis, C.S.P., of the *Catholic World*, had the same worries. Alfred E. Smith told the American Liberty League that the choice was plain: one could have either communism or constitutional government.... Many others stressed communism ... [including] Brooklyn priest Edward Lodge Curran of the International Catholic Truth Society [who] leaned heavily on this argument.[262]

Yet another conservative critique came from Father Edmund A. Walsh, S.J., one of the founders of Georgetown University's School of Foreign Service and surely the man who accomplished the most in the school's development. Born of Irish immigrant heritage in the Dorchester Heights section of South Boston in 1885, he entered the Jesuit Novitiate in Frederick, Maryland, and was ordained at Woodstock College, also in Maryland, in June 1916. During his

[262] Ibid., 269.

years of formation, he had taught at Georgetown and was once
again assigned there after ordination. In 1918, he was asked by the
university to establish the School of Foreign Service, the first of
its kind in the United States. Its purpose was to train diplomats,
businesspersons, bankers, and traders, primarily educating them
on international relations.

Father Walsh directed the Papal Famine Relief Mission to Russia
in 1922 and later worked on behalf of the Vatican to resolve the
long-standing issues between church and state in Mexico in 1929.
After the Allied victory in World War II, he served as consultant
to the U.S. chief of counsel at the Nuremberg Trials. Walsh had
a first-class geopolitical mind, and, based on his firsthand experiences in Russia so soon after the 1917 revolution, he was staunchly
anti-communist:

> [He] is largely remembered today in connection with Sena-
> tor Joseph McCarthy. Indeed, in March 1950, columnist
> Drew Pearson accused Walsh of prompting McCarthyism
> by suggesting that the Senator emphasize communism in his
> 1952 reelection campaign. Pearson claimed that McCarthy's
> famous speech at Wheeling, West Virginia, in February 1950,
> in which he claimed to have a list of communists in the
> State Department, was the result of Walsh's advice. Because
> Walsh refused to publicly respond to the charges, the story
> gained credence to the point where nearly every biography
> of McCarthy has cited Walsh as his mentor.[263]

Father Walsh was unenthused about Roosevelt and his New
Deal policies. He believed firmly that individualism, not compulsory

[263] McNamara, Patrick, *A Catholic Cold War: Edmund A. Walsh, S.J.,
and the Politics of American Anticommunism.* (New York: Fordham
University Press, 2005), xii.

government intervention, was the guiding force to freedom and prosperity. Many in the United States, due largely to the dire economic circumstances of the late twenties and early thirties, temporarily put aside their distrust of government expansion, feeling that *something* had to be done. As difficulties diminished during FDR's first term, and the administration's domestic agenda became still more expansive, Walsh and many American Catholic conservatives became increasingly alarmed. In the Jesuit's case, a letter he wrote to Roosevelt's secretary of commerce, Daniel Roper, is telling. He was objecting to a speech given by a member of FDR's brain trust, Rexford Tugwell, to a group of Midwestern farmers that was very divisive, and could be, in his judgment, construed as incitement to "nothing less than class warfare":

> The abuses of capitalism, which no one has condemned more openly than I have, will be cured only by the Christian principles of persuasion and an enlightened social consciousness. All attempts to do it by compulsion run counter to the experience of psychologists and those familiar with the stubborn instincts of "human nature."[264]

This was also his position in foreign affairs, especially official recognition of Russia on the part of the United States. As early as 1924, upon returning from Russia, Walsh had a lengthy visit with Charles Evans Hughes, secretary of state under Calvin Coolidge. He laid out as clearly as possible conditions in Russia as he had observed them, and, though his opposition to recognition was well known, he never expressed his opinion directly to Secretary Hughes, or, for that matter, years later to President Roosevelt. However, he spent several years on the lecture circuit, in the classroom, and in writing, trying to enlighten the country to the true

[264] Ibid., 87.

desires and intentions of the communists. He knew well Lenin's basic philosophy: Charge with a bayonet; if you encounter mush, proceed; if you encounter steel, retreat.

In 1933, Father Walsh was invited to the White House to confer with Roosevelt. Ironically, it was the same day that the president had informed the media that he had sent an invitation to the Soviet government to send a representative to Washington for the purpose of negotiating an agreement that would result in official diplomatic recognition. Biographical studies clearly show the vast difference in thinking between FDR and Georgetown's famed Jesuit:

> One phase of the interview he calls "particularly revealing", namely, the president's seemingly off-hand attitude toward the whole matter in question. He said at the time, "In reply to certain observations I had made respecting the difficulty of negotiating with the Soviets, he answered with that disarming assurance so disarmingly characteristic of his technique in dealing with visitors, 'Leave it to me, Father, I am a good horse dealer'". This visit terminated with a request from the President, asking Father Walsh to prepare a report for him relative to religious liberty in Russia, and a second one regarding the background and the personality of Maxim Litvinov, the Soviet negotiator then preparing to leave Moscow for Washington. The two reports requested were prepared and returned to the President before Litvinov arrived in Washington. The first contained a full account of the so-called religious liberty in Russia and of the so-called provision made for it in the Soviet Constitution. The most important part of this report is couched in a warning, calling for some specific guarantee of action before recognition was granted, and stating what the results would be if no such guarantee were exacted. The wisdom written into that

report became more and more evident with the passing of the years.[265]

League of Extraordinary Businessmen

The most significant collective conservative opposition to FDR and his policies came from a group formed during his first term, with a special eye on the presidential election of 1936. They called themselves the American Liberty League but, for all their initial hopes, fell short of their objective for a variety of reasons. The League had its official beginnings at the National Press Club Building in Washington, D.C., in August 1934, when scores of newspapermen were called in for an important announcement. The point person was Jouett Shouse, a former chairman of the executive committee of the Democratic Party. Prior to this, Shouse had worn many hats: He was a newspaper editor in Kentucky, a stock broker, a legislator, and a congressman from Kansas (after relocating there in 1911). He had served briefly as assistant secretary of the Treasury during Woodrow Wilson's administration and was for years a

[265] Louis J. Gallagher, S.J., *Edmund A. Walsh, S.J. : A Biography* (New York: Benziger Brothers, 1959), 92–93. Gallagher includes commentary on the day of dedication of Georgetown's School of Foreign Service Building: "The new building was dedicated with a schedule of all day ceremonies on Monday, the thirteenth of October, 1958. President Dwight D. Eisenhower was guest of the University at the morning exercises, during which he assisted Archbishop O'Boyle of Washington at the laying of the cornerstone and then unveiled a bronze bust of Father Walsh. ... After receiving the University's degree of Doctor of Laws, *honoris causa*, the President gave a brief but very interesting eulogy of Father Walsh, and took occasion to congratulate the Society [of Jesus] and the University on the work being done at this school in providing the country with soldiers of peace." Ibid., 207.

powerful force in Kansas politics. By now well established, he was described as "charming, confident, eloquent, persuasive ... a born leader of men."[266]

Governor Alfred E. Smith, by now far separated from Roosevelt in his political views, also persuaded his close political and personal friend, John J. Raskob, to become involved. Raskob had recently retired from the directorship of General Motors to become chairman of the Democratic National Committee. A former Republican, Raskob had no particular affinity for politics, had limited acquaintances with Democratic leaders, and did not want the League to get off on the wrong foot; with this in mind, Raskob asked Shouse to take over the active leadership, and the latter agreed.

Raskob had been born in the Erie Canal town of Lockport, New York, in 1879. He had been a financial executive and businessman for DuPont prior to joining General Motors and was the builder of the Empire State Building in Manhattan. A lifelong devout Catholic, he was of German and Irish decent, and, once hired by Pierre Du Pont as his personal secretary, relocated to Delaware. In 1928, he had supported fellow Catholic Al Smith for the presidency, but by 1932, when Roosevelt received the nomination, Raskob quickly resigned as national party chairman.

Whatever Catholic cause approached him for a contribution, he and his wife, Helena, could always be counted on. Described as a "committed, faithful and generous Catholic whose childhood and youth had in so many ways been sustained and enriched by the Church,"[267] he was always open to such appeals as the Irish

---

[266] George Wolfskill, *The Revolt of the Conservatives: A History of the American Liberty League: 1934–1940* (Boston: Houghton Mifflin, 1962), 21.

[267] David Farber, *Everybody Ought to Be Rich: The Life and Times of John J. Raskob, Capitalist* (New York: Oxford University Press, 2013), 207.

Fund, the Catholic Orphans Fund, the Catholic Hospital Fund, and many more. In the 1920s, the Vatican was experiencing financial difficulties: "Postwar bond failures and bank crises in Europe had hit the church's investments hard, and the 'Peter's Pence' donations that Catholic churches around the world contributed to the Vatican were down as well."[268] Raskob contributed very generously and, with eight other wealthy American Catholic laymen, became a Knight of Malta. In 1927, while he and Helena were on a Eoropean tour, they visited the Vatican, were thanked personally by Pope Pius XI for their generosity, and were given a tour of Vatican City State by the young, "charming, energetic American priest"[269] Francis J. Spellman. The association would only be strengthened in later years.

With such a background, it is easy to see why this magnate would be attracted to the Liberty League. While no friend of Roosevelt, his thinking on joining the League was quite specific:

Raskob genuinely believed that he was not fighting Roosevelt and the New Deal. He was just trying to move the president back toward the temperate, pro-business, pro-sound currency policies that Raskob believed had once charactericzed the Roosevelt Administration.... Raskob, like many others, desperately wanted to believe that he knew where Roosevelt really wanted to lead the nation. He seemed to think that the aspect of the protean, shape-shifting New Deal that he had fixed his gaze on back in the first months of 1933 was the real and true New Deal. Everything else done in the name of the New Deal—what Raskob saw as the anti-business, pro-labor, market-regulating, anticapitalist aspects—were dangerous deviations. The right mixture

[268] Ibid., 213.
[269] Ibid., 214.

of political pressure and public education, Raskob hoped, would bring the Roosevelt administration around.[270]

This was an apt description of many who pledged allegiance to the American Liberty League; others, however, went further in their protest and were very doubtful that FDR or his administration could be brought back to (what they perceived as) reasonableness. Though its official launch was in Washington in the summer of 1934, Raskob privately launched the League at a "posh dinner" at the Metropolitan Club in New York City. Among the guests were: John W. Davis, the Democrats' nominee for president in 1924, a lawyer fiercely loyal to Wall Street and the country's largest corporations, and one who despised the New Deal; Irénée Du Pont, who, along with her husband, Pierre, had a dislike of administration policy to match Davis's; Al Smith; the broker E. F. Hutton; and "a half dozen other leading financiers and industrialists."[271] Walter Crysler, a close friend of Raskob, also joined the League. At its first official press conference, Shouse spoke for the entire group when he said that the League "is definitely not anti-Roosevelt.... We want to try to help the administration."[272]

Shortly into its existence, the League had developed a unique configuration:

It is perhaps no exaggeration to say that not in the history of the country did one organization marshal so much prestige, wealth, and managerial skill to undo a president as the Liberty League did in the fight against Roosevelt and the New Deal. At the time, the 1930's, the Liberty League was the most articulate spokesman of what (for lack of a better

[270] Ibid., 297.
[271] Ibid., 299.
[272] Ibid., 300.

term) may be called political conservativism. It was a time-
honored creed, a creed with impressive credentials, one that
needed no apologies. Yet the Liberty League probably did the
cause of conservatism a disservice. Almost from the outset
(with no little help from the Administration), it was made
to look ridiculous, or dangerous, and sometimes both.[273]

Some historians felt the organization was too rich: In the 1930s,
for rich men publicly to decry Roosevelt as a false savior, or to say
that the New Deal was little short of deceptive socialism, simply
accentuated the gap between the haves and the have-nots. "Regardless of party and regardless of region, today, with few exceptions, members of the so called Upper Class frankly hate Franklin
Roosevelt," *Time* magazine reported in April 1936, and the May
issue of *Harper's* ran an article by Marquis Childs that claimed
that most of the upper economic classes were beginning to share
"a consuming personal hatred" for FDR.[274]

> In their thesaurus of hate, Roosevelt was a "renegade Demo-
> crat," an "extravagant," "destructive," "vacillating," [and]
> "unprincipled charlatan." A "cripple," an "invalid" lack-
> ing physical stamina, a captive, psychologically, who was
> morally "weak," intellectually "shallow," unbelievably "gull-
> ible," [and] a "dupe"(surrounded by "radicals," "crackpots,"
> "quarterbacks," and "foreign-thinking brain-trusters, some
> of whom were better known in Russia than in the United
> States").... From Newport to Miami, from Wall Street to
> Park Avenue, in country club locker rooms, the cathedral-like
> hush of bank offices, in board rooms and carpeted law offices,

---

[273] Wolfskill, *The Revolt of the Conservatives*, viii.
[274] Ibid., 107. Marquis Childs was a contemporary author, syndicated
columnist, and journalist.

in hotel suites and cabin cruisers the broad stories passed: Roosevelt was an inveterate liar, immoral ... a syphilitic, a tool of Negroes and Jews, a madman given to unprovoked gales of immoderate laughter, an alcoholic, a megalomaniac dreaming his dreams of dictatorship.[275]

This may be a little exaggerated, but it is the way one historian viewed the League's assessment of Roosevelt. Whatever blame may be ascribed to them, Leaguers sincerely believed that Roosevelt, if he continued on the same road, was surely moving in the direction of dictatorship. The belief was widely held that the chief executive was a Marxist, one who "surrounded himself with reds and pinks," instead of carrying out the mandate of the American people. Governor Alfred E. Smith was convinced that the battle lines were clearly drawn: "There can be only the clear, pure, fresh air of free America, or the foul breath of communistic Russia." Charles I. Dawson, a federal judge in Louisville, was even clearer than Al Smith:

Does any man or woman within the sound of my voice doubt that the President hopes, if re-elected, he will have the opportunity within the next four years to place upon the Supreme Court enough judges holding his own constitutional views to change the whole current of constitutional construction in this country? Do any of you doubt that if such an opportunity is presented, that is exactly what he will do?[276]

Dawson was clearly anticipating Roosevelt's abortive attempt to pack the Supreme Court with fellow liberals in 1937. In fact, the fear of destroying the U.S. Constitution through such maneuvering

[275] Ibid., 107–108.
[276] Ibid., 115–116.

was another issue at the heart of the concern of many Leaguers. Chamber-of-commerce audiences were particularly ripe for hearing such maledictions; for example, a group in Washington were told by a speaker that it

> was not Ulysses S. Grant who effected the near-destruction of "States' Rights," but rather the man who invented "Federal Aid." ... [The speaker] meant that it was largely through federal aid that the central government was gradually and insidiously invading those areas properly reserved for the states.[277]

While the major activities of the Liberty League occurred in 1933 to 1936, the presidential campaign of that last year became their central focus and, in many ways, their last stand. By 1936, John J. Raskob had become the public face of the League, and he and many others were exceedingly vocal in their opposition to the administration; they criticized the Tennessee Valley Authority, the farm subsidy programs, FDR's open support for organized labor, and various forms of big government spending. For his part, Roosevelt openly welcomed their criticism, knowing full well the degree of his support on the political left as well as with the rank-and-file American voter who had benefited, in one fashion or another, from New Deal legislation. Speaking to an enormous group of supporters in Madison Square Garden during the campaign, the president said:

> "We know that Government by organized money is just as dangerous as Government by organized mob. Never before in all our history have all these forces been so united against one candidate as they are today. They are unanimous in

[277] Ibid., 117. The speaker of the evening was Fitzgerald Hall, president of the Nashville, Chatanooga, and Saint Louis Railway, and a member of the Liberty League's advisory council.

their hate for me—and I welcome their hatred. I should like to have it said of my first Administration that in it the forces of selfishness and of lust for power met their match. I should like to have it said of my second administration that in it these forces have met their master." Raskob and the Liberty League had no answer for that kind of rhetoric.[278]

Roosevelt could obviously dish it out as well as he could take it, and his convincing margin of victory over the GOP's candidate, Governor Alfred M. Landon of Kansas (whom Alfred E. Smith and most Leaguers supported), appeared to diminish severely the League's chances of convincing the American people that they were right and FDR was seriously wrong. Why did the League fail? Many Americans were quick to blame corporate America for what happened to the economy in 1929, and to the average voter, Roosevelt seemed to offer a reasonable alternative: If the economy was incapable of restoring itself, moderate government intervention (which was all Roosevelt was talking about in 1932) seemed the obvious solution. If this was un-American, then the same could be said of the New Nationalism of FDR's cousin Theodore or Woodrow Wilson's New Freedom. In addition, Roosevelt came across as a close friend and confidant of the people, especially in his famous Fireside Chats. In the end,

> the League failed because the people, rightly or wrongly, regarded it as the executor of a bankrupted estate, the medicine man selling worthless stump water. The League failed because it represented economic and political conservatism at a time when both were out of style. In the 1930's the political pendulum was swinging, had swung, and the arc it was describing was toward the Left.... Meanwhile they

[278] Farber, *Everybody Ought to Be Rich*, 309.

Toil and Transcendence

[the Liberty Leaguers] took what comfort they could in the
thought that they had forced some restraint and temperance
on the Administration; that without the Liberty League the
New Deal would have been far more radical than it was.
"This was its great contribution," said Jouett Shouse.[279]

(In)famous Father Coughlin

In many ways, a far more significant opposition to Roosevelt, both
domestically and internationally, came from a Catholic clergy-
man whom history has called the "Radio Priest," Father Charles
E. Coughlin, pastor of the Shrine of the Little Flower in Royal
Oak, Michigan, in the Archdiocese of Detroit. When Roosevelt
finally succeeding in having Father Coughlin silenced, he seemed
to prove the fears of many of the Liberty Leaguers — that in his no-
opposition-tolerated approach, FDR might well have had dictato-
rial dreams. His apparent relations with the Catholic Church and
several of its best-known prelates, apparently marked by nothing
but cordiality, were challenged, and a very different Roosevelt, to
say the least, came to the forefront.

Born in Hamilton, Ontario, in 1881, Coughlin attended St.
Michael's College in Toronto, run by the Basilian Fathers, and
later entered their community, being ordained a Basilian priest in
1916. After teaching for a number of years at Assumption College
in Windsor, Ontario, he departed the community when proposed
revisions to their constitution would have changed their rule from a
society of common life to a more monastic rule. He was incardinated
in the Diocese of Detroit, taking a number of parochial assignments
before being assigned pastor in Royal Oak, a congregation of some
twenty-five families in a largely Protestant Detroit suburb.

[279] Wolfskill, *The Revolt of the Conservatives*, 261–262.

In 1926, the same year as his appointment, he began broadcasting on radio station WJR. His first work was a series of catechetical instructions for children, but later he began responding to the work of the Ku Klux Klan in Royal Oak, specifically the frequent cross burnings inspired, it seems, by the growing fear that Catholics would start to populate Royal Oak in significant numbers. When WJR was purchased by a larger company, its owner, recognizing Coughlin's talent, suggested that he begin addressing political topics.

By January 1930, the increasingly well-recognized priest began a series of attacks on socialism and Soviet communism. It was at this same time that charges of anti-Semitism began to be leveled against him, and one historical commentator has observed that "it was probably Coughlin's anti-Semitic vitriol that ultimately reserved him a special niche in the pantheon of American history."[280]

Several factors contributed to accusations against him: He felt, for example, that Nazism, very correctly associated with the fiercest form of anti-Semitism the human mind could imagine, was created in response to communism.

> Imbued with this idea [national socialism], be it right or wrong—an idea that spread rapidly, particularly since 1923 when Communism was beginning to make substantial advances throughout Germany—a group of rebel Germans under the leadership of an Austrian-born war veteran—Adolf Hitler by name—organized for two purposes. First, to overthrow the existing German government under whose

---

[280] Charles F. Gallagher, "A Peculiar Brand of Patriotism: The Holy See, FDR, and the Case of Reverend Charles E. Coughlin," in Woolner and Kurial, *FDR, the Vatican, and the Roman Catholic Church*, 269.

Toil and Transcendence

jurisdiction Communism was waxing strong and, second, to rid the Fatherland of Communists whose leaders, unfortunately, they identified with the Jewish race. Thus Naziism was conceived as a defence mechanicism against Communism and was ushered into existence as a result of Communism. And Communism itself was regarded by the rising generation of Germans as a product not of Russia, but of a group of Jews who dominated the destinies of Russia.[281]

Coughlin then listed twenty-five Jewish surnames of the advisers surrounding Vladimir Lenin, seemingly giving credence to the view he attributed to the Nazis, though he did note that it must be "emphasized that these Jews were not religious Jews. They were haters of God, the haters of religion."[282] Coughlin added:

Thus, it is my hope that the thousands of erudite, sincere Jews in this nation, together with all informed Christians, will recognize that as long as misguided Jews and gentiles both, and in such great numbers, continue to propagate the doctrines of anti-God, anti-Christ, anti-patriotism and anti-property, so long there always will exist some defensive mechanism against Communism. Today it is Naziism in Berlin. Tomorrow it will be some other "ism" in New York. But always it will be characterized by persecution.[283]

In yet another publication, Coughlin wrote an article attempting to answer the question of why Jews were persecuted throughout the world. Here, he relied on the Roman Jesuit publication *La*

---

[281] Charles E. Coughlin, "*Am I an Anti-Semite?*: 9 *Addresses on Various "Isms" Answering the Question* (Royal Oak, MI: Shrine of the Little Flower, 1939), 37.
[282] Ibid., 38.
[283] Ibid., 42.

Civiltà Cattolica, and he answered it was due to the causes and movements with which Jews have been associated:

> Coming to the topic to which the document invites us, to the Jewish peril that threatens the whole world by its pernicious infiltration and evil influences, especially among the Christian nations and more particularly among the Latin Catholics, where the blindness of the old liberalism has particularly favored the Jews, while it persecuted the Catholics ... this peril becomes every day more and more threatening.... We have denounced it, furnishing documents, proofs and facts of the frequent and undeniable alliance with Masonry ... or other sects and societies camouflaged as patriotic but in reality fluctuating towards or tending in fact to the subversion ... of the modern civil and religious society.... We have tried ... in the question of Bolshevism,... to show clearly ... how great has been the responsibility and the preponderance of the misguided generation of Jews in the Russian revolution as well as already in the French, and in the more recent one in Hungary.... We cannot understand why it is protected by governments which pretend to oppose resolutely all such Masonic, liberalistic, Socialistic and Communistic propaganda....[284]

With such editorializing, it would have been extremely difficult, if not impossible, for Coughlin to escape charges of anti-Semitism. Serious as these accusations were, however, they did not concern the Roosevelt administration nearly as much as Coughlin's criticisms of the president's domestic and foreign policy iniatives did. Initially, the radio priest was a staunch supporter of Roosevelt,

---

[284] Charles E. Coughlin, *An Answer to Father Coughlin's Critics* (Royal Oak, MI: Shrine of the Little Flower, 1940), 102–103.

coining the phrase "Roosevelt or Ruin" during the 1932 campaign. He felt the New Deal was the remedy to the country's ills, and as time progressed, he became known for his comment that the "New Deal is Christ's deal." In 1934, he testified before a Congressional Committee that if the New Deal policies did not become reality in all their fullness, a revolution worse than the French Revolution could overtake the United States. While Coughlin was always given to hyperbole, he and Roosevelt did become rather friendly associates: "Coughlin looked to Roosevelt for great things[;] Roosevelt looked to Coughlin for Catholic votes."[285]

Coughlin's frustration, in fact, was that New Deal agencies and programs seemed to be moving at a slow pace and not accomplishing what they set out to do. By the fall of 1934, the Detroit priest's support for FDR had abated substantially, and he founded his National Union for Social Justice, which, in the end, could count hundreds of thousands of members. He had also begun publication of a journal-type newspaper, *Social Justice*, which appeared on newsstands weekly, sold for ten cents, and contained articles not only by Coughlin, but by senators, governors, congressmen, well-known citizens, and churchmen — anyone who was sympathetic with any or all of his aims. Finally, there was his Sunday-afternoon nationally syndicated radio broadcast, estimated by some historians to have reached thirty million listeners per week.

With all this clout, Father Coughlin was beginning to cause concern among some members of the American hierarchy. Those who wanted him silenced realized that, short of Vatican intervention (which never became a reality), only his immediate ecclesiastical superior, Bishop Michael Gallagher of Detroit, had real authority.

---

[285] Charles J. Tull, *Father Coughlin and the New Deal* (Syracuse: Syracuse University Press, 1965), 239.

And at no point in the radio priest's career did Gallagher oppose him. Indeed, on Sunday, April 21, 1935, the bishop made a nationwide radio broadcast:

> I pronounce Father Coughlin sound in doctrine, able in its application and interpretation. Freely I give him my *imprimatur* on his written word and freely I give my approval on the spoken word. May both be circulated throughout the land. Under my jurisdiction, he preaches the just codes of the Old Law and Its Commandments. He teaches Christ and the Fathers and the Doctors of the Church. He preaches the Encyclicals and applies them as he has been ordered to do. Father Coughlin preaches the doctrine of *social justice* to all. Remember the words of St. Paul: "There is neither Greek nor Jew, bond nor free, male nor female, but you are all one in Christ Jesus our Lord."[286]

By the 1936 presidential election campaign, the National Union for Social Justice had grown to the point that it fielded its own presidential candidate, Congressman William Lemke of North Dakota. While earning no electoral votes, his popular-vote total was a non-negligible nine hundred thousand. The irritation Coughlin was creating was growing within the administration, and with Roosevelt himself. In the Church, Cardinal William O'Connell of Boston was no Coughlin admirer, though Boston's colorful mayor, Michael Curley, called it "the strongest Coughlinite city in America." In New York, Cardinal Patrick Hayes had one of his diocesan priests write a pamphlet "debunking anti-Semitic canards of the kind being published in Coughlin's *Social Justice*," while *Commonweal*'s George N. Schuster complained that "men who have studied least are listened to most." Monsignor John A. Ryan, no friend of Coughlin,

[286] Coughlin, *An Answer to Father Coughlin's Critics*, foreword.

wrote a critical article for the *Catholic Charities Review* on "Quack Remedies for a Depression Malady."[287]

Behind the scenes, activity on Coughlin grew more urgent. Detroit at this time was a suffragan see of the Archdiocese of Cincinnati, whose archbishop was John T. McNicholas, O.P. At the apparent request of a number of his episcopal colleagues, the archbishop became the liaison on the issue with Archbishop Pietro Fumasoni-Biondi, the apostolic delegate to the United States, and later his successor, Amleto Cicognani. McNicholas was to ask Gallagher in Detroit to have Coughlin cease his attacks on Roosevelt. Gallagher also informed Coughlin that the delegate did not want him naming names on his broadcasts. The entreaties apparently fell on deaf ears, and Coughlin went full steam ahead.

Cicognani later asked McNicholas if the National Catholic Welfare Conference (forerunner to the NCCB) might issue a statement that Father Coughlin was exercising his constitutional freedom of speech in stating his views but was not speaking on behalf of the Catholic Church in the United States. McNicholas wanted to save the Vatican the ordeal of publicly censuring Coughlin, but at the same time, he realized that he could not go over the head of the Bishop of Detroit. Despite such maneuverings, and Coughlin's formation of a third party to challenge the president, Roosevelt continued to gain favor among Catholic voters. It was at the same time that the relatively new Bishop Francis Spellman, a close friend of Vatican secretary of state Cardinal Eugenio Pacelli, was coming into Roosevelt's orbit. Spellman wrote to and later visited Cicognani to inform him of FDR's annoyance with Coughlin, and, as the election campaign was progressing in the fall of 1936, James A. Farley, chairman of the Democratic National Committee, urged Roosevelt to obtain a statement from Chicago's Cardinal Mundelein that he

---

[287] Hennesey, *American Catholics*, 274–275.

saw nothing of a communistic nature in the administration. The Chicago cardinal had, in fact, issued a statement falling short of a specific endorsement of Roosevelt, rather stressing how grateful Catholics in the United States should be for all the economic assistance they received from New Deal policies.[288]

In January 1937, Bishop Gallagher died. Father Coughlin claimed that his bishop's dying wish was that he continue his work on radio, which he did for a time. Shortly thereafter, however, it was announced that the bishop of Rochester, Edward A. Mooney, was to succeed Gallagher in Detroit, and that the see was to be raised to an archdiocese. By 1946, Mooney would be made a cardinal. Mooney was not nearly as favorably dioposed to Father Coughlin as his predecessor had been, and a set of events were set in motion within the Church—but clearly also at the strong urgings of the administration—that would bring Coughlin's career to a conclusion.

The Roosevelt administration argued that the First Amendment's protection of free speech did not necessarily apply to broadcasting, since it was a "limited national resource," and thus susceptible to regulation. With the radio priest very much in mind, it was decreed that broadcasters would now be required to seek operating permits. Father Coughlin's application and appeal were denied. In order to work around the scheme, he purchased air time and played his talks by transcription. This put significant strain on his organization's financial resources, and when he continued his attacks, more often now about foreign affairs, the National Association of Broadcasters adopted more stringent rules on the sale of radio time to those who were broadcasting controversial material. Further, they required manuscripts to be submitted in advance for clearance, under the threat of losing their licenses.

[288] Fogarty, "Roosevelt and the American Catholic Hierarchy," 16–20.

Toil and Transcendence

The loss of franking privileges that had previously allowed *Social Justice* to be mailed throughout the country, and to many parts of the world, followed the Japanese attack on Pearl Harbor in December 1941. Coughlin had been, up to then, a staunch isolationist, but this view was increasingly seen as unpatriotic, even favoring the enemy. Doubtless at Roosevelt's urging, the attorney general, Francis Biddle, contacted Frank Walker, the postmaster general, to deny *Social Justice* the privileged rates it had enjoyed: The prohibitive cost increase caused the magazine to cease publication. Added to this was a directive that Cardinal Mooney, under pressure from the Roosevelt administration, gave to Coughlin to cease all political activity over the airwaves or in writing. To his credit, Father Coughlin immediately complied, stating publicly that it was and always would be a priest's duty to yield to his bishop in obedience. He remained pastor of the Shrine of the Little Flower until his retirement in 1966, and he died in 1979 at age eighty-eight.

Father Coughlin's major support came from working-class Irish and Germans in the East and the Midwest who were spellbound by his eloquent and persuasive oratory. His isolationism was shared by millions of his fellow countrymen. The "voluminous catalogue of human misery could easily have embittered a man of Coughlin's emotional nature"; still, "there is no reason to question his genuine sympathy for the poor."[289] True, the overwhelming historical interpretation of the radio priest has been negative—for his belief that nationalization of currency was the solution to the nation's economic woes, for his perceived anti-Semitism, and, above all, for his audacity in taking on the New Deal and its architect, Franklin D. Roosevelt. Still, to many Catholics of a faith-filled era, he was a true, real, priestly priest, who tried to address the nation's

---

[289] Tull, *Father Coughlin and the New Deal*, 242–244.

severest economic crisis up to that point in its history, as well as an international situation growing more fearful with each passing day.

Literary Luminaries

Much else was transpiring in the Church in America during these years, especially in the Catholic literary world, not to mention the field of social work. Catholic writers such as Frances Parkinson Keyes and Phyllis McGinley were very popular. Mrs. Keyes, born in Charlottesville, Virginia, began writing articles for publications such as the *Atlantic Monthly* and *Good Housekeeping*, then moved on to novels set against such backgrounds as her native Virginia, Louisiana, France, England, and South America. As a widow, she purchased the Beauregard House in the French Quarter of New Orleans, where she produced many of her works. Her conversion to Catholicism came about, no doubt, from living in the very French Catholic atmosphere of New Orleans, and it is discernible in several of her books. As a Catholic, she wrote excellent biographies of Saint Ann, Saint Thérèse of Lisieux, and Saint Bernadette Soubirous.

Phyllis McGinley, who was given Notre Dame's prestigious Laetare Medal, was born and educated in Utah but moved east as a young woman. She spent many years in Larchmont, New York, and began her literary career as a copywriter and poetry editor for *Town and Country* magazine. She went on to write light verse and poetry that reflected her strong Catholic Faith. Her works were often included in Catholic high school English texts, and, in later years, she wrote books for smaller children. One of her many collections of poetry included *The Love Letters of Phyllis McGinley*, which won her the Pulitzer Prize for poetry.[290]

[290] Glazier and Shelley, *The Encyclopedia of American Catholic History*, 880–881.

Toil and Transcendence

Saint Louis Jesuit Father Daniel A. Lord, an activist for morality in media, accomplished much in his life. Of English and Irish extraction, he was born in Chicago, entered the Missouri Jesuit province, and was ordained to the priesthood in 1923. As a young priest he taught English at Saint Louis University and its high school before branching out into his life's work. He believed that "literature, motion pictures and the performing arts were effective means of communicating moral values in society," and as such, he worked diligently for years to establish moral codes for entertainment. His influence was to be found in the Hays Code, which governed motion-picture content, as well as the particulars of the famous pledge Catholics took each year during Lent to abstain from all offensive films. This came from the Legion of Decency, along with Catholic ratings for all motion pictures that appeared in diocesan newspapers throughout the country.

Father Lord also began the Summer Schools of Catholic Action in 1931 and served for many years as editor of the *Queen's Work*, the organ of the Sodalities of the Blessed Virgin Mary in the United States. Part of this was the Catholic Students' Mission Crusade (CSMC), remembered by generations of Catholic students, for its famous song:

> An army of youth, flying the standard of truth,
> We're fighting for Christ the Lord.
> Heads lifted high, Catholic Action our cry
> And the cross our only sword.[291]

Queen's Work pamphlets, largely an apologetic tool, were found in Catholic bookstores throughout the country as well as on pamphlet racks in Catholic churches. Millions of copies were circulated and sold; Father Lord was equally commited to working among

---

[291] Hennesey, *American Catholics*, 258.

young Catholics, with a primary concern "to raise [their] level of religious, social, and ethical consciousness that they might act in socially responsible ways."[292]

Yet another author, educator, editor, and well-remembered Catholic name was George N. Schuster. Born into a German Wisconsin family, Schuster was a 1915 graduate of the University of Notre Dame. He saw action during the First World War and, fluent in German, served for a time translating intercepted German communiqués. Upon his return, he assumed a teaching position at Notre Dame, where he also received his master's in English and served for four years as chairman of the English Department. He earned his doctorate at Columbia University, while he was teaching at St. Joseph's College for Women in Brooklyn and serving on the editorial board of the new magazine *Commonweal*. He became president of Hunter College in New York, where he opened a School of Social Work, and admitted men for the first time to the largest women's college in the country. Schuster later returned to Notre Dame as assistant to President Theodore M. Hesburgh, C.S.C., and did much to establish the Center for the Study of Man in Contemporary Society.

George Schuster wrote more than twenty books in his lifetime, along with scores of scholarly articles. Fiercely Catholic and quick to defend the Church, he seemed to waver in his position on *Humanae Vitae* in the late sixties—indicative of liberal leanings discernible in much of his writing. He resigned, for example, from *Commonweal* in 1937 over the publication's support of General Francisco Franco. Several Catholic colleges honored him in his life, including Fordham University and his alma mater with its Laetare Medal.

[292] Glazier and Shelley, *The Encyclopedia of American Catholic History*, 815.

Toil and Transcendence

Catholic Radicals

One of the most significant happenings in the American Church during these years was the founding of the Catholic Worker Movement by Dorothy Day, in company with Peter Maurin. Dorothy Day was born in Brooklyn in 1897, but it was not until she was living in Chicago as a young girl that she began to entertain favorable notions about Catholicism. At the same time, she read Upton Sinclair's novel *The Jungle,* and her social consciousness began to be stirred. She took long walks around Chicago's poorest neighborhoods and developed a lifelong attraction to areas most people would tend to avoid. As a young woman, she moved to New York, where she found a job as a reporter for the *Call,* the city's only socialist daily paper. This was followed by similar work for the *Masses,* a publication opposing American entry into the First World War. Throughout the course of her life, "her conviction that the social order was unjust changed in no substantial way from her adolescence until her death, though she never identified herself with any political party."[293]

Her religious development was slower. As a child, she had attended services at an Episcopalian church, but in her New York years, she grew into the habit of making lengthy visits to St. Joseph's Church in Greenwich Village. Catholic liturgy and discipline strongly attracted her, and, because of its immigrant makeup, she began to feel that the Catholic Church was the church of the poor and the downtrodden. In her younger years, Dorothy had had an abortion,[294] which she vividly portrayed in her novel *The Eleventh*

---

[293] Ibid., 414.

[294] It was in part because of that abortion that New York's John Cardinal O'Connor, when he formally introduced her cause for sainthood, stated that she would be a particularly strong advocate and intercessor for young women who had experienced abortion or for

Virgin. Later, she entered into a common-law relationship with For-
ster Batterham, an "anarchist opposed to marriage and religion."[295]
She became pregnant by Batterham, gave birth to daughter Tamar,
and immediately had the little girl baptized a Catholic. Shortly
thereafter, she broke with Batterham and was formally received
into the Catholic Church in 1927. In 1932, Dorothy traveled to
Washington, D.C., to report for the Catholic publications *Commonweal* and *America* on the hunger march through the capital.
This, it seemed, readied her all the more for her life's work.

That same year, she met Peter Maurin, a French immigrant
much older than she, who had once been a Christian Brother; they
connected through his friendship with George Schuster. Day and
Maurin shared the goal of establishing a Catholic newspaper that
would enunciate Catholic social teaching, along with developing
a concrete plan for a peaceful transformation of society. From these
notions, the *Catholic Worker* was begun in 1932, and by the end
of the year, one hundred thousand copies were being printed each
month. The publication "expressed dissatisfaction with the social
order, and took the side of labor unions, but its vision of the ideal
future challenged both urbanization and industrialism."[296]

Besides the newspaper, the Catholic Worker Movement became
a practical reality at the same time. Houses of Hospitality began to
spring up in different parts of the country: It made little difference
why someone showed up at their doors; all were welcome for as
long as they chose to stay. The movement also experimented for
a time with farm communes.

---

those contemplating one. O'Connor, until his death in 2000, was
perhaps the leading pro-life spokesman in the American hierarchy.

[295] Glazier and Shelley, *The Encyclopedia of American Catholic History*,
414.
[296] Ibid., 415.

Day, Maurin, and the Catholic Worker Movement were always committed to pacifism and nonviolence, based solidly on Scripture and many of the Church's social teachings. In 1936, the *Catholic Worker* refused to take sides in the Spanish Civil War, and after Pearl Harbor, the paper continued to stress pacifism, carefully stressing that opposition to the war had nothing to do with supporting America's enemies. After the war emerged "the cold war, the nuclear-armed welfare state, and a series of smaller wars in which America was involved,"[297] all of which grieved Day. On her seventy-fifth birthday in 1955, the Jesuit publication *America* devoted an entire issue to her, calling her the individual who best exemplified "the aspiration and action of the American Catholic community during the past forty years." Notre Dame, in awarding her the Laetare Medal, thanked her for "comforting the afflicted and afflicting the comfortable."[298] By her death in 1980, many had seen her saintly qualities shine forth, and these admirers were little surprised when the Church opened the investigation into her cause.

The United States and the Holy See

Franklin Roosevelt's administration is remembered as much for the Second World War as for its domestic policies. As a prelude to the growing conflagration, the pragmatic president saw the value in some sort of diplomatic relations with the Holy See. He set a plan in motion that he officially announced to the American public on Christmas Eve 1939. The principal players in this story were Secretary of State Cordell Hull and his assistant secretary, Sumner Welles. Early in the fall of 1939, the president asked Hull to look into the possibility of establishing a special mission to the Vatican

[297] Ibid., 416.
[298] Ibid., 417.

for the purpose of mutual discussion on the problem of refugees from war-torn countries. Hull and Wells were essentially diplomats, but Roosevelt, the consummate politican, wanted to avoid any semblance of *formal* diplomatic relations, especially with the election year of 1940 soon to be upon him, and the anti-Catholicism that surely would be stirred up throughout the country at the mere thought of such a plan.

Soon thereafter, FDR invited Cardinal Spellman to the White House to discuss his plan; following that meeting, Spellman contacted the apostolic delegate, Archbishop Cicognani, who, in turn, contacted Pius XII's secretary of state, Cardinal Luigi Maglione. The communiqué noted that the president was scheduled to go on radio at the same time as the pope to congratulate the Catholic University of America on its fiftieth anniversary. Also contained, though, was the president's desire to establish some sort of diplomatic ties in the near future. A special mission would not require congressional funding, Spellman assured Maglione; if it were established as a successful enterprise for several years, however, Congress might be induced to appropriate funds for a permanent mission. This would, of course, according to Spellman, have to wait more than forty years.

Roosevelt had some candidates in mind to fill the post, but at the top of the list seemed to be Myron C. Taylor, an Episcopalian and former board chairman of U.S. Steel who enjoyed the favor and friendship of a number of members of the American hierarchy. It did not hurt that he was an independently wealthy man who owned a private villa in Florence, from where Rome would be an easy commute for meetings, audiences with the Holy Father, and the like.

Pius XII took an eager interest in events up to this point and conveyed to Roosevelt through his secretary of state how mutually advantageous such a relationship would be at that moment in history. Two additional White House meetings took place between the president and the archbishop of New York, and shortly before the official announcement was made, notice was sent to the presidents of the Jewish Theological Seminary and the Federal Council of Churches, a Protestant group. Roosevelt's argument was that the arrangement would strengthen his own base of moral support, possibly even allowing him to avoid an all-out war. Despite FDR's efforts, though, several Protestant denominations did object: Methodists, Presbyterians, Lutherans, Baptists, and Seventh-day Adventists were the most vocal in their criticism.

But FDR pressed forward, and Myron Taylor was given the title "extraordinary ambassador"and presented his credentials to Pius XII on February 27, 1940. Over the next several years, he visited the Vatican on several occasions; Harold Tittman, his administrative assistant, was chargé d'affaires, and often represented Taylor, especially when he was ill. Taylor continued his mission in the Truman administration, retiring in 1950. Taylor, for all purposes, was treated as any ambassador would be, though Roosevelt continued to maintain that he was not one. He was paid from a special White House fund, and his name was never formally submitted to the U.S. Senate for confirmation.[299]

Topics often discussed by Taylor and the pope or his secretary of state ranged from freedom of religion and freedom of communication to arms reduction and freedom of trade between nations. These were neutral points, ones which Taylor and Vatican officials could largely agree on. For its part, the Holy See appeared glad not to grant the U.S. full diplomatic relations, thereby giving Roosevelt a good deal of leeway he could enjoy only under the present arrangement. Nonetheless, the president had instructed Taylor to discuss certain specifics:

[299] Hennesey, *American Catholics*, 278.

"COUGHLIN" was listed as a topic in bold faced letters. Roosevelt understood Samuel Stritch "to be somewhat of a Fascist," while "Spellman seems to be very good." The president also learned that Washington would be erected into an Archdiocese and as the first Ordinary he stressed that it is important that he be a reputable and liberal-minded Bishop. Bishop Bernard J. Sheil, who was understudy to Cardinal Mundelein "would be an agreeable choice." Roosevelt added to the agenda for Taylor's discussion the anti-Jewish sentiment in Baltimore, Brooklyn and Detroit which "is said to be encouraged by the church" and which in turn "automatically stirs up anti-Catholic feeling and that makes a general mess." ... Maglione condemned the anti-Semitism Roosevelt claimed existed with church support ... and promised if Taylor would draw up a protest, Cicognani would be instructed to investigate. On Coughlin [Secretary of State] Maglione said he was ready to investigate the question. But on the appointment of Sheil to Washington, Maglione side-stepped the question and stated that the appointment properly belonged to the Consistorial Congregation. The president's mentioning of Sheil as a possible candidate for Washington, however, may very well have left the new Archdiocese under the administration of Roosevelt's outspoken foe, Archbishop Curley, until the latter's death in 1947; it may also have prevented Sheil's advancement beyond Auxiliary Bishop of Chicago. The Holy See may have been willing to accept a compromise on establishing full diplomatic relations with the United States, but it would not allow the compromiser to intrude into strictly ecclesiastical affairs.[300]

[300] Fogarty, "Roosevelt and the American Catholic Hierarchy," 263–264.

Toil and Transcendence

A *Third Term*

American involvement in the Second World War had its beginnings well before the appointment of Taylor: When the president finally made up his mind about intervening has been open to historical interpretation for years. What is certain is that his decision was made before the attack on Pearl Harbor, and the diplomatic events leading up to it show the United States in an increasingly defensive posture.

While Europe and Asia roiled in the first years of the war, Roosevelt was engaged in a political campaign at home for an unprecedented third term in the White House. By now, Roosevelt had little to fear from his opposition, so popularly entrenched was he in the American psyche; nevertheless, many felt three terms for any president was too much, especially since the tradition of two terms had been set by George Washington. Roosevelt's Republican opponent was Wendell Willkie, a native of Indiana. Willkie was a lawyer for Firestone who had returned to private practice and represented, among other clients, electric utility companies. In 1939, he had accepted a position as counsel for Commonwealth & Southern Corporation (C&S), a utility holding company. He soon assumed leadership of the company, and when FDR announced the formation of his Tennessee Valley Authority, which would supply power in competition with C&S, Willkie testified against the scheme before Congress, the public, and the courts. Though a longtime Democratic activist, he changed his registration in 1939 and waited in the wings, willing to be a compromise candidate should the GOP Convention become deadlocked. Never having held an elective office, Willkie was nonetheless nominated on the sixth ballot over such candidates as New York Governor Thomas E. Dewey and Ohio Senator Robert A. Taft, whom many felt too conservative and isolationist.

Roosevelt won a resounding victory, carrying thirty-eight of the nation's forty-eight states. During the campaign, however, there was some worry among the Democrats about Catholic votes—especially among the more isolationist Irish and Italians. One reason for this was the vocal opposition to FDR's foreign policy from Joseph P. Kennedy, ambassador to the Court of St. James and former head of the Securities and Exchange Commission. Many prominent Americans, such as Henry Luce of the Time Life empire, encouraged Kennedy to come out against Roosevelt when he returned to the United States. Rumors began to fly that Kennedy, one of the most high-profile Catholics in the United States at the time, might well endorse Willkie.

> On Sunday, October 27 [1940] Kennedy landed in the United States and then went to Washington for dinner with the president and a small group at the White House. Roosevelt tried to charm Kennedy, but the ambassador declared that he was "damn sore at the way I have been treated" in being bypassed or ignored on important diplomatic matters. The president expressed sympathy—and then came the straight politics. By the ambassador's account, Roosevelt pledged to support his son Joseph P. Kennedy, Jr. for Massachusetts governor in 1942 if Kennedy endorsed FDR; by the account of Kennedy's son John F. Kennedy, the president intimated that the ambassador himself might be the democratic presidential nominee in 1944; by the account of the president's son James, FDR warned that should Kennedy desert FDR and support Willkie, his sons' careers would be badly damaged. Whatever the understanding or the reason, Kennedy agreed to give a radio speech on Tuesday, October 29, endorsing FDR's reelection.[301]

[301] Jeffries, *A Third Term for FDR*, 158.

Toil and Transcendence

What impact Kennedy's endorsement had can only be speculated. An analysis of the 1940 vote did shed considerable light on voting patterns, especially religious and ethnic:

> Jews and Catholics, many of relatively recent immigrant background in 1940, were much more likely than white non-Southern Protestants, largely old stock, to vote Democratic. (Southern Protestants who voted, mostly white, were overwhelmingly Democratic.) Outside the South, white Catholics voted some seventy percent for FDR, while Protestants about thirty percent ... [and] Jews voted about ninety percent for Roosevelt. Protestants accounted for some two-thirds of Willkie supporters outside the South, but for little more than two-fifths of FDR's. Catholic and Jewish voters together constituted about one-tenth of non-Southern Willkie voters, about three-tenths of FDR's.... Voting by religious groups reflected not only ethnicity, but also socioeconomic status: among white voters outside the South FDR won only about one-fifth of the high-socioeconomic status Protestants, about half of low-socioeconomic status Protestants; he won some two-fifths of high-socioeconomic status Catholics, three-forths of low-socioeconomic status Catholics. Religion thus helped shape the division of the vote, but apparently not so importantly as ethnicity and class.[302]

The War

World War II was fought in three theaters: Europe, the Pacific, and North Africa. Each of these areas held concern for the Church, but perhaps none more so than Europe. There, perhaps the greatest

---

[302] Ibid., 175–176.

concern of the American hierarchy, and, for that matter, of bishops throughout the world, was the the safety of Vatican City, the outlying city of Rome, and, most of all, the person of the Holy Father.

In September 1943, New York's Archbishop Spellman went to see Roosevelt at the White House. He was extremely concerned for the safety of the Eternal City and the pope, since the Germans were within days of occupying the city. Up to now, Spellman had not been in any way critical of FDR's handling of the war. At this meeting, he "found the president extraordinarily frank about the chances of American forces being able to stop two hundred Russian divisions from doing whatever Stalin pleased, at a time when the United States did not yet have a single boot on mainland Europe." Spellman came away from the hour-long audience disappointed at the president's "laissez-faire" attitude. As Roosevelt put it to Spellman, Europeans will simply have to endure Russian domination, with the hope that, in one or two decades, they will be able to live well with them.

Spellman, who had spent so many years at the Vatican earlier in his career, wondered at the despairing view of the president regarding the future of Europe: the very cradle of Western civilization and the home of so many Christians. Roosevelt had always been against "spheres of influence" in the world but was now talking of "an agreement among the Big Four. Accordingly, the world will be divided into spheres of influence: China gets the Far East; the U.S., the Pacific; Britain and Russia, Europe and Africa. But as Britain has predominantly colonial interests it might be assumed that Russia will predominate."[303]

On July 19, 1943, the Americans bombed Rome. As expected, an immediate crisis came about in U.S.-Vatican relations. Weeks

---

[303] Nigel Hamilton, *Commander in Chief: FDR'S Battle with Churchill, 1943* (New York: Houghton Mifflin Harcourt, 2016), 360–364.

earlier, on May 19, 1943, Pius XII had written Roosevelt "pleading that he recognize the sacred character of the city and spare the civilian population." The president replied that he appreciated the pope's concern for the safety of the people, and he assured the pope that "Americans are among those who value most the religious shrines and the historical monuments of Italy." At the same time FDR told Pius that his countrymen were "likewise united in their determination to win the war which has been thrust upon them and for which the present government of Italy must take full responsibility." Roosevelt did promise that bombings would be limited, as much as possible, to military targets, and that American aviators had been informed "as to the location of the Vatican and have been specifically instructed to prevent bombs from falling within the Vatican City."[304]

Vatican City itself had pursued a policy of neutrality during the war. Although Rome was occupied by Germany in 1943 and by the Allies in 1944, Vatican City itself was never seized. The Lateran Treaty of 1929 with Italy recognized the sovereignty of Vatican City, declaring it a neutral country in international relations and requiring the pope to abstain from mediation unless requested by all parties. Thirty-eight nations had come to recognize the legitimacy of this sovereign state, which had a diplomatic corps of thirteen ambassadors and twenty-five ministers. Despite this, Vatican City was bombed twice during the war: first, on November 5, 1943, southwest of St. Peter's Basilica, causing damage but no fatalities; and second, on March 1, 1944, on the margins of the city-state, causing the death of one person and the injury of another.

The papal palace at Castel Gandolfo, some fifteen miles south of Rome in the Alban Hills, had been the summer residence of the popes for centuries. Part of the concordat with the Italian

[304] Fogarty, "Roosevelt and the American Catholic Hierarchy," 37–38.

government guaranteed the Holy See this residence in perpetuity. It was designated part of the territory of Vatican City-State and would enjoy extraterritorial status from then on. In 1938, when Hitler made an official state visit to Rome to meet with Mussolini and all of the Eternal City was bedecked with Nazi flags, Pope Pius XI and his secretary of state withdrew to Castel Gandolfo, refusing to meet with the German dictator, whom he had sharply criticized. The following year, Pacelli, the new Pope Pius XII, made an appeal to the entire world from the summer residence; he said that nothing was ever lost by peace, but war might well be the ruination of the world. These words were quickly forgotten, and by 1943 German soldiers began occupying Rome and deporting Roman Jews.

Castel Gandolfo was used as a shelter for those who were targeted; several hundred Jews were kept hidden there and provided with kosher foods. In October 1943, the Vatican dispatched a contingent of papal guards to stand guard in front of the residence. These were strengthened by additional volunteers until this Vatican property was protected by thousands. By the spring of 1944, thousands of people had taken advantage of the security of the palace, which was considered safe from attack. Nonetheless, on February 10, an American bomb fell on the residence while a crowd of people were gathering for the daily distribution of milk, and the following day, some five hundred bodies were discovered under the rubble. As could be imagined, this placed a great strain on relations between the White House and the American hierarchy. Cardinal Cicognani, the apostolic delegate, wrote to the U.S. State Department, and Cardinal Spellman, heretofore a friend of Roosevelt, wrote to the president and stated :

> After my several talks with you and my repeated assurances
> to the Holy Father of our desire to show him every respect,
> I feel I must do something to comfort him, and others who

reverence him and are pained to see his home at Castel Gandolfo bombed by our airmen, … while the Vatican states that "no German soldier has been admitted within the borders of the neutral Pontifical Villa and that no German military whatsoever are within it at present." There are only helpless and homeless people refuged there.[305]

Two days later, speaking at a Memorial Mass for the Knights of Columbus in St. Patrick's Cathedral, Spellman drew an interesting comparison, hoping and praying that "as Britain once spared the Holy City of Mecca, military ingenuity will overcome 'military necessity' which would destroy the Eternal City of Rome, the citadel of civilization."[306] Unfortunately, this would not come to pass.

The cordial relations between the president and the hierarchy ultimately ran upon the shoals of the problem of the bombing of Rome. Here [FDR] apparently failed to see the religious sensitivities of the American hierarchy and its Catholic people. Whether he was misled by some of his advisers or simply had to respond to military necessities, he confronted a problem analogous to what Wilson had faced in regard to the Irish problem. What had begun in 1933 as a close alliance between Roosevelt and American Catholics ended in 1944 with the feeling among Catholic prelates that the president subordinated the interests of Catholics to transitory military expediency influenced by British policy.[307]

Despite the rift between the White House and the American Catholic hierarchy, Cardinal Spellman must be credited for his

[305] Spellman to Roosevelt, February 20, 1944, cited in Fogarty, "Roosevelt and the American Catholic Hierarchy," 37.
[306] Ibid.
[307] Ibid., 38–39.

exceptionally high degree of patriotism and the part he played to instill such feeling even deeper into American Catholics. His Christmas visits to American troops serving in all theaters of the war became legendary, and decades after the war had ended, in 1967, it was during the preparations for yet another overseas trip that he died suddenly. Spellman cautioned against those who "do not lift their gaze above the present dark horizon to the light of vision from above," fearing that such individuals "may easily succumb to defeat and to despair." He added that "only the soul with supernatural vision can hope to endure. Faith is the lost horizon which we must find and the world must find." The cardinal felt two battles must be won in every human life—the battle of life for the salvation of our immortal souls and, for Americans especially, the battle for the country's life.

> It will be our honor to have a part in this victory, a victory not alone of arms over the forces of those who would destroy us, but also a victory for the freedom of righteous people everywhere, because ... in the words of President Roosevelt, "the vast majority of the members of the human race is on our side. Many of them are fighting with us. All of them are praying for us. For in representing our cause we represent theirs as well—our hope and their hope for liberty under God."[308]

The final major military act of the Second World War was the dropping of atomic bombs on the Japanese cities of Hiroshima and Nagasaki. Roosevelt, after winning his fourth term, had died suddenly at his summer White House in Warm Springs, Georgia,

[308] Francis J. Spellman, *The Road to Victory: The Second Front of Prayer* (New York: Charles Scribner's Sons, 1942), 37, 110, 112. The cardinal also wrote *What America Means to Me*, a further insight into his patriotism.

on April 12, 1945, and was succeeded by his vice president, Harry Truman. By August 1945, it was known to all observers that Japan had lost the war. The country was split, however, between those who wanted to surrender immediately and those who wanted to continue the fight despite all odds. Most historians agree that Truman had several options: continue conventional bombing; invade Japan; demonstrate the bomb on an unpopulated island; or drop the bomb on an inhabited Japanese city. Truman chose the last option, vaporizing hundreds of thousands of Japanese civilians, but seemingly sparing the lives of innumerable soldiers who would fall in an assault on the islands.

Polling showed that 53.5 percent of the American public supported Truman's decision to drop the bomb on Hiroshima and Nagasaki. Considering the size of the American Catholic population, reaction was minimal. The American bishops remained silent, as did a large majority of Catholic newspapers. Some did express an opinion: *America* felt that immediate moral judgments were too difficult to call; Dorothy Day in the *Catholic Worker* said, "We have created destruction"; *Commonweal*, a decidedly liberal publication, was highly critical; and, strangely, Pat Scanlan's *Brooklyn Tablet*, faithfully on the right of most issues, sided with their colleagues at *Commonweal*.[309]

The Aftermath

One of the more positive developments for Catholics in the postwar era came with the passing of the Servicemen's Readjustment Act of 1944, more popularly referred to as the G.I. Bill. It provided for a subsistence allowance, tuition, and supplies for returning veterans, allowing them to pursue educational opportunities. It is estimated

---

[309] Hennesey, *American Catholics*, 281–282.

that seven and a half million veterans took advantage of it. As a result, Catholics began attending college in unprecedented numbers, and with their advanced educational attainment, significant employment opportunities opened up; the flight to the suburbs occurred; and a more educated generation had the chance to pass on to their offspring even more opportunity. It sounded wonderful in the late forties and throughout the fifties, but in subsequent decades, this ticket to respectability would result in all sorts of difficulties, not the least of which was the loss of the practice of the Faith among younger generations.

At the beginning of 1950, when Myron Taylor announced his departure from his position at the Vatican, *Century* magazine seemed to project a cautious optimism that America's ties with the Holy See might be at an end. The publication was one of the leaders in warning of the danger of the United States becoming involved with the Vatican in any way. The *Washington Post*, however, joined several Catholic publications in favoring the selection of a permanent successor to Taylor, but a bit of time would elapse before the Truman administration would take any sort of action. In the fall of 1951, though, Truman surprised many when he announced his selection of General Mark Clark to be sent to the Senate for confirmation as full ambassador to the Holy See.

Clark was a veteran of both world wars and in 1945, at age forty-eight, became the youngest officer ever to be promoted to the rank of four-star general. An Episcopalian whose mother was Jewish, he became a close friend of Dwight D. Eisenhower when the two were young cadets at West Point. He served as a deputy commander of the Civilian Conservation Corps (CCC) in Omaha and taught between wars at the U.S. Army General Command and General Staff School, and later at the Army War College. Among his associates were Matthew Ridgeway and Walter Bedell Smith, an active Catholic and Eisenhower's secretary in Europe. Clark's

many military promotions were recognition of his contributions to the European theater of war.

Clark had an excellent wartime rapport with Pius XII, apologizing to the Holy Father on one occasion for the noise made by American troops in Rome. The pope was said to have replied to the general that whenever he came with the intention of liberating Rome, he could make as much noise as he wanted. Noise was made domestically, however, when the announcement was made of Truman's intent. The pope was reported to be very pleased with Clark's selection, but

> Truman announced the ambassadorial appointment to "Vatican City State" and not to the Holy See. The Catholic hierarchy felt this specification to be a severe affront to the supreme pontiff. Domestic critics were similarly unimpressed by this distinction, which they perceived to be legalistic dodge intended to get around constitutional difficulties with appointing an ambassador directly to the Roman Catholic Church.[310]

Many Senators who were up for reelection in 1952 kept silent on the issue, scared to offend large sections of their constituencies either way. *Century* wrote a strong editorial rallying against the appointment and even had the article reproduced as a pamphlet, which was circulated throughout the country. The *New Republic* reported that the Senate Foreign Relations Committee had received some fifty thousand letters about the proposed appointment, with "scarcely more than 50" favorable to the idea. All of this proved

[310] Michael H. Carter, "Diplomacy's Detractors: American Protestant Reaction to FDR'S 'Personal Representative at The Vatican,'" in Woolner and Kurial, *FDR, the Vatican, and the Roman Catholic Church*, 194.

the success of Protestant leaders' opposition; the consistency of their letters was well described by *Newsweek*:

> Many were mimeographed; many were in the form of petitions.... [The mail] consisted primarily of temperate discussion of the proper relationship between church and state, and there were very few expressions of Klan-type bigotry. There was evidence that many of the letters were a sort of church community enterprise, probably motivated as much by dutiful response to pastors as by burning personal convictions.[311]

Clark withdrew his name from nomination, and the papal mission staff was transferred to the Italian consulate. No successor was named, nor was the issue given serious consideration for more than three decades, when another American president would raise the question of full diplomatic relations with the Vatican and submit his nomination to the Senate for an ambassador. This time, the effort would be successful.

[311] Ibid.

5

∞

The Church of the Fifties

The Heyday

If the 1920s were a return to "normalcy" after the First World War, the 1950s were an even more impressive period of stability, growth, affluence, peace, patriotism, religious fervor, and an abiding belief in the greatness of America. The economic growth of the decade was led by an increase in manufacturing and home construction, the latter tied to the flight to the suburbs. The Cold War helped to create a politically conservative climate, with anti-communism a driving force in American political life. A continuous state of political, military, and economic tension existed between the Soviet Union and its satellite nations on the one hand, and the United States and its western allies on the other. Underground shelters to protect (probably in vain) from nuclear attack became common, and corresponding drills were demonstrated on television and practiced by those whose fears were very real.

Some historical commentary has described the decade as the Catholic Church's Indian Summer—a sort of lull before the storm. But the idea of a coming storm was, at the time, about as far away as one could imagine in the American Catholic mind.

> In 1950 … the Catholic Church in the United States was at a higher peak of success than she had ever reached before

or has reached since. American Catholicism — awkward and unsure of itself it was, but like an adolescent bursting with vitality and newfound strength — wanted only an opportunity to test how strong it had bcome.[312]

Perhaps a more particularized version of the state of things, one that underscored the prevailing optimism of the era, noted that

in the last years of Pius XII [pope from 1939 to 1958], the Catholic community prospered in the United States. Between 1912 and 1963, the country's Catholic population had nearly tripled, from 15,015,569 to 43,851,538. Between 1954 and 1963, almost half of this increase was accomplished — over twelve million.... Seminaries and convent motherhouses blossomed across the nation to handle large numbers of applicants. The silent Trappists peaked at over one thousand monks and nuns in 1956. The summer of 1956 saw 408 young men begin their training as Jesuits. By 1965 their religious order had 8,393 American members, nearly a quarter of its world membership.... Other communities experienced similar developments. In 1954 there were 158,069 religious sisters, the mainstay of the church's extensive system of schools, hospitals and charitable institutions. Their numerical peak year was 1965, when they totaled 181,421. The 8,752 religious brothers of 1954 had grown to 12,539 by 1966. Seminarians increased from 32,344 in 1954 to 48,992 in 1964. The 46,970 priests of 1954 had become 59,892 by 1966.... A national sample by the University of Michigan Survey Research Center in 1957 found

---

[312] Russell Shaw, *American Church: The Remarkable Rise, Meteoric Fall, and Uncertain Future of Catholicism in America* (San Francisco: Ignatius Press, 2013), 97.

67 percent of Catholic men and 75 percent of Catholic women attending Mass regularly, and another 14 percent and 13 percent respectively, attending often. National Opinion Research Center staffers concluded that Catholic church attendance ran at about 70 percent. A survey carried in the *Catholic Digest* of 1953 found strong evidence of personal devoutness and acceptance of church teachings. Only in two areas were the percentages of those agreeing with standard teaching appreciably lower: while 99 percent believed in the existence of God, 89 percent in Christ's divinity, and 85 percent in personal immortality, only 51 percent accepted that divorced persons who remarried were "living in sin," or that "mechanical birth control" was wrong.[313]

The Church seemed to be flourishing in just about every way it could. The theological turmoil of the sixties, the massive collapse of the priesthood and religious life, the pervasive culture of death, the scandals in the priesthood of later decades, and the averse effect of a more prosperous lifestyle: All these seemed unimaginable.

Postwar Politics

Domestically, the communist threat appeared to be growing with each passing year. Perhaps the episode that most entrenched this notion in the American psyche was the Alger Hiss case in 1948.

Hiss was an American government official who was accused of spying for the Soviet Union. He had begun as a government attorney during Roosevelt's administration; served briefly at the Justice Department as temporary assistant to the Nye Committee, investigating alleged profiteering by military contractors during

[313] Hennesey, *American Catholics*, 286–287.

the First World War; and gradually worked his way into the State Department, working under Secretary of State Cordell Hull. He became an assistant to Assistant Secretary of State Francis Sayre, the son-in-law of Woodrow Wilson, and then special assistant to one of Hull's advisers on Far Eastern affairs. He served as executive secretary of the Dunbarton Oaks Conference, which drew up plans for the future United Nations, and was a member of the U.S. delegation attending the Yalta Conference, later claiming that he had been responsible for assembling background papers and documentation necessary for the meeting's success. In short, he was a well-placed bureaucrat and diplomat of the New Deal era.

In early August 1948, Whittaker Chambers, a former U.S. Communist Party member, testified under subpoena before the Committee on Un-American Activities that Hiss had secretly been a communist while in federal service, a charge that Hiss categorically denied. The hearings brought a young Congressman from California into the public eye: Richard M. Nixon broke the Hiss case open, ensured that Hiss was convicted of perjury related to espionage, easily won a Senate seat from California in 1950, was selected by General Dwight D. Eisenhower as his running mate on the Republican ticket in 1952, was defeated for the presidency in 1960, staged one of the greatest political comebacks ever eight years later, and, after five and a half years in office, in 1974 became the first president of the United States to resign.

All this, of course, was in the future. Back in 1948, the Hiss case riveted the nation, especially Chambers's testimony indicting his former friend. If Alger Hiss appeared a suave, neatly dressed, articulate speaker with his clipped words and impressive manner, Chambers was the opposite; though he was disheveled in appearance and monotonous in speech, his brilliance shone through. Several years later, Chambers reflected on the communist menace in the aftermath of the Hungarian Revolution of 1956. His musings in the conservative journal *National Review* captured America's fear for the future. Though he embraced Christianity fully only as an adult when he became a Quaker, he believed that "Christianity's tidings of great joy was that it had banished Fate from the world...."

No longer was a man's Fate fixed and shaped irreversibly by the stars he happened to be born under, so that his life was predestined to be just so, and not otherwise.... This was the glad tidings — that Fate was overthrown. The hopeless entrapping ring was broken. Man himself could break it, since every individual soul was divinely precious. Armed with this knowledge, man was free at last, first of all from Fate; then free to make of his destiny what he would and could. In our century, Fate has returned to the world, and possessed the minds of millions who, submitting to its thrall or acting in its name, seek to extend its dominion. This time Fate has returned in the guise of History. It may be put (very loosely) like this: History is shaped by the action and interaction of great imperial forces. Men merely enact it. If they act, prevailingly, in the direction of the main lines of force, its momentum carries them along to success; and we are invited to call such men great, wise, and even very good. Those who, out of folly, ignorance or stubborn principle, resist the main lines of force, History exterminates mercilessly. They are in the way; and what does a ragweed, for example, have to do with mercy, when a million pollen grains may be wasted to bring a single seed to fruition? The process is impersonal."[314]

---

[314] *National Review,* November 8, 1958, in *The Whittaker Chambers Reader: His Complete National Review Writings, 1957–1959* (New York: National review, 2014), 54–55. In his time, Chambers was said to have written the finest articles on religion ever published in *Time.*

Toil and Transcendence

In this environment, Dwight D. Eisenhower, supreme allied commander of American forces in Europe during the Second World War, seemed just the person America was looking for to steer confidently the ship of state. He handily captured the Republican nomination and presidential election in 1952. In this stridently anti-communist era, the administration had a strong ally in the Catholic Church, whose public opposition could be traced to at least 1933, when FDR's administration officially recognized the legitimacy of the Soviet Union. It appeared, in many Catholic minds of those days, that the government was bestowing its blessing on Marxism and that its leaders were little concerned with the persecutions being endured by the Russian Church, not to mention Catholics in Soviet satellite countries. Even as liberal a Catholic publication as *Commonweal*, known for its many pro-Roosevelt stands, expressed severe reservations about the president's choice.

Behind the Iron Curtain

Stories quickly emerged from the Soviet bloc that shocked the consciences of many, especially American Catholics. The first involved the arrest and imprisonment of Archbishop Aloysius Stepinac of Yugoslavia. The prelate had been staunchly opposed to Marshal Tito's communist regime and spoke out forcefully. He was arrested in September 1946 on trumped-up charges and one month later received a sentence of sixteen years' imprisonment. By the end of the year, a rally in Philadelphia numbering some forty thousand gathered to protest the persecution of the Church in Yugoslavia and specifically to demand the release of Archbishop Stepinac. Cardinal Spellman addressed a similar gathering in New York, asking for the prayers of the Catholic faithful for the archbishop and calling for the construction of a high school in the archdiocese named in his honor. New York Catholics raised four million dollars in less than one year, and the high school became a reality in White Plains, Westchester County. The archbishop ultimately served only five years of his sentence and was placed under house arrest for the remainder of time: His movements were very limited, and he was continually under close surveillance. He died in 1960.

Another dry martyr was Cardinal József Mindszenty of Hungary. He had opposed the attempts of the Hungarian communist regime to reduce the Church, and when it became obvious to authorities that he would not be silenced, he was arrested the day after Christmas 1948 and charged with treason, subversion, and spying. Six weeks before his incarceration, the cardinal wrote a pastoral letter to his people following government criticism of public displays in honor of Our Blessed Mother. Such displays were held, Mindszenty said, to strengthen the centuries-old devotion of the Hungarian people to the Mother of God, particularly in those challenging times.

> The country is condemned to silence and public opinion is made a mere frivolous jest. Democratic "freedom of speech" in this country means that any opinion that differs from the official one is silenced. If any man dares to raise his voice in contradiction, he is dismissed from his position for criticism of democracy, or he is punished in other ways.... I look on calmly at this artificial whipping up of the waves. In the place where I stand, not by the grace of any party, but by the grace and confidence of the Holy See, seething waters are not an extraordinary phenomenon. History lives in change.... I stand for God, for the Church and for Hungary. This responsibility has been imposed on me by the fate of my nation which stands alone, an orphan in the whole world. Compared with the sufferings of my people, my own fate is of no importance. I do not accuse my accusers. If I

am compelled to speak out from time to time and to state the facts as they are, it is only the misery of my people and the urge of truth which force me to do so.[315]

Mindszenty was a close friend of Cardinal Spellman, who deeply respected and admired his Hungarian counterpart. When the cardinal called for a day of prayer throughout his archdiocese for the Hungarian patriot and saint, more than one thousand Boy Scouts paraded down Fifth Avenue; later the same day, a Rosary rally was held on the campus of Fordham University in the Bronx, during which three thousand students joined in prayer for the cardinal's safe deliverance. Some time later, through the good offices of the Eisenhower administration, the cardinal was granted asylum in the American embassy in Vienna, Austria.

Television Talker

When one thinks of the surge of anti-communism in the American Church in this era, one immediately thinks of the work of then-Monsignor Fulton J. Sheen. Sheen was born in El Paso, Illinois, in 1895, studied at Spalding Academy in Peoria, and completed his theological studies for the priesthood at the major seminary in Saint Paul, Minnesota. He was ordained in St. Mary's Cathedral, Peoria, on September 20, 1919, and assigned briefly to do graduate work at the Catholic University of America. While there, he confided to a faculty adviser that he would like to study in an institution where he would thoroughly learn contemporary thought, in order to be able to respond effectively to it. The adviser said his choice was clear: He must study at the Catholic University of Louvain in Belgium, and specifically at its famed Institute of Philosophy.

[315] József Cardinal Mindszenty, *Memoirs* (New York: Macmillan, 1974), 318–319.

With the permission of his superiors, Sheen went to Belgium and studied under the famed Father Leon Noel (whose last name, Sheen often observed with a smile, was the reverse of his first). At the completion of his graduate studies, he was awarded the agrégé en philosophie, a degree beyond a simple doctorate, which qualified him to teach in the philosophy faculties of many European universities. To win this degree, his scholarly dissertation was *God and Intelligence in Modern Philosophy*, to which a foreword was written by the Catholic convert and brilliant apologist G. K. Chesterton. Upon completion, he returned to his Diocese of Peoria, where, to test his obedience, his bishop assigned him to a poor inner-city parish, St. Patrick, where he made many converts and brought many more back to the active practice of the Faith.

Sheen was eventually assigned to the philosophy faculty at Catholic University, where he would spend the next twenty-five years teaching while giving instruction classes to prospective converts in both Washington and New York City. In the early years, he became a regularly featured presenter on *The Catholic Hour*, a radio program sponsored by the National Council of Catholic Men. As the years progressed, he would author sixty-four books, among the best known of which are *Peace of Soul*, *Lift Up Your Heart*, *Three to Get Married*, *Calvary and the Mass*, *Moods and Truths*, *Victory over Vice*, and, surely his magnum opus, the *Life of Christ*.

In 1950, he was named the national director of the Society for the Propagation of the Faith and, the following year, auxiliary bishop of New York. He served in these positions until 1966, when he was appointed, ever so briefly, bishop of Rochester. Through the fifties, prior to his becoming an ordinary, he hosted an Emmy Award–winning television program, *Life Is Worth Living*, beginning on the DuMont Television Network and later moving to ABC. During these years, he became the face of Catholicism in the United States. After his resignation from his diocese in 1969,

Toil and Transcendence

his liberty and popularity made him a popular retreat master for priests throughout the country as well as in England and Ireland.

One of Sheen's earliest successes, though, was as a writer and lecturer against communism. He began teaching a course at Catholic University on the basic philosophy of the ideology and its errors and fallacies. From these lectures came the book *Communism and the Conscience of the West*. As early as 1935, he addressed an audience of forty-three thousand in Cleveland and dramatically predicted an unprecedented conflict between atheistic communism and faith:

> In the future there will be only two great capitals in the world: Rome and Moscow; only two temples, the Kremlin and St. Peter's; only two tabernacles, the Red Square and the Eucharist; only two hosts, the rotted body of Lenin and the Christ Emmanuel; only two hymns, the Internationale and the Panis Angelicus—but there will be only one victory—if Christ wins, we win, and Christ cannot lose.[316]

One very particular fruit of Sheen's crusade against communism was the story of the return to the Faith of Louis Budenz. Budenz was born into a Catholic family in Indianapolis, but he abandoned the Faith in favor of communist doctrine, rising in the ranks to become editor of the *Communist Daily Worker* in the United States. As Budenz related the story, whenever Sheen's voice came over the radio, he went into a veritable rage and turned off the machine immediately or asked the woman with whom he was living to do so. Years went by, and finally a meeting was arranged between the two men in New York City. Sheen's command of his subject matter, especially his knowledge of the Russian Constitution, overwhelmed Budenz, and, in a moment of hope, Sheen told Budenz he really

---

[316] Cited in Thomas C. Reeves, *America's Bishop: The Life and Times of Fulton J. Sheen* (San Francisco: Encounter Books, 2001), 100.

wanted to talk to him about his soul. From that initial encounter came Budenz's reception back to the Church — along with his girlfriend, who became his wife and practiced the Faith alongside him. Budenz taught at Fordham University in later years, became very popular on the Catholic lecture circuit, and recounted his entire journey in a best-selling book, *This Is My Story.*[317]

Hunting Commies

If anything, anti-communism was even more prominent among the laity than the clergy — especially in political life. The most famous exemplar was the junior senator from Wisconsin, Joseph Raymond McCarthy. Born into an Irish Catholic family in Grand Chute, Wisconsin, in 1908, he faithfully practiced his Catholicism throughout his life, though, by his own admission, was not one to wear his religion on his sleeve. McCarthy's college and law school were both completed at Marquette University in Milwaukee, though one Jesuit biographer feels the training of the Society of Jesus was not clearly discernible in the senator's life.[318]

After military service, he quickly got into politics, challenging the entrenched progressive senator Robert M. La Follette for the Republican nomination in 1946. Following a surprise upset, he easily defeated his Democrat opponent, Professor Howard McMurray, a "mild and thoughtful liberal."[319] Even at this early juncture, McCarthy, seen as the most aggressive campaigner the GOP had

---

[317] By coincidence, Douglas Hyde and his wife in England also became Catholics; the interest here is that each had converted separately without the other's knowledge.

[318] Donald F. Crosby, S.J., *God, Church, and Flag: Senator Joseph R. McCarthy and the Catholic Church, 1950–1957.* (Chapel Hill: University of North Carolina Press, 1978), 27–28.

[319] Ibid., 30.

produced in years, accused McMurray of having communist affiliations. The Democrats in Appleton, Wisconsin, McCarthy's home area, decided to retaliate. They contacted Bishop Bernard Sheil, auxiliary of Chicago, an ardent Roosevelt supporter and just as ardent McCarthy foe, and persuaded him to make a public statement condemning political candidates who smeared their opponents with the communist label while not being able to "meet the issues head on."[320]

The first few years of McCarthy's Senate career were relatively lackluster—until February 9, 1950, when he gave a talk to the Republican Women's Club of Wheeling, West Virginia. During his remarks, he produced a paper on which he claimed were listed the names of some two hundred communists working in the State Department. (Since no recording was made of the talk, the number has always been a matter of dispute.) In that moment, McCarthy's real career was launched. The question of the senator's sincerity in this matter has remained an open one. In an interview with former White House aid Frank Gannon, Richard Nixon, who had known McCarthy for years and had often served as the Eisenhower administration's designated critic of many of the senator's tactics, said that initially he felt McCarthy had jumped on the bandwagon of a hot-button issue but, as time progressed, became deeply commited to the cause of stamping out domestic communism, supposed or real.

McCarthy was taken aback by the overwhelming media response to his Wheeling speech, especially the incessant criticism that he was constantly revising his charges and figures. A few weeks later, the senator gave a detailed, five-hour analysis of eighty-one "loyalty risks," likely given him from a three-year-old list compiled for the House Appropriations Committee.

[320] Ibid.

McCarthy's attacks were spirited, to say the least, and he was accused of blurring the line between those listed as merely inclined toward communism and those considered full-fledged communists. As the accusations expanded, the Senate Committee on Foreign Relations agreed to form a subcommittee headed by Senator Millard Tydings of Maryland to conduct a full study. Many Democrats were angered over McCarthy's attacks on the State Department of a Democratic administration and hoped to use the hearings to discredit him. After the hearings were concluded and McCarthy failed to come up with the sort of particulars many hoped he would, the Tydings committee concluded that the McCarthy claims were both a fraud and a hoax, devised to confuse and divide the American people.

At the beginning of his second term, McCarthy was named chairman of the Senate Committee on Government Operations, a rather mundane appointment meant to lower his profile. The committee, however, included the Senate Permanent Subcommittee on Investigations, whose directives were vague enough for McCarthy to use for his own investigations of communists in government. He appointed Roy Cohn as chief counsel and Robert F. Kennedy as an assistant counsel to the subcommittee.

Perhaps the best remembered investigation of this subcommittee was its ill-fated inquiry into the United States Army, which begn with an inquiry into Army Signal Corps Laboratories at Fort Monmouth, New Jersey. After several weeks of scrutiny turned up nothing, the senator began to focus on the case of Irving Peress, a New York dentist drafted into the Army in 1952 and promoted to major the following year. Peress was a member of the American Labor Party and had declined to answer questions about his political affiliation on a loyalty review form. Subpoenaed, Peress refused to answer McCarthy's questions, claiming his Fifth Ammendment rights. Subsequently, McCarthy demanded that Secretary of the

Toil and Transcendence

Army Robert T. Stephens court-martial Peress. Immediately, Peress asked that his pending discharge from the Army be made effective immediately, and he was given an honorable separation. With McCarthy's blessing, "Who promoted Peress?" became a rallying cry among anti-communists and McCarthy supporters.

The following year, 1954, the U.S. Army accused McCarthy and his chief counsel, Roy Cohn, of improperly pressuring the Army to give favorable treatment to a former aid to McCarthy and a friend of Cohn, G. David Schine, who was then serving in the Army as a private. The subcommittee, usually headed by McCarthy, was in this instance headed by Senator Karl Mundt; after questioning thirty-two witnesses, its conclusion was that McCarthy had not exercised any improper influence on Schine's behalf but that Cohn had engaged in what they termed "unduly persistent and aggressive efforts."

These hearings, especially a confrontation between McCarthy and Joseph Nye Welch, the Army's legal counsel, began a slow but steady stream of events leading to the U.S. Senate's final vote to censure McCarthy on two specific counts. After this, the senator lived out his days much more quietly, still carrying on his crusade against communists in government and especially criticizing President Eisenhower for his selection of William Brennan to be an associate justice of the Supreme Court: McCarthy was the only senator to vote against Brennan's confirmation. McCarthy's health began to fail rapidly, and hospital stays caused by cirrhosis of the liver became more frequent. He was also reported to have taken doses of morphine to the point of addiction. His death at Bethesda Naval Hospital in 1957, at age forty-eight, was followed by a state funeral attended by seventy senators, more than one hundred priests, and two thousand others at St. Matthew's Cathedral in Washington. Burial followed in St. Mary's parish cemetery in Appleton, Wisconsin.

McCarthy and the Church

As Joe McCarthy increasingly became a household name, and his popularity (or infamy) grew, he became yet another flashpoint for anti-Catholicism. One of the earliest examples came when he married Jean Kerr, a former assistant in his office, in St. Matthew's Cathedral in Washington. The *Brooklyn Tablet* covered the event in rich detail, attesting to the very large crowd of attendees, all of whom were proud to be called McCarthy's friends. The problem occurred when the celebrant of the nuptial Mass read the inscription from a papal blessing from Pope Pius XII to the newly married couple — very common at Catholic weddings, but quite foreign to the Protestant mind. "Did this mean that the Pope himself had put his solemn imprimatur on McCarthy's career? Many liberals in Washington wondered about the meaning of the 'special blessing' from Rome."[321]

The fact that the Catholic Church in the United States had never been stronger, and that Her numbers were constantly growing, gave some of the country's non-Catholic population cause to worry. Many of these hostilities ended up being lobbed against McCarthy's style, rhetoric, and accusations. Paul Blanchard, an author, lawyer, socialist, and assistant editor of the *Nation* magazine, was known as an outspoken critic of Catholicism. In 1951, he articulated Protestant fears in saying that McCarthy's "campaign of disgraceful vilification" against his enemies had received "wide acclaim" in the Catholic press. McCarthy's activities had probably done more "to discredit American democracy in Europe than any event in American politics in recent years."[322]

Reverend Robert McCracken, pastor of the fashionable Riverside Church in New York City, warned his congregation in February

[321] Crosby, *God, Church, and Flag*, 39.
[322] Ibid., 124.

1954 that the Wisconsin senator was a member of a church that "has never disavowed the Inquisition, that makes a policy of censorship, that insists on conformity."[323]

To America's Catholics it must have seemed especially galling that the Protestant Bishop who most often blamed the church for McCarthy was himself an ex-Catholic. The offending prelate, Bishop James Pike [dean of the Church of Saint John the Divine in New York City] had received his college education from the Jesuits at the University of Santa Clara in northern California. He had renounced Catholicism, however, and had entered the Episcopal church, rising eventually to the top of that denomination's leadership. On 21 March 1954 Pike exchanged pulpits with Francis B. Sayre, Jr., Dean of the Washington Cathedral in the nation's capital, and both men used the occasion to ask why the Catholic church had not formally condemned McCarthy. By implication, at least, the two clerics were blaming Catholicism for McCarthy but hinting that the Catholic hierarchy's silence on the Senator was somehow sinister and malign. Inspired perhaps by the solemnity of the occasion, both prelates condemned McCarthyism as spiritually destructive and viciously undemocratic.[324]

Many Protestants believed that McCarthy enjoyed tremendous Catholic support because he was one of their own; others genuinely feared that the whole purpose of McCarthy's campaign was eventually to run for the White House. McCarthy had publicly expressed the view that his religion, at that time, would almost certainly have precluded a successful run for the presidency; this

[323] Ibid., 136.
[324] Ibid., 137.

was far from calming, however, to a deeply entrenched Protestant mindset.

Many liberal Catholics were of a similar mindset as Protestants. George N. Schuster, then president of Hunter College in New York City, became the first college president to denounce McCarthy, and the fact Schuster was a Catholic was not lost on the secular press. Schuster felt the time had come when colleges should examine the senator's activities "with the utmost objectivity, calm and chilly resolution," adding that "the day on which the senator is summoned before the bar of American history and social science will not be the least revealing of his career." A few months later, the senator insinuated that *Commonweal* had once harbored a writer who was "a security risk and a Communist sympathizer." When the magazine challenged him to make a public correction, he responded not by answering their challenge but by asserting that the publication was not worthy of the title Catholic: "So that there will be no doubt in your mind as to how I feel about your magazine, I feel that you have done and are doing a tremendous disservice to the Catholic Church and a great service to the Communist Party."[325]

To be sure, many prominent Catholics were in McCarthy's corner. He could readily count on support from such publications as the *Brooklyn Tablet, Ave Maria,* and *Columbia,* the official magazine of the Knights of Columbus. Richard Ginder, well-known columnist for *Our Sunday Visitor,* was also a staunch defender, making the claim that "the Senator would not have so many enemies if he were a high ranking Protestant and a Mason."[326] The *Tidings,* official newspaper of the Archdiocese of Los Angeles, faithfully reflected the pro-McCarthy sentiments of its archbishop, Cardinal James Francis McIntyre. Catholic Boston was the metropolitan area

[325] Ibid., 120–121.
[326] Ibid., 125.

Toil and Transcendence

where the senator's support was strongest, and in New York, many interested onlookers were curious what position Cardinal Francis Spellman took. Undoubtedly the most powerful member of the American hierarchy in his time, his presence at a Communion breakfast sponsored by the Holy Name Society of the New York City Police Department, at which McCarthy was principal speaker, was taken as a vote of support.

Spellman's first direct statement, though, came in August 1953, when newspaper reporters asked him what he thought about the senator. "He is against communism and he has done and is doing something about it," Spellman replied somewhat blandly. "He is making America aware of the dangers of communism." Two months later, the cardinal defended McCarthy against his liberal critics. Responding to the charge that McCarthy had abused the civil rights of those he accused of being communists, the cardinal asserted firmly that neither the McCarthy investigating committee nor any other congressional committee had violated such liberties. "Anguished cries and protests against McCarthyism" will not deter America from trying to root communists out of the government, he promised. Spellman paid no attention at all when his opponents accused him of advocating McCarthyism.[327]

McCarthy invited many critiques, pro and con. At the height of his career, a probing analysis was made by fellow conservative thinkers, trying to unravel the meaning of it all. Their findings were summed up succinctly:

> McCarthyism ... is a weapon in the American arsenal. To the extent that McCarthyism, out of ignorance or impetuousity or malice, urges the imposition of sanctions upon persons who are *not* pro-Communist or security risks, we

[327] Ibid., 133–134.

should certainly oppose it. When persons about whose loyalty or security reliability there is *no* reasonable doubt are
flushed from government service for security reasons, those
responsible should be criticized and held to an account-
ing both at the polls and before investigating committees.
Whenever the anti-Communist conformity excludes well
meaning Liberals, we should, in other words, go to their
rescue. But as long as McCarthyism fixes its goal with its
present precision, it is a movement around which men of
good will and stern morality can close ranks.[328]

Rumblings in Indochina

One area of foreign policy in the fifties with which McCarthy likely
would have been in agreement was the work of the Eisenhower
administration to stop the growth of communism in what was
then called French Indochina — that is, Vietnam. The president's
views on most matters of foreign policy were shaped by his secretary of state, John Foster Dulles; according to Sherman Adams,
Eisenhower's chief of staff, the two men spoke at length on the
telephone most days, and "there was never much doubt about who
was responsible for the foreign policy of the United States."[329]

Dulles, the son of a Presbyterian minister, had grown up in a
small town in Upstate New York. Indeed he was descended from

[328] William F. Buckley Jr., and L. Brent Bozell, *McCarthy and His Enemies: The Record and Its Meaning* (New Rochelle, NY: Arlington
House, 1954), 335.
[329] *The Influence of the Catholic Church on the Eisenhower Administration's Decision to Directly Intervene in Vietnam — Soviet Communist
Containment, South Vietnamese Policy, Indochina, Southeast Asia*
(Washington, D.C.: U.S. Government, U.S. Military, Department
of Defense, 2015), 35.

several generations of ministers, many of them overseas missionaries. His desire to halt the spread of communism intersected with that of the Catholic Church. He has been described as a "moral absolutist" who felt that the atheistic nature of communism alone deserved the attention of all concerned Americans: "Soviet Communism starts with an atheistic, Godless premise. Everything else flows from that premise."[330] Dulles's son, Avery, converted to Catholicism while a student at Harvard, was professed in the Society of Jesus, and was ordained a Catholic priest. He would rise to be recognized as one of the Society's most prominent theologians and was honored by the Church by being named to the Sacred College of Cardinals, even though he was never ordained a bishop.

Meanwhile, New York's Cardinal Spellman was serving as military vicar of the armed forces and had over the years visited American troops in many parts of the world. In this role, he became quite friendly with such personalities as Eisenhower and Generals Mark Clark, George Patton, and Douglas MacArthur. Through these contacts, Spellman came to know British prime minister Winston Churchill and French president Charles de Gaulle. Spellman's anti-communist credentials had long been established and were in complete conformity with Pope Pius XII. The pope had long supported the administration of President Ngo Dinh Diem in Vietnam, at least in part because the president's brother, Bishop Ngo Dinh Thuc, later archbishop of Hue, had been a friend since the days of his service in Rome. Pius was very concerned about the losses the Church would suffer should communism spread in Asia, and when Diem found himself in the position of supporting either the French or the communists in Vietnam, his choice was clear. A trip to the United States would further cement relations with the West.

[330] Ibid., 37.

During his soujourn in America, President Diem visited with several prominent Catholics, including General William Donovan, the director of the Office of Strategic Services during World War II. Senators Mike Mansfield and John F. Kennedy were also brought into Diem's orbit. Cardinal Spellman and Diem became friends largely through the latter's brother, Bishop Thuc, who had studied with Spellman in Rome. The political support Diem received in the United States matched the perceptions of the State Department, who saw the invaluable assistance the Catholic community in Vietnam could produce. The department thought, however, that the Catholics in Vietnam were ambiguous in their position toward communism and wanted to gain some political momentum by energizing the Catholic community to recognize the communist threat. Before Diem even came to America, the State Department in Vietnam considered his family to be the leaders of Vietnamese Catholics, and so there was a desire to use Catholicism to generate support for anti-communist operations, with Vietnamese Catholics as a political base.[331]

In 1953, Foster Dulles's brother Allen became director of the Central Intelligence Agency, successor to the Office of Strategic Services (OSS). Through the years, Dulles often called on Cardinal Spellman to serve as an unofficial representative of the U.S. government, especially in Latin America. The two Dulles brothers had been lifelong friends with General Donovan; "Wild Bill," as he was affectionately known, had grown up in a staunchly Irish Catholic household, went to Niagara University, and had thought of studying for the priesthood. He maintained strong Catholic ties as head of the OSS and was rewarded by Pius XII in 1944 with the Grand Cross of the Order of Saint Sylvester in a private ceremony in the Vatican. Donovan also had close personal ties to Eisenhower and was an early supporter of President Diem. He served as honorary

[331] Ibid., 40.

chairman of the American Friends of Vietnam, a largely Catholic lobbying group who supported South Vietnam, and especially Diem, in the struggle against communism.

The Dulles brothers, working together as the head of the CIA and the secretary of state, were thus very tied in to Catholic opinion and Catholic causes. All of these connections among the Dulles brothers, Donovan, Eisenhower, and the Church facilitated the transformation of mutual views of communism between the Vatican and the Eisenhower administration into what would become a "professional" relationship in organizing policy toward South Vietnam.[332]

In his attempt to prevent communist North Vietnam from taking over the South, Eisenhower's policy, after the defeat of the French colonial army at the battle of Dien Bien Phu in 1954, was to take the lead in projecting Western power in Vietnam. The 1954 Geneva Accords said that the future of Vietnam was to be decided by popular election, an agreement neither the United States nor South Vietnam signed. Ho Chi Minh, however, was forced to sign them because of pressure from the Soviet Union and China. In 1955, Eisenhower, fearing a future Vietnam under the North Vietnamese communist, sent a Military Assistance Advisory Group to train the army of the Republic of Vietnam. With the 1960 creation of the Vietcong, a communist guerilla force in the South, the U.S. committed combat forces to Vietnam. If it weren't for Eisenhower's support of the Catholic Diem, there would have been no support for the South, and they would have crumbled before the Vietnam War ever got started.

Catholic Intellectual Life

Closer to home, a monumental article on American Catholic intellectualism was published by Monsignor John Tracy Ellis of the

---

[332] Ibid., 42.

faculty of Catholic University of America. Born in Seneca, Illinois, in 1905, he received his doctorate from the same university where he served much of his academic life. Ellis rose to become the dean of American Catholic Historians, served as executive secretary of the American Catholic Historical Association, and was editor of the *Catholic Historical Review* for more than twenty years. His many works qualified him for the academic dictinctions he received, yet he never lost the essential priestly quality given him at ordination. In 1955, Ellis published an article in *Thought*, a scholarly journal published at Fordham University, on the lack of true intellectualism found in the Church in the United States. To say the least, the article sent shock waves through the Catholic intellectual community.

Ellis began by citing an observation of Denis W. Brogan, professor of political science at the University of Cambridge, that "in no Western society is the intellectual prestige of Catholicism lower than in the country where, in such respects as wealth, numbers, and strength of organization, it is so powerful."[333] Fully agreeing with Brogan, Ellis began by indicting the long-standing anti-Catholic bias the first English settlers had brought to Jamestown, one which "requires no elaborate proof for any educated American."[334] For those of the household of faith, this meant that the American intellectual climate, where it did exist, was unfriendly to Catholic thought and ideas. Added to this was the makeup of the Catholic Church in the United States, especially in the nineteenth century: The immigrants who poured into the country were, for the most part, uneducated and necessarily preoccupied with the rudiments of making a living. It was, Ellis

---

[333] Cited in John Tracy Ellis, "American Catholics and the Intellectual Life," *Thought* 30 (June 1955): 353.
[334] Ibid.

contends, a rare Catholic man who could make any headway in the world of higher education.

Furthermore, historically Americans have been wary of scholars and academicians. Alexis de Tocqueville, in his early nineteenth-century observations of the United States, said that Americans "do not fear distinguished talents, but are rarely fond of them."[335] Interestingly, Ellis cites a commencement address given by Orestes Brownson, a somewhat controversial yet brilliant nineteenth-century convert to Catholicism, at Mount St. Mary's College in Emmitsburg, Maryland, where he urged his listeners to resist this very American tendency, "the grand heresy of our age."[336]

The author saw the beginnings of an American Catholic educational elite in many of the original English Catholic settlers in Southern Maryland in the 1630s, the early French Sulpicians who came to provide seminary education in the new nation, and the mid-nineteenth-century converts who formed an American equivalent of the Oxford Movement. To emphasize his point, Ellis turned to an idea of Archbishop John Ireland in his work *The Church and Modern Society*:

> This is an intellectual age. It worships intellect. It tries all things by the touchstone of intellect.... The Church herself will be judged by the standard of intellect. Catholics must excel in religious knowledge.... They must be in the foreground of intellectual movements of all kinds. The age will not take kindly to religious knowledge separated from secular knowledge.[337]

---

[335] Cited in ibid., 356.

[336] Cited in ibid. Interestingly, among the graduates in that class was John La Farge, who was to become a nationally recognized artist, and Silas M. Chatard, the fifth bishop of Vincennes, Indiana.

[337] Cited in ibid., 359.

Though there were a few Catholics who could identify with this, it would sound foreign to the ears of most. Catholic intellectual life was helped, according to Ellis, by generous donations made by Catholics who gradually accumulated fortunes and bequeathed large endowments to Catholic educational institutions, with an obvious case being the Caldwell sisters of Kentucky and their generosity to Catholic University. Even so, American Catholic clergy rarely pursued advanced degrees in the humanities; rather, they placed far greater emphasis on "what are the professional and vocational aspects of higher education, since they serve a practical end in their diocesan chanceries, charities, and offices of the superintendents of schools, than might otherwise be the case."[338]

Nor did Ellis notice any difference in this regard between diocesan and religious priests. "Would it not be reasonable to expect," he queried, "that in religious orders, whose aims and energies are devoted in good measure to school work, that intellectual distinction would be fairly common?"[339] He did admit, though, that religious priests through the years had made significant intellectual contributions to such publications as the *American Catholic Quarterly Review* and the *American Ecclesiastical Review*, both of which owed their origins to diocesan priests. The *New York Review*, one of the most scholarly of all, was another that Ellis praised.

To the Church's discredit, though, a revival in Scholastic philosophy seemed to be far more evident on secular campuses, while Catholic colleges and universities were more apt to be engrossed in a "mad pursuit of every passing fancy that crossed the American

[338] Ibid., 368.
[339] Ibid., 372.

educational scene."[340] The author went on to indict competing graduate schools that were poorly financed and filled with mediocre personnel. Professors at Catholic institutions who had been granted rank and tenure rarely pursued any further scholarly inquiry in their respective disciplines. Curiously, Ellis also found fault with a Catholic educational system that saw the school as "an agency for moral development, with an insufficient stress on [its] role as an instrument for fostering intellectual development."[341] In the end, Ellis felt that

> The major defect ... lies elsewhere than with the unfriendly attitude of some of those outside the Church. The chief blame, I firmly believe, lies with Catholics themselves. It lies in their frequently self-imposed ghetto mentality which prevents them from mingling as they should with their non-Catholic colleagues, and in their lack of industry and ... habits of work.... It lies in their failure to have measured up to their responsibilities to the incomparable tradition of Catholic learning of which they are the direct heirs.[342]

Needless to say, these observations met with mixed reviews in the American Catholic intellectual community. Nonetheless, what Monsignor Ellis likely did not realize was that the same year his article was published, 1955, an intellectual movement was originating that would clearly meet many of the criteria he felt were lacking up until then. While the American conservative movement was not limited to Catholics,[343] its founder, William F. Buckley Jr., met the Catholic criteria in every respect.

[340] Ibid., 374.
[341] Ibid., 377–378.
[342] Ibid., 386.
[343] Ellis likely would have favored this, given his emphasis on Catholics' mingling with their counterparts of other denominations.

A New Movement

Born in New York City in 1925, he was the son of Aloise Steiner and William Frank Buckley, a Texas-born lawyer and oil developer. Schooled in Paris, the Jesuit preparatory school of St. John's Beaumont in England, and at Yale University, Buckley rose to be an American public intellectual and conservative author. In 1951, he wrote *God and Man at Yale*, a work that became a classic within the conservative movement in the United States. One author has described the book as "written in the American-Apollonian style," exhibiting "something of Mencken's rakish offhandedness, and of Belloc's British dash."[344] Buckley lost no time indicting his alma mater:

> Yale is a private university, therefore, responsibility for her governance devolves constitutionally on her alumni (broadly speaking, Christian individualists) — not on her administration (mainly capitalist Christian gentlemen, who, unfortunately, are disposed to tolerate agnostic and atheistic collectivists on the faculty and to condone secular collectivism and agnosticism in the curriculum, where they go mostly unchallenged). The university, founded by Christians and individualists, has historically subscribed to a traditional "value orthodoxy" at odds with her present commitment to "laissez-faire education" and the shibboleth of "academic freedom," tantamount to institutional acquiescence in moral relativism and social collectivism. Yale still subscribes to orthodoxy; but hypocritically, by lip service, or simply in the sense that the university maintains limits within which

[344] Chilton Williamson Jr., *The Conservative Bookshelf* (New York: Kensington Publishing, 2004), 163. The references here are to H. L. Mencken, an American author, and Hilaire Belloc, a British Catholic apologist and historian.

faculty members (and students) must restrict their opinions if they expect to be tolerated by the Yale community. These limits, latitudinarian as they may be, are "prescribed by [social and intellectual] expediency, not principle"—prescribed, that is, by none other than the reigning *liberal* orthodoxy, which runs wholly counter to the traditionalist orthodoxy officially espoused by Yale! For this reason, it is necessary *not* that limits be set to the Yale curriculum, to free speech, and to academic freedom in its other forms (since, manifestly, limits already exist); rather, the existing limits should be *narrowed* to conform with Yale's stated historical mission, described by President Charles Seymour as "the upraising of spiritual leaders."[345]

Buckley's book did not begin the conservative movement in the United States—its origins in the twentieth century are traceable at least to the Liberty League's opposition to Franklin D. Roosevelt. It did, however, shape American conservative thought in the post–World War II years, until the time of Ronald Reagan's administration in the 1980s.

Buckley's Catholicism shaped his entire life; he was known to recite the Rosary daily for more than seventy years, and he much preferred what today is called the Extraordinary Form of the Church's Liturgy—that is, the Latin Mass—sometimes offered for him right in his home in Sharon, Connecticut. At times, he had to wrestle with Church teachings he found difficult to accept,[346]

[345] Ibid.

[346] One such example was *Humanae Vitae*, St. Paul VI's encyclical letter of 1968 defending life and reiterating the Church's official opposition to the use of contraception to regulate or limit birth. In his spiritual autobiography, Buckley writes of the encyclical: "The orthodox observation, as I view it, is that it is expected that the faithful will sin, seventy times seven times. But the church has much

but, in the end, he yielded. A slight glimmer of his faith, especially his Marian devotion, comes from a reaction experienced after a pilgrimage to Lourdes:

> Those who seek relief from the quandary — *if it wasn't a natural cause that effected the cure, what did?* — will need to come up with a superforce of some sort. Who was it at the grotto in 1858? Allah? The skeptics run the risk of being ambushed by: God/Christ/the Immaculate Conception. The whole Christian package.[347]

In 1955, Buckley founded *National Review*, a semimonthly magazine focusing on news and commentary on political, social, and cultural affairs. It was to be a vehicle for many conservative Catholics to be published, and more often than not, it reflected Catholic thinking on the issues of the day. The magazine served as a rallying point for conservative writers and conservative thought in general, which, up until then, had been somewhat scattered. More than any other cause, strident anti-communism found a home in the pages of *National Review*. To be sure, in the fifties, publications such as *Time*, *Reader's Digest*, and the *Saturday Evening Post* carried many articles and editorials strongly condemning communism and the effects it would have on American society if not contained. Most effectively, though, Buckley's new magazine brought this thought together and raised it to a higher intellectual plane. In addition, Buckley hosted hundreds of television interviews on the

---

to ponder when, after pronouncing a practice anathema, the flock ceases even to wince. A sense of the sinfulness of an act is hugely important to the moral order. In its absence, there is a terrible void." William F. Buckley Jr., *Nearer, My God: An Autobiography of Faith* (New York: Doubleday, 1997), 200.

[347] Ibid., 157. Here Buckley is referring to the case of a French woman, Marie Bailly, who was miraculously cured at the grotto.

Toil and Transcendence

program *Firing Line*, where guests from all walks of life, liberal and conservative, were given a forum to express their views and engage in a spirited conversation with the host.

Heyday of Catholic Apologetics

Yet another sign of the strength of American Catholicism in the 1950s was the number of converts who were received into the Church. This was one of the highest priorities of the Church: She who possessed the fullness of truth was filled with a strong evangelistic fervor to share that truth with as many people as possible. This attitude, which had always been present in the Church in the United States, received a special burst of adrenaline in the nineteenth century from the writings of Father Isaac Hecker, founder of the Paulists, and continued through the decades. One of the classic books of instruction was Fort Wayne, Indiana, archbishop John Francis Noll's *Father Smith Instructs Jackson* as well as an enormously popular work by Notre Dame's Father John A. O'Brien, *The Faith of Millions*.

Perhaps the single best-known convert instructor, of course, was Bishop Fulton J. Sheen. In the fifties, Sheen was at the height of his popularity; his Emmy Award–winning program, *Life Is Worth Living*, made Sheen a household name and brought him—and the Faith—to the attention of millions. It would be impossible to calculate how many were brought to the Church through his broadcasts and books. Some who were received into the fullness of faith, however, were particularly well known, and their conversions were well noted.

Clare Boothe Luce was, without doubt, one of Sheen's best-known students. The wife of Henry Luce, founder of an empire that would come to include such publications as *Time*, *Life*, *Sports Illustrated*, and *People* magazines, she was a distinguished author and writer of Broadway plays, not to mention a Congresswoman from Connecticut and a United States ambassador to Italy. Bishop Sheen felt that never in his life had he been so privileged to instruct anyone who was as "brilliant and scintillating in conversation as Mrs. Luce."[348]

As to Clare's ultimate conversion:

> It finally took two world wars, the overthrow of several dozen thrones and governments, the Russian revolution, the swift collapse, in our own time, of hundreds of thought-systems, a small number of which collapsed on me, the death of millions, as well as the death of my daughter, before I was willing to take a look at this extraordinary institution, the Catholic church."[349]

It had been her daughter's death that stimulated her to discuss religion with then-Monsignor Sheen. She became irate at Sheen's mention of the goodness of God, asking why, if God was so good, He had taken her daughter in an automobile accident. Sheen replied: so that she, Clare, might now be taking the first steps needed for conversion. She feared her own death, and whether she would merit an afterlife, and wanted to rid herself of her burden of sin.

Maisie Ward, wife of Frank Sheed, themselves Catholic publishers and friends of Clare, described Clare's state in 1945 and 1946 as exemplifying "the sharp cry of hunger when a diet of stones is set upon the table."[350] Many of her friends tried to dissuade her from becoming a Catholic. When she finally mustered the courage to tell her husband, "he was speechless. All his entrenched Presbyterian hostility to the Church of Rome surfaced. He was chagrined at not

[348] Cited in Connor, *Classic Catholic Converts*, 180.
[349] Sylvia Jukes Morris, *Price of Fame: The Honorable Clare Boothe Luce* (New York: Random House, 2014), 157.
[350] Ibid., 153.

having been informed sooner."[351] Conveniently or not, Mr. Luce was out of town on the day of Clare's reception into the Church. On February 16, 1946, with only a few friends present, Sheen received Mrs. Clare Boothe Luce into the Catholic Church in St. Patrick's Cathedral in New York. The following day, she made her First Holy Communion and received the sacrament of Confirmation. As a sign of gratitude, she commissioned a celebrated artist to paint a portrait of Monsignor Sheen against a background of the shrine of Our Lady of Lourdes. To this day, it is one of the most recognizable depictions of Venerable Sheen.

Heywood Broun was another interesting convert. Born in Brooklyn in 1888, he became a popular American journalist, working as a sportswriter, newspaper columnist, and editor in New York City. He founded the American Newspaper Guild and was best remembered for his writing on social issues and championing the cause of the downtrodden. From 1919 to 1929, he was a member of the Algonquin Round Table, or Algonquin Wits—literary types who met in the famous Forty-Fourth Street hotel in Manhattan to discuss a wide variety of topics. Known for his disheveled appearance, he was often likened to an unmade bed. Politically a socialist, he made an unsuccessful run for Congress in 1930 on the slogan that he'd "rather be right than Roosevelt." He was married twice and lived most of his life as an agnostic.[352] Not long before his death, and, by his own admission, fearing to die in his sins, he decided to take instruction in the Catholic Faith; he was strongly attracted to Catholicism as the first of all professions of Christianity, as well as the one ecclesial body providing him the sort of discipline he felt he needed in his life.

[351] Ibid., 155.
[352] Broun and his first wife, Ruth Hale, became the parents of Heywood Hale Broun, a long-time sports commentator on CBS, as well as a sportswriter, author, and actor.

The most famous modern proselytizer was Monsignor Fulton
Sheen, whose radio pastorals, his burning eyes and magnetic
presence, his erudition as a Church philosopher had made
him a famous figure among Broun's contemporaries. Monsignor Sheen had a reputation of converting or bringing
back to the altar rail "hard cases," doubting intellectuals,
Manhattan sophisticates.... Monsignor Sheen's celebrity
as a missionary to the elect naturally attracted Broun, who
liked to go first class when it came to important things.[353]

On May 23, 1939, Broun was baptized. He made his First Holy
Communion in the Lady Chapel of St. Patrick's Cathedral on Pen-
tecost Sunday and was the first person confirmed by Archbishop
Francis J. Spellman in his role as archbishop of New York, making
Broun feel "he was being accorded the red-carpet treatment."[354]
After Broun's funeral in St. Patrick's, which was thronged with lit-
erary types, politicians, Cabinet members, and the like, Monsignor
Sheen, who had preached the sermon, reminisced:

> I preached his eulogy ... and in the course of the sermon told
> the reasons he gave for wanting to become a Catholic. The
> next day the Communist *Daily Worker* carried the headline:
> "Monsignor Sheen reveals the secrets of the confessional."
> What were given, of course, where the reasons Mr. Broun
> gave me when I first met him.[355]

A famous witness at the House Un-American Activities Committee was Elizabeth Bentley, an American spy and member of
the Communist Party in the United States who served the Soviet

[353] Richard O'Connor, *Heywood Broun: A Biography* (New York: G. P.
Putnam's Sons, 1975), 212-213.
[354] Ibid., 213.
[355] Cited in Connor, *Classic Catholic Converts*, 179.

Union from 1938 until 1945, when she defected. She became widely known after her testimony on Capitol Hill, and in 1952, she became an informer for the FBI, paid for her frequent appearances before congressional committees. She exposed two networks of spies, ultimately naming more than eighty Americans whom she claimed engaged in espionage. In 1948 Monsignor Sheen instructed her and received her into the Catholic Church; later, she, like Louis Budenz, became a popular lecturer to Catholic groups on the communist threat.

Similar was the case of Bella Dodd, a lawyer for the Communist Party who was well known in labor-union circles in New York City. On one occasion, while she was in Washington testifying before the House Un-American Activities Committee, Senator McGrath from Rhode Island suggested that she contact Monsignor Sheen, who was then at Catholic University teaching courses on communism. Dodd did so and made an appointment. When they met, the priest noticed a certain sadness in her: He later recollected that just as doctors can detect maladies in the human body, so often priests are able to detect the same in souls.

> While we knelt silently, she began to cry. She was touched by grace. Later on, I instructed her and received her into the Church. With Marx behind her, she began teaching law first in Texas and later at St. John's University in Brooklyn.[356]

Television viewers who faithfully watched *Life Is Worth Living* in the 1950s were familiar with its theme song. It was called the "Vienna March," but it had been put into waltz time. Many musicians would consider this a difficult task, but for Fritz Kreisler, one of the world's great violinists, it was all in a day's work. Kreisler and

[356] Ibid., 172.

his wife, Harriet, were both converts of Fulton Sheen, and their conversion came about in an indirect way.

Bishop Sheen received a phone call from a woman asking if he would visit her uncle. The man's wife had recently committed suicide, and he was despondent. He was not home on the day Sheen came to call, so the bishop, making conversation, asked the elevator operator who lived in the apartment across the hall. When he learned it was Fritz Kreisler, he knocked and immediately began a conversation. Despite his enormous musical prestige, Kreisler, because of his German birth, faced much discrimination in the United States during the First World War, and several of his concert engagements had been canceled. In the very different climate of 1939, he had moved to the United States permanently and, four years later, became a citizen. No sooner had the Kreislers met Sheen than they began taking instructions from him. The bishop noted what a serious student of the Faith Kreisler was: If an Old Testament reference was given to him, he would read it in Hebrew; if a New Testament one, he would read it in Greek.

> I was a very close friend of the Kreislers from the time of their reception into the Church, and it was tragic to see Fritz in his last days, blind and deaf from an automobile accident, but radiating a gentleness and refinement not unlike his music. I visited them every week for some years until the Lord called them from the Church Militant to the Church Triumphant, where I am sure the music of Fritz Kreisler is in the repertoire of heaven.[357]

These are some of the many testimonials of faith in a faith-filled era. Much was to change in the decade that followed, presenting the Church with challenges unimaginable just a few years earlier.

---

[357] Ibid., 178. Kreisler died in New York City in 1962.

Toil and Transcendence

The entire world would seem to be turned upside down by events in the 1960s and beyond—and yet the Barque of Peter, tossed as it would be, survived well, and, as the Lord tells us, will perdure till time is no more.

6

∞

The American Church
in the Turbulent Sixties

Setting the Stage

A study of the Catholic Church in the United States in the 1960s must begin with the monumental presidential election of 1960. As America entered a new decade, the Church brought with it the tremendous strength of faith characteristic of the preceding years: Vocations were flourishing; church attendance was high; Catholicism seemed to have taken its rightful place in the nation. But a Roman Catholic had not, up to this point, been elected president of the United States.

The candidates who secured their parties' nomination for the White House that year were John Fitzgerald Kennedy for the Democrats and Richard Milhous Nixon for the Republicans. Both men had come to Congress together in 1946—Nixon from a conservative district in Southern California, and Kennedy from a liberal district in Massachusetts. Both were eventually elected to the U.S. Senate, and Richard Nixon assumed the vice presidency under Dwight D. Eisenhower.

Kennedy was born in Brookline, Massachusetts, in 1917, the son of Ambassador Joseph P. and Mrs. Rose Fitzgerald Kennedy. On his mother's side, he was the grandson of John Fitzgerald, or "Honey Fitz," as he was often called, an early Catholic mayor of

Toil and Transcendence

Boston. His father had amassed a tremendous fortune as a stock market and commodity investor and later rolled over his profits by investing in real estate and a wide range of industries across the United States. His son, the future president, graduated from Harvard in 1940 before joining the U.S. Naval Reserve the next year. During World War II he commanded PT boats in the Pacific theater, earning the Navy and Marine Corps Medal for his service. Unlike Alfred E. Smith from 1928,

> [Kennedy] received, as he later said, a thoroughly secular education "from the elementary grades to Harvard." Not surprisingly, his religious knowledge was scanty and super-ficial. Yet on January 20, 1961, he concluded his inaugural address with these ringing words: "With a good conscience our only sure reward, with history the final judge of our deeds, let us go forth to lead the land we love, asking His blessing and His help, but knowing that here on earth, God's work must truly be our own." Whether JFK wrote that or Ted Sorenson or somebody else, the fact remains that John F. Kennedy spoke the words with the nation and the world watching and listening, and he deserves credit for that.[358]

Rather than coming from one of the wealthiest families in America, Richard M. Nixon was born in Yorba Linda, California, in 1913 to a devout Quaker family who in later years ran a grocery store and gas station. His hopes of college in the East were dashed by the Depression, so he attended Whittier College, a Quaker school in Whittier, California. He graduated from Duke Law School in 1937 and returned to California to practice law. He moved to

---

[358] Russell Shaw, *Catholics in America: Religious Identity and Cultural Assimilation from John Carroll to Flannery O'Connor* (San Francisco: Ignatius Press, 2016), 110. Ted Sorenson was a one-time speech writer for Kennedy, both before and during his presidency.

Washington, D.C., in 1942 to work for the federal government and served on active duty in the Navy Reserve during World War II. At age forty, he became the second youngest vice president in history.

By all historical standards, Nixon should have been an American media hero. He was a natural candidate for laurels in the grand old tradition of self-help, of pulling yourself up by your own bootstraps. He came from nowhere. His family background was respectable but obscure. He worked his way through an unfashionable college. He had no money except what he earned by his own efforts. He had, to begin with, no influential friends or connections. His life was dominated by a passionate desire to serve in public office, sometimes masquerading as brutal ambition, and by his patriotism and love of country, which knew no bounds. He was an autodidact and voracious reader, always trying to better himself, intellectually as well as professionally. He combined this earnest cultural endeavor with solid campaigning and administrative skills, which brought him early and continuing success, and with a modest private life which was morally impeccable.[359]

The Evangelists

We may have entered into the modern age by 1960, but as Arthur Schlesinger Sr. observed, anti-Catholicism is the most deep-seated bias in American history. As such, it was next to impossible that the question of religion would not be raised during the campaign: Not only was it raised, but it became a significant issue, strongly impacting the race. To understand what transpired in 1960, it is important to see the face of American religion as it then existed.

[359] Johnson, *A History of the American People,* 707.

Toil and Transcendence

The two leading figures of the era were Dr. Billy Graham, often referred to as "America's pastor," and Dr. Norman Vincent Peale, just as forcefully termed "America's Minister to Millions."

Billy Graham, more properly William Franklin Graham Jr., was born in Charlotte, North Carolina, in 1918 and died just a few months short of age one hundred in 2018. A Southern Baptist by birth, Graham rose to become perhaps the best-known and most influential preacher of a pure, evangelical Christianity, which few of any Christian persuasion could find fault with. A man of sincerest convictions, he was known all over the world for his evangelistic "crusades," which brought millions to Christ. He was a close friend, confidant, and spiritual adviser to the majority of American presidents of his lifetime, and continued his ministry until illness and old age overtook him. Those who criticized him would be few and far between, and many, including Catholic clergy and members of the hierarchy, were counted among his friends.

Norman Vincent Peale was of a different stripe. Born in Ohio in 1898 and surviving until the age of ninety-five, he was for years minister of the Marble Collegiate Church at the corner of Fifth Avenue and Twenty-Ninth Street, New York City. He was of the Dutch Reformed tradition and was more of a motivational speaker than a preacher. One of his books, *The Power of Positive Thinking*, was one of the best sellers in the fifties in Protestant America. Peale was the author of many similar titles, usually with the same theme and always popular. By the fifties, his church in New York had a national reputation:

> By 1954 ... he was named one of the country's twelve best salesmen. His congregation was now at capacity; black and white photographs capture lines of expectant New Yorkers waiting to hear him preach. *Life* magazine reported that his church was "jammed twice every Sunday with 2,400

people, including many seated in two overflow chapels which carry the service on close[d]-circuit television. Hundreds are turned away."[360]

In the summer of 1960, Billy Graham had invited a number of evangelicals to Montreux, Switzerland, for a discussion of their common mission. As Graham expected, the meeting turned into a discussion of the forthcoming American presidential campaign. Peale attended at Graham's invitation because of his concerns about Kennedy's Catholicism. Both men had significant contacts among wealthy businessmen and politicians and were close friends of Nixon, who, with his wife, Pat, had often attended church services at Peale's church while he was a young naval officer based in New York.[361]

Graham and Peale were not exactly theologically kindred spirits; Graham's message was more Gospel-driven, Peale's the seminal self-help manual. As for their political instincts, if Graham wrestled with how to balance the demands of his ministry to reach out to all, and the desires of his heart to help his friend get elected, Peale showed less ambivalence. During the West Virginia Primary, he had gone to Charleston and declared that it was essential to talk about Kennedy's Catholicism. He was planning to come out squarely for Nixon in a Sunday sermon in October, when it would

---

[360] Christopher Lane, *Surge of Piety: Norman Vincent Peale and the Remaking of American Religious Life* (New Haven: Yale University Press, 2016), 85.

[361] In December 1968, not long after Nixon had been elected president, his daughter Julie married David Eisenhower, grandson of Dwight D. Eisenhower at the Marble Collegiate Church, with Peale officiating.

have the greatest impact, and his wife had already looked into what it would cost to print 350,000 copies of it.[362]

As a result of the Switzerland meeting, Graham encouraged Nixon to speak far more about religion, to let the country know what he really believed, and to establish himself firmly on the basis of his Quaker heritage. The point wasn't to directly attack Kennedy's Catholicism but to reassure jittery Protestants about the alternative. President Eisenhower, himself a religious man, also leaned on his vice president to mention God more in his speeches. Nixon, on the other hand, had always felt very uneasy about wearing his religion on his sleeve: He believed religion to be entirely personal, a relationship between the believer and his God. He often spoke of Hannah Milhous, his mother, whom he described as a "Quaker saint," firmly holding to the belief that when praying, one should go to one's room, close the door, and pray in private.

Graham, for his part, was no religious bigot. Writing to Nixon during the course of the campaign, he said "it wasn't just that bigotry was wrong, it was stupid."

The open attacks by Protestants ... were serving mainly to solidify the Catholic vote. At all costs you must stay a million miles away from the religious issue at this time. I read a very dangerous letter yesterday. A Protestant leader said that he had established underground communication with the Republican National Committee. Even if it were true, I was shocked to see it in a letter for fear that if it ever got into the wrong hands it would do the Republicans great damage.[363]

---

[362] Nancy Gibbs and Michael Duffy, *The Preacher and the Presidents: Billy Graham in the White House* (New York: Center Street, 2007), 87.

[363] Ibid., 89.

Few realized that throughout his life, Graham was a registered Democrat. Being from the South, this was understandable in those years—and, to his credit, during the campaign, he wrote to John Kennedy promising that in the ensuing months he would not cause trouble; and, though he would very likely vote for Nixon, if JFK were elected he would give him his "wholehearted support."[364]

Though the Montreux meeting was clandestine, another gathering of Protestants held in Washington, D.C., and also meant to be private, backfired. The meeting was closed to the press, but two reporters managed to slip into an adjoining sound booth and to hear the entire proceeding. Peale was there and was heard saying that the entirety of American culture was at stake if a Catholic were elected president—not that the nation would collapse, but that it would be drastically changed. He openly questioned whether Kennedy, or any Catholic, could possibly function as president totally free from Vatican control. Other attendees were Daniel Poling, editor of the very Protestant *Christian Herald* and a long-time Kennedy foe, and Billy Graham's father-in-law, L. Nelson Bell, who felt Protestants in the United States were too soft on Catholicism: "The antagonism of the Roman church to Communism is in part because of similar methods."[365] The reaction was blistering. Columnist Murray Kempton inveighed against the bland spiritual flavor of the Eisenhower era and the "priests of the empty temple," including both Graham and Peale: "We have been afflicted with a state religion which is so diluted as to be no religion at all," he wrote, "and whose true conviction was abstracted neatly by Peale when he said of the Quaker birth of his candidate, Richard Nixon: 'I don't know that he ever let it bother him.'" He noted that Graham, the "Pope of lower Protestantism," was more discreet than Peale in public, but

[364] Ibid., 86.
[365] Ibid., 91.

"Graham certainly prays Republican; he has prayed at the White House and Gettysburg with the President and totes his good friend the Vice President around to Bible conferences."[366]

During the ill-fated Washington event, Nixon had been hospitalized with a serious knee infection. A few days after his discharge, he appeared on *Meet the Press*. The Republican candidate had not known of the meeting, and, had he been informed, likely would have disapproved of it. On television he attested to his opponent's loyalty, patriotism, and service to his country, lamented the fact that the election could possibly be decided on the basis of the religious issue, and clearly said that he would not raise the issue at all during the campaign (which promise he kept), instructing his staff "not to discuss religion, not to raise it, not to allow anybody to participate in the campaign who does on that ground."[367]

Kennedy's Catholicism

Kennedy, since his Senate days, had had to address the question of his Catholicism on different occasions. In March 1959, *Look* magazine commissioned one of their writers to produce an article titled "A Catholic in 1960." Kennedy happily cooperated; he was clearly presidential timber long before this and by 1959 was the likely front-runner for his party's nomination. In a series of interviews he expressed support for "public policies that were contrary to church pronouncements,"[368] and the interviewer, summarizing Kennedy's positions, wrote:

> "Whatever one's religion in his private life may be," [Kennedy] asserts, "for the officeholder nothing takes precedence

---

[366] Ibid., 91–92.

[367] Ibid., 92.

[368] Marlin, *American Catholic Voter*, 249.

over his oath to uphold the Constitution and all its parts —
including the First Amendment and the strict separation of
church and state. Without reference to the presidency," he
adds, "I believe as a senator that the separation of church and
state is fundamental to our American concept and heritage
and should remain so."[369]

The Catholic reaction to this, while predictably favorable in
some quarters, was not universally so. The *Indiana Catholic and
Record* said that "young Senator Kennedy had better watch his
language," and Kennedy speechwriter and adviser Ted Sorenson said
that in the *Look* article, Kennedy had come across as "a poor Catholic, a poor politician, a poor moralist and a poor wordsmith."[370] It
mattered little, though: Kennedy's star only brightened in the off-
year election of 1958, which brought many gains for the Democrats,
both in the House and the Senate, as well as several new governors,
at least four of whom were Catholics.[371]

Two years later, JFK steamrolled to his party's nomination, and
in his acceptance speech in Los Angeles on July 15, 1960, he
candidly admitted that his party was taking a risk nominating a
Catholic. But he praised his party for placing its confidence in the
American people and their ability to render a "free, fair judgment."
He hoped no American, considering the very real issues facing the
country in 1960, would waste his or her franchise by voting for
or against him on the basis of his creed, and he concluded with
the assurance that "my decisions on any public policy will be my
own — as an American, a Democrat and a free man."[372]

[369] Ibid.
[370] Ibid., 250.
[371] The major reason for the gains was a recession, which, of course,
voters blamed on the party in office.
[372] Ibid., 253.

Toil and Transcendence

Nixon was keenly aware of Kennedy's strength. From the outset, he had "no doubts whatever on this score: I believed that Kennedy's religion would hurt him in states he could afford to lose anyway, and that it would help him in states he needed to win."[373]

> I knew that I personally would never raise the question.... I did not believe it to be a legitimate issue. There were several questions as to Kennedy's qualifications for the presidency, but I never at any time considered his religion in this category.... I felt that the nation had come a long way in terms of both political sophistication and religious tolerance since the election of 1928 — which Al Smith probably would have lost in any event but in which the margin of his defeat was increased by the effect of the religious issue.... The most convincing argument ... that Kennedy's religion would be helpful rather than harmful to him, came from his own campaign organization. During the 1956 Democratic Convention, Kennedy's staff prepared and circulated a memorandum filled with past election statistics to show that a Catholic candidate on the national ticket could assure a Democratic victory — not despite but rather because of his religion.[374]

Nixon very honorably kept his promise of not allowing religion to surface during the campaign. As the campaign was in its final weeks, Nixon recalls:

> Kennedy and I were co-speakers at Cardinal Spellman's annual Alfred E. Smith Memorial Dinner. Kennedy spoke first and read a speech which delighted this distinguished audience with its wit but also irritated them with an incredible

---

[373] Richard M. Nixon, *Six Crises* (New York: Doubleday, 1962), 330.
[374] Ibid., 331.

display of bad judgment. At this strictly nonpolitical, non-partisan affair, he proceeded to raise what were obviously partisan political overtones. When I then spoke extemporaneously, all I had to do to top his performance was to avoid any statement that smacked of partisanship. The effect was easily predictable. He received polite applause. I received a prolonged ovation. Kennedy himself referred ruefully to this incident when we met in Miami immediately after the election. He was discussing voting patterns among Catholics and he pointed out that economics rather than religion primarily determined how people voted. And then he added with a smile, "You saw how those wealthy Catholics reacted at the Al Smith Dinner in New York."[375]

For his part, Kennedy tackled the issue head on with an address to several hundred Protestant ministers in Houston, Texas. The session ran for one hour: Kennedy explained his position for thirty minutes, then took questions for the rest. Many of the queries revealed deeply rooted Protestant prejudices — some even taking excerpts from old Catholic encyclopedias that had referenced Catholic persecutions of Protestants centuries ago in Europe. Perhaps the best remembered portion of JFK's address was this:

I believe in an America where the separation of church and state is absolute — where no Catholic prelate would tell the President (should he be a Catholic) how to act, and no Protestant minister would tell his parishioners for whom to vote — where no church or church school is granted any public funds or political preference — and where no man is denied public office merely because his religion differs from the president who might appoint him or the people who

[375] Ibid., 380.

might elect him. I believe in an America that is officially neither Catholic, Protestant nor Jewish—where no public official either requests or accepts instructions on public policy from the Pope, the National Council of Churches or any other ecclesial source—where no religious body seeks to impose its will directly or indirectly upon the general populace or the public acts of its officials—and where religious liberty is so indivisible that an act against one church is treated as an act against all.[376]

Kennedy's statement, while praised by many in 1960, has been a topic of discussion ever since. In March 2010, fifty years after the address, Philadelphia archbishop Charles Chaput gave an address at Houston Baptist University quite critical of the position Kennedy had taken so many years earlier. He described Kennedy's speech as "sincere, compelling, articulate—and wrong."[377] The candidate was not wrong about the patriotism of Catholics, "but wrong about American history and very wrong about the role of religious faith in our nation's life."[378] Chaput wanted to look at the problems in what Kennedy said, reflect on what a proper approach to politics and public service might look like, and finally examine where Kennedy's speech had lead the country.

The archbishop felt that Kennedy's stated belief in an America where the separation of church and state was absolute was

[376] Cited in Marlin, *American Catholic Voter*, 254. In addition to the question of aid to parochial schools, Kennedy also mentioned the topic of birth control as one in which he would, as president, not be affected by the teachings of his Church.

[377] Archbishop Charles J. Chaput, O.F.M., Cap., "The Vocation of Christians in American Public Life" (address at Houston Baptist University, March 1, 2010), EWTN, https://www.ewtn.com/catholicism/library/vocation-of-christians-in-american-public-life-3681.

[378] Ibid.

shrewd, especially in light of the distrust of Catholics in the United States. But:

> The trouble is, the Constitution dosen't say that. The Founders and Framers didn't believe that. And the history of the United States contradicts that. Unlike revolutionary leaders in Europe, the American founders looked quite favorably on religion. Many were believers themselves. In fact, one of the main reasons for writing the First Amendment's Establishment Clause — the clause that bars any federally-endorsed Church — was that several of the Constitution's Framers wanted to protect the publicly funded *Protestant* Churches they *already had* in their own states. John Adams actually preferred a "mild and equitable establishment of religion," and helped draft that into the 1780 Massachusetts Constitution. America's Founders encouraged mutual support between religion and government. Their reasons were practical. In their view, a republic like the United States needs a virtuous people to survive. Religious faith, rightly lived, forms virtuous people. Thus, the modern, drastic sense of the "separation of Church and state" had little force in American consciousness until Justice Hugo Black excavated it from a private letter President Thomas Jefferson wrote in 1802 to the Danbury Baptist Association. Justice Black then used Jefferson's phrase in the Supreme Court's *Everson v. Board of Education* decision in 1947.[379]

One year later, Chaput pointed out, the Catholic bishops responded to the decision, stating that it had forced the nation's public institutions into an "indifference to religion and the exclusion of cooperation between religion and government."

[379] Ibid.

Toil and Transcendence

Kennedy referenced the 1948 bishops' letter in his Houston comments. He wanted to prove the deep Catholic support for American democracy. And rightly so. But he neglected to mention that the same bishops, in the same letter, repudiated the new and radical kind of separation doctrine he was preaching.[380]

Kennedy's position, then, amounted to the privatization of religious belief. Now, to Kennedy's credit, he said he would resign the presidential office if his duties should ever require him to violate his conscience. "But in its *effect*, the Houston speech did exactly that," according to the archbishop. "It began the project of walling religion away from the process of governance in a new and aggressive way."[381] The way of the Founders—the cooperation between church and state—according to Chaput, is not the work of politicians, nor of clergy. It is rather something that belongs to lay believers, "who live most intensely in the world." It does not consist in theories about social or economic justice, but "in a relationship with Jesus Christ; and it bears fruit in the justice, mercy and love we show to others because of that relationship."[382]

Yet another Catholic writer, Russell Shaw, has admitted that "while no one expects politicians in a pluralistic democracy to translate doctrine into law, neither can religious believers turn their backs on their faith-based convictions about right and wrong."[383]

Many Catholic politicians have followed the path marked out by JFK in Houston. Catholic officeholders and candidates who lend support to causes like legalized abortion and same-sex marriage are in effect following his lead. Now as

[380] Ibid.
[381] Ibid.
[382] Ibid.
[383] Shaw, *Catholics in America*, 111–112.

then, however, the issue isn't taking orders from the pope and the bishops—something those supposedly power-hungry ecclesiastics neither expect nor want—but how to apply moral principles grounded in faith to real world politics. John Kennedy's innovative and influential approach lay in giving assurances that he wouldn't even try. We are still living with the consequences.[384]

Cardinal Richard Cushing, archbishop of Boston from 1944 until 1970, was a close friend and spiritual confidant of the entire Kennedy family. Reminiscing after the president's death, he said that

President Kennedy wore his religion, like his patriotism, lightly, and, again like his patriotism, he felt his religion profoundly. It was as natural for him to be a good Catholic as it was to be a good American, and neither loyalty ever encumbered his buoyant spirit. The many spiritual references that became part of his public utterances never gave the impression of being something added; they were part of the text in a vital and integral fashion, just as they were part of the man himself. He had his favorite scriptural readings, and they were almost uniformly those passages which emphasized courage, and home, and confidence in God. They were the texts of youth and destiny.... I remember well his father telling me, some months after the inauguration, that there had not been a night since he assumed office when "Jack" failed to spend some moments on his knees in prayer before closing the long day that is the duty of the President.... I was close to John Kennedy at those moments of his life which were most meaningful—his marriage, the family christenings, the death of his infant children. I can testify

384 Ibid., 112.

that he was a man of strong religious commitment, that his grace of style, his boundless courage, his patient suffering, his self-assurance and the warmth of his affection—all these were firmly rooted in a faith that was anchored beyond this world, truly in God Himself.[385]

Many decades later, another prelate related a very different impression. Philip Hannan was an auxiliary bishop of the Archdiocese of Washington during Kennedy's presidency and, in many ways, served in the same capacity as Cushing—a friend and spiritual confidant. Years later, when he had retired as archbishop of New Orleans, Hannan looked back on the unique relationship he had enjoyed with the president and Mrs. Kennedy, but the reflection was more realistic than what was portrayed in the media in 1960. It is important to know how enamored the Washington press corps was with Kennedy; even if it had been an era of far greater scrutiny into the private lives of the nation's public figures, Kennedy may still have come out unscathed due to the deference of the press. As it was, Archbishop Hannan noted with regret that the Kennedy boys had grown up watching their father flaunt his extramarital relationships, though "by the time he was elected to office, Jack, presumably was a grown man, independent of his father—except in their shared ambition to make him president."[386] Becoming even more specific, the archbishop wrote:

---

[385] Daughters of St. Paul, comp., *Richard Cardinal Cushing in Prose and Photos* (Jamaica Plain, MA: Daughters of St. Paul, 1965), 138–139. Cardinal Cushing was also, for many years, a good friend of Richard Nixon. When Nixon called on the cardinal in Boston in 1955, after the vice president's first trip to Latin America, he greeted him with the Spanish word *tocayo*, which means in effect "your name is the same as mine." Nixon, *Six Crises*, 456.

[386] Archbishop Philip Hannan, *The Archbishop Wore Combat Boots: Memoir of an Extraordinary Life* (Huntington, IN: Our Sunday Visitor, 2010), 202.

By nature, Jack was neither particularly tender, nor affectionate, at least publicly. However, I never doubted that, despite their differences, Jack and Jackie's relationship was based on a deep, if complicated love—made more so by Kennedy's reported philandering. Let me say up front that I, like the vast majority of Americans, knew nothing about Jack Kennedy's infidelities, which, sinful and reprehensible, caused his wife enormous embarrassment and pain. In those days the mainstream media never reported on the personal life of the President; and though it's unimaginable now, no one ever told me about the rumors. When criticized for not upbraiding him on the subject, I can only respond honestly that, under the circumstances, I was the last person to learn about it. No responsible report about his actions was ever given to me. The ideal place for dealing with this problem, of course, would have been the confessional, but Jack never asked me to hear his confession. If he had, and he had confessed infidelity, I would have counseled him to immediately amend his life. If his excuse (as I imagine it might have been) was that he had a compulsion, I simply would not have accepted it—which is perhaps why he didn't come to me. Jack did not really want to hear what I had to say to him on the subject.[387]

Kennedy's assassination in Dallas on November 22, 1963, left the nation stunned by its horror, by the sight of a young president struck down in the very prime of his life. His assassination left an indelible mark on the American psyche and, decades later, contributes to the ongoing Kennedy mystique. Perhaps it was William F. Buckley Jr., a Kennedy antagonist, who said it best:

[387] Ibid., 201.

Toil and Transcendence

The grief was spontaneous and, in most cases, wholly sincere. Not because Mr. Kennedy's policies were so universally beloved, but because he was a man so intensely charming, whose personal vigor and robust enjoyment of life so invigorated almost all who beheld him. The metabolism of the whole nation rose on account of the fairyland quality of the First Family. After all, no divine typecaster could have done better than to get JFK to play JFK, Jackie to play the First Lady, and the children to play themselves. The assassination of President Kennedy was the act presumably of a madman, heir to the madmen who killed Lincoln and McKinley, and, for that matter, Christ, reminding us that the beasts are always with us, and that they continue to play roles in history, and in human affairs. Even his most adamant political opponents acknowledged the personal courage Mr. Kennedy showed during his young and dazzling lifetime. Now, no doubt, he would desire that his countrymen also act heroically, by enduring their grief; and by demonstrating to his bereaved family not only their compassion, but also their fortitude.[388]

A Modern Church?

A friend once quipped that it would take a century to return to normalcy after President Kennedy and Pope John XXIII—an exaggeration, to be sure, but one with a core of truth. While Kennedy could have had no knowledge of what the remainder of the sixties had in store, he is often seen as representative of hopeful new beginnings

---

[388] William F. Buckley Jr., *A Torch Kept Lit: Great Lives of the Twentieth Century* (New York: Crown Forum, 2016), 19–20. This eulogy appeared in *National Review* on December 10, 1963.

that become disasters. When the "New Frontier" and "Camelot"
passed away, so did the "promise" people read into such mystagogy,
and a rebellious spirit was unleashed in the country, finding its way
into religion and politics particularly. As to Saint John XXIII, his call
for the Second Vatican Council later unleashed upon the Church
something the saintly pontiff never dreamed of, and it underscored
the belief of many historians that the Church generally does spend
at least a century recuperating from major upheavals.

Pope John, a deeply pious man, had "an invincible optimism
that the final purposes of God must be for good and that in the
end, whatever the obstacles they might meet upon their way, those
purposes would be achieved."[389] In fact, optimism about the council's objectives and conclusions seemed to permeate much of the
Catholic world in its immediate aftermath:

> For four hundred years the Church had been an army on
> the defensive. Attacked first by positive Protestantism and
> afterwards by infidelity, the ecclesiastical authorities had
> thought, naturally enough, that their first task was to pre-
> vent the disruption of Christendom in Europe and to defend
> the faithful against its attacks. After four centuries it had
> to be recognized that Catholic unity in that old sense had
> irrevocably perished. There was no chance that Protestant
> bodies would prove to be but temporary aberrations and
> that the people of those countries would return to their
> medieval uniformity. There was equally no chance that the
> challenges of modern invention and modern thought would
> be easily refuted by the quotation of a few sentences from
> St. Thomas Aquinas. On the other hand, while the day of

[389] Christopher Hollis, *The Achievements of Vatican II* (New York:
Hawthorn Books, 1967), 16.

Toil and Transcendence

Catholic countries as such had passed, the intermixture of peoples and the improvement of communications offered to Catholicism an opportunity to make its message a world-wide message to a degree that it had never previously been and imposed upon the Church an obligation to restate its teaching in a way that would make it appear revelant to modern man and his problems. Of course, as with all the great turning events of history, this was an event that did not suddenly and unexpectedly emerge out of a clear sky on one particular day. Things happen like that in plays or novels but not in reality.[390]

On January 25, 1959, Pope John spoke of a "New Pentecost" when he announced the council that would open just short of four years later. He hoped for "nothing less than the conversion of the world, something that required Catholics to put aside the defensiveness that had characterized the Church since the Counter-Reformation."[391] Cardinals, meanwhile, were already to be found in liberal and conservative camps; many strains of thought and trends in moral theology, philosophy, and especially biblicial studies had been competing for years, and now a chance to determine the course of the Church for generations had arrived. The Council was both the Church going out to the world and, at the same time, the world coming into the Church.

When Pope John succeeded he inherited problems created by the changing nature of the world. When he called for an *aggiornamento*, he was not wantonly inventing problems. A new world required new solutions. Pius XII, his predecessor,

---

[390] Ibid., 108–109.
[391] James Hitchcock, *History of the Catholic Church* (San Francisco: Ignatius Press, 2012), 475.

had recognized this as clearly as he, and under Pius XII ... we had seen the beginnings of liturgical reforms, and in other ways the shape of things to come was beginning to show itself. What had not been suggested under Pius was that these reforms should be introduced by means of a Council. That was John's original contribution. How far John foresaw the detailed shape that the Council would take, and how far he foresaw what its purpose would be, we cannot say.[392]

We can see this in the historical background of some of the Council's major documents. The decree on Revelation, *Dei Verbum*, for instance, had its origins in evolving biblical scholarship. In the early twentieth century, Leo XIII authorized the establishment of the École Biblique, a Dominican "school of the Bible" in Jerusalem; he also set up the Pontifical Biblical Commission to encourage and oversee these studies. Pius X went on to establish the Pontifical Biblical Institute in Rome under the Jesuits, and Pius XII gave at least qualified endorsement to biblical scholarship, reminding Catholics that although the Bible was divinely inspired, it was written through human agencies.

Liturgically, decades of study also developed before Vatican II. The liturgical movement, which sought to study the history of pre-Tridentine worship and apply it to the present moment, largely began in Benedictine monasteries in Germany and Belgium and was brought to the United States and implemented at Saint John's Abbey in Collegeville, Minnesota. Monsignor Romano Guardini, the German-Italian theologian and spiritual writer who died in

---

[392] Hollis, *The Achievements of Vatican II*, 20. Curiously, the *aggiornamento* to which Hollis refers took on a quite different meaning not very long after the Council's close. A later understanding of the term came to mean the nebulous "spirit of Vatican II," far different from the Council's original intent.

1968, had become over the years the most important theologian of the liturgical movement. At the same time, the German Benedictine Odo Casel, who died in 1940, explained the Church's Liturgy as "not only the continuation of the sacrifice of Calvary, through which the faithful receive grace, but as a divine mystery into which the faithful fully enter, in order to die and rise with Christ."[393]

Even the ecumenical movement had antecedents: In the 1920s, Cardinal Désiré Mercier of Malines, Belgium, conducted the "Malines Conversations with the Anglicans." The Holy See did little more than tolerate these, and nothing of substance came from them, except perhaps the thawing of some ice that had formed since Leo XIII's declaration that Anglican orders were "absolutely null and utterly void." There was also some informal ecumenism between Catholics and Protestants during World War II in Germany, the Netherlands, and France, in opposition to the Nazis.

In its attempts to read the signs of the times, the Council issued by far the longest, and perhaps the most sweeping, of its decrees, *Gaudium et Spes*, the Pastoral Constitution on the Church in the Modern World. Its agenda was broad:

It attempted to deal with all aspects of the modern world: the human sense of alienation, the economy, war and peace, the family.... [It] mandated economically developed nations to help poorer ones; condemned the arms race and all wars against civilians, made blunt reference to the "plague of divorce," and the "abominable crime" of abortion, judged deliberately childless marriages to be a tragedy, and reminded the faithful of the church's condemnation of artificial birth control.[394]

[393] Hitchcock, *History of the Catholic Church*, 485.
[394] Ibid., 489.

It appears that many of the Council fathers, upon returning to their dioceses, seemed unclear of the Council's intent and meaning. In retrospect, little or no catechesis was given to the Catholic faithful about any of the conciliar degrees; in particular, no training or preparation was given prior to implementing the Constitution on the Sacred Liturgy, *Sacrosanctum Concilium*. In most instances, bishops left the implementation not only of matters liturgical but of all conciliar teaching in the hands of lay and cleric "experts." In most cases, the results were devastating.

A culture of dissent began to develop and metastasize in the Council's aftermath. American Catholic opinion was generally formed by the popular press, especially by the author Xavier Rynne, a pseudonym of the American Redemporist Francis X. Murphy, who authored a series of reports in the *New Yorker* "depicting Vatican II as a titanic struggle pitting heroic liberals against dastardly conservatives, with the church's future course at stake."[395] An almost immediate reaction came from the French Thomist philosopher Jacques Maritain, then living in the United States. In his work *The Peasant of the Garonne*, he deplored what he found to be "a widespread abandonment of values like asceticism, mortification, and penance, along with virginity and chastity, and their replacement by a simple-minded immanentism."[396]

Controversial theologians such as the Dutch Dominican Edward Schillebeeckx, the German Redemptorist Bernard Häring, to a lesser extent the German Jesuit Karl Rahner, and perhaps most abrasive of all, Hans Küng all demanded that the Church adapt Herself to a changing culture. On the other side, such theologians as Henri de Lubac, Jean Daniélou, Jacques Maritain, Hans Urs von Balthasar, and Joseph Ratzinger began to protest strongly what they perceived to be distortions of the Council.

---

[395] Shaw, *Catholics in America*, 112.
[396] Ibid., 112–113.

Toil and Transcendence

Practically, the most obviously damaging effect of the Council was the mass exodus of priests and sisters from their vocations. Most notable among male communities in this regard was the Society of Jesus. At the end of the Council, their international membersip stood at thirty-six thousand; by 2010, it was well below twenty thousand. Women's religious communities seemed to suffer more devastating effects than men's. Most Church historians would agree that, prior to the Council, women's communities led far more austere lives than did priests. At the same time, they had had less formal education than their male counterparts. As the twentieth century progressed, this began to change, with the advent of graduate summer courses in theology for sisters. The famed Belgian Cardinal Leo Suenens wrote an influential book urging sisters to come out of their cloisters, and subsequent "renewalists" predicted tremendous revitalization of religious life in the United States if religious would modify or discard their traditional habits, abandon their rigorous forms of discipline, and return to the supposed original charisms of their founders and foundresses.

The most celebrated "renewal" story in the United States was that of the Immaculate Heart Sisters of Los Angeles, whose program of *aggiornamento* was guided by the prestigious psychologist Carl Rogers (d. 1987), a one-time student for the Protestant ministry who had developed a negative attitude toward religion. The Immaculate Heart "renewal" was a paradigm for many others that followed: favorable publicity, optimistic expectations, the use of fashionable techniques of "behavior modification" and a personal villain (Cardinal James F. McIntyre [d. 1979]). The community soon fell apart. Many sisters left; those who remained split into opposing factions; there were few new members; and most apostolates were abandoned. In time, the community virtually ceased to exist.[397]

In liturgical matters, aberrations abounded everywhere. In catechetics, the traditional approach to teaching the Faith was abandoned in favor of a new emphasis that promised to "inculcate in [students] a lively personal faith, through Bible study, liturgy, and many other things, paying close attention to the psychology of the students and the pedagogical methods appropriate to their ages."[398]

In biblical studies, the historical-critical method came into its own, and priests, sisters, and laypeople seemed almost to worship at the feet of the leading exegetical gurus of the day. The Gospels, for instance, were now understood under the influence of skeptical secular commentators to have been composed long after the death of Christ, largely by local communities to justify their own distinctive beliefs, while emphasizing certain stories from the life of Christ at the expense of others. At first, it was suggested that the infancy narratives might not be historical; then the bodily Resurrection of Christ was seriously questioned. Everything, it appeared, was up for grabs. This is not to say, however, that many of the exegetes of this school were not themselves very holy men. It is also not to say that every word written in this vein destroyed personal faith. As with so many academic disciplines, much that was true and honest and helpful also emerged that expanded understanding of the genuine circumstances of the development of Scripture.[399]

---

[397] Hitchcock, *History of the Catholic Church*, 502.

[398] Ibid.,498.

[399] In later decades, Pope Benedict XVI, Joseph Ratzinger, was of the opinion that as a disciplinary approach to Scripture, the method had outlived its usefulness. The theologian Hans Urs Von Balthasar was of the opinion that it was in no way a useful approach to the sacred text.

Toil and Transcendence

Moral relativism, self-fulfillment, and the "lived experience" all became touchstones of contemporary moral theology. Much of this would come to fruition at the end of the sixties, with the controversy over Pope Paul VI's encyclical *Humanae Vitae*. The French paleontologist and Jesuit Pierre Teilhard de Chardin and his "omega point," at which all differences in being would converge, "a Christogenesis [birth of Christ] that was the ultimate fulfillment of creation," was widely read and enthusiastically accepted, though he has since been criticized for his understanding of salvation "as a wholly natural process in which sin, and therefore the need for redemption, was transcended and the universe underwent a kind of pantheistic divinization."[400]

War in Vietnam

The sixties saw the initial outbursts of these intellectual phenomena that would remain with the Church for decades. But even as the Council dominated Catholic news, there was much more that American Catholics concerned themselves with in this decade—especially their nation's involvement in the seemingly endless conflict in Southeast Asia.

America's involvement stretched over twenty years (1954–75). American military personnel began to serve there in 1954 and the last fifty were evacuated on April 20, 1975. In all, 8,762,000 Americans performed Vietnam-era military service: 4,386,000 Army, 794,000 Marines, 1,740,000 Air Force, and 1,842,000 Navy. Of these, about two million servicemen actually fought in Vietnam or operated offshore. There were 47,244 U.S. battle-deaths in all services,

[400] Hitchcock, op. cit., 496.

153,329 hospitalized wounded, 150,375 "lightly wounded", and 2,483 missing.... Vietnamese losses were calamitous. About 300,000 civilians were killed in South Vietnam and 65,000 in North Vietnam. South Vietnamese forces lost 223,748 killed and 570,600 wounded. North Vietnamese casualties were estimated at 6,660,000 killed, the number of wounded being unknown. The war's direct expense to the United States was $106.8 billion.[401]

It was in the Kennedy and Johnson administrations that events really began to unfold. Early in his presidency, Kennedy sensed that Southeast Asia would become very problematic. But after his Bay of Pigs fiasco in Cuba, he hesitated before deciding for further involvement elsewhere.[402] Nevertheless, in November 1961, he did send 7,000 troops to Vietnam, "the critical step down the slippery incline into the swamp."[403] The next step was to get rid of Diem, a man Kennedy's vice president, Lyndon Johnson, once described as the "Churchill of Southeast Asia."[404] Kennedy, because of his failure to achieve immediate success in Vietnam, seemed to blame Diem.

Ngo Dinh Diem was born into a prominent and devout Catholic family in 1901 and was educated at French-speaking schools. Early on, he thought of following his brother, Ngo Dinh Thuc, into the priesthood, but he finally settled on a career in civil service. His brother would eventually become archbishop of Hue in central Vietnam. Diem served the Vietnamese emperor in a

[401] Johnson, *A History of the American People*, 732.
[402] The Bay of Pigs was an abortive effort to free the island of Cuba from communist control. Insurgent rebels staged a military effort, but Kennedy, relying on advice from the liberals in his own party, failed to provide the rebels with sufficient aircover. They were easily outmaneuvered and quickly defeated.
[403] Johnson, *A History of the American People*, 734.
[404] Ibid.

number of ministerial posts but became increasingly convinced that the emperor was a tool of the French. Diem favored a third way: anti-communist and anti-colonialist. He founded the Can Lao Party to support his political doctrine but, lacking the upper hand, went into exile for some years before returning in July 1954 to be appointed prime minister of Vietnam. During these years of exile, a true picture of the man gradually appeared:

> During his two-year stay in America, Diem lived in Maryknoll Mission Society seminaries in upstate New York and New Jersey. Diem embraced the Maryknoll way of life, doing the same menial chores as the seminarians. Visitors of high import in American politics were stunned to see Diem taking out the garbage, washing the floors, and doing other lowly labors without complaint. Plainly, the man was seeking political power not for his own aggrandizement but out of dedication to God and his fellow men, whom he wished to serve. Diem greatly impressed Francis Cardinal Spellman, Archbishop of New York, who introduced him to everyone he knew in Washington who might help him. As a result, Diem made friends with Supreme Court Justice William O. Douglas, Senator Mike Mansfield, and the rising political star Congressman John F. Kennedy. What seems to have appealed to these Washington power brokers, apart from Diem's Catholicism, was his resolute stand against both Communism and French colonialism.[405]

Kennedy was influenced in his declining view of Diem by two advisers who strongly disliked the Vietnamese leader: Averell Harriman, then serving as assistant secretary of state for Far Eastern

[405] Geoffrey Shaw, *The Lost Mandate of Heaven: The American Betrayal of Ngo Dinh Diem, President of Vietnam* (San Francisco: Ignatius Press, 2015), 36–37.

affairs, and John Kenneth Galbraith, a prestigious Havard economist whose unflinching support of Kennedy in the 1960 presidential
race won him an appointment as ambassador to India. Harriman
had visited Vietnam in 1961 and felt that Diem was to blame for
the ongoing insurgency. Some of his observations may have been
based on Diem's favoritism of Catholics and disdain for Buddhists.
In any event, Harriman concluded that "there is no solution that
does not involve a change in government."[406] Both Harriman and
Galbraith were at odds with Frederick Nolting, a careerist at the
State Department whom Kennedy had appointed ambassador to
South Vietnam shortly after he assumed the presidency. At one
meeting in the White House, Nolting was prohibited by Harriman
from giving his views on the grounds that Nolting had been too
friendly with Diem. Kennedy overruled Harriman and listened
carefully to the other side of the story.

Meanwhile, Dean Rusk had been appointed secretary of state
by Kennedy in 1961. A Southerner, he was never fully accepted
by many in the administration. As a result, he would often defer to
men who had been on the scene for years and, more importantly,
were members of the Eastern liberal establishment.

> To powerful Democrat diplomats Bowles, Galbraith, and
> Harriman, President Diem stood in the way of their reso-
> lution to the conflicts in Southeast Asia, with his defiant
> stance against their demands to reform his government. . . .
> Anyone who supported Diem, such as Nolting and Colby,
> were cast in an unfavorable light by the Harriman group,
> which had direct access to President Kennedy. Outside the
> Washington "in-crowd," Nolting found that he had little
> means to explain or to defend his and Diem's actions. Indeed,

[406] Ibid., 147.

Nolting came to realize that President Kennedy was basing his perceptions of the situation in Vietnam more on reports from his friends and the news media than on the official reports sent to him by his embassy in Saigon.[407]

An interesting counterpoint to the narrative of the Harriman group came from Senator Mike Mansfield, then Senate majority leader and an influential member of the Senate Foreign Relations Committee. Mansfield had made a trip to South Vietnam at the end of 1962 and reported that

> relations between the American and Vietnamese governments were excellent but for the negative news reports. The concern of the Kennedy administration, Mansfield said, was that the difficulties the South Vietnamese government was having with Western reporters, particularly Americans, was reflecting negatively on the Diem government back home.[408]

As time wore on, those who defended Diem in Washington became more and more shut out of meetings within the administration, especially Ambassador Nolting. Henry Cabot Lodge, a Republican from one of the most blue-blooded families in the

---

[407] Ibid., 153. William Colby, a future director of the Central Intelligence Agency under Richard Nixon and Gerald Ford, was, in the Kennedy years, serving as the CIA's deputy chief and then chief of station in Saigon until 1962. Both he and Nolting were strong partisans of President Diem. Chester "Chet" Bowles was a former governor of Connecticut, and later Congressman, long known for his support of liberal programs in education and housing. Under Kennedy, he succeeded Galbraith as United States ambassador to India. By 1960, he had become an influential foreign-policy adviser to Kennedy and was known to be a liberal intellectual. He, Harriman, and Galbraith had considerably more influence with President Kennedy than did the Diem supporters.

[408] Ibid., 166.

country, soon succeeded him. At a September meeting attended by Attorney General Robert Kennedy, Secretary of Defense Robert McNamara, CIA director John McCone, Harriman, Colby and several others, the deep chasm that had developed was apparent. Robert Kennedy said the conflict in Vietnam would go better without Diem; McNamara immediately disagreed, saying the government had been trying to overthrow Diem but had no compelling alternative. Harriman said that Diem, "by persecuting Buddhists, had made it impossible for the United States to back him. Diem had to be removed ... because he had gravely offended the world community."[409]

In the end, this thinking prevailed. Diem and his brother Nhu, his closest political adviser, attended Mass at St. Francis Xavier Church in Saigon on November 2, 1963. After Mass, they were outside in the Grotto of the Blessed Virgin Mary when they were kidnapped and secured in a personnel carrier. The vehicle was driven away, and "the executioner ... cut out their gallbladders while they were still alive and shot them."[410]

Three weeks later, Kennedy was dead himself. The next five years of Lyndon Johnson's presidency saw the war drag on, with the chief executive continuing it in a "desultory" fashion until August 1964, when North Vietnam attacked an American destroyer conducting electronic espionage in the Gulf of Tonkin. The subsequent Gulf of Tonkin Resolution, easily passed by both houses of Congress, in effect gave the President the right to prosecute the war without further authorization:

> He was fighting an election campaign against Senator [Barry] Goldwater, who openly advocated the bombing of North Vietnam. Johnson sensed the public would be unhappy about

[409] Ibid., 264.
[410] Ibid., 267.

getting into "another Korea" and played down the war during the campaign. In fact if anything he advocated a "peace" line during the campaign, just as Wilson had done in 1916 and Roosevelt in 1940. Then, having won his overwhelming victory he did the opposite—again like Wilson and Roosevelt. In February 1965, following heavy US casualties in a Vietcong attack on a barracks, he ordered the bombing of the North.[411]

The move was controversial—some held that the United States should have occupied the North with infantry and that the American people would have backed such a move. But the conflict continued, and the American people became wearier and wearier. The seemingly limitless bombing attacks never produced the desired effect, and reports in the American press continually gave the impression that America was fighting a hopeless war. American successes were little reported, while North Vietnamese and Vietcong victories were played up. One Catholic chaplain candidly admitted:

> What has astonished me most has been the frequency of misquotation of essential documents pertaining to the war. Entire arguments have been built on such misquotations. I am not talking about mere chance references by the unsophisticated. Scholars, writers, clergymen, Congressmen and professional diplomats have argued forcefully and persuasively, but unwittingly, on the basis of "facts" that have been born of misquotations. I honestly believe that a tremendous amount of misunderstanding has resulted from this single problem and that much of the heated debate between equally sincere people has been predicated on such misunderstanding.

[411] Johnson, *A History of the American People*, 734–735.

The same chaplain was quick to add, however, that he did not believe in "a national conspiracy of the press, or in widespread malice on the part of journalists." He did not believe that politicians who favored or opposed administration policy on the war were engaging in "party politics," "any more than I believe that all peace marchers are draft dodgers or Communists."[412]

A war-wearied president told the American people in March 1968 that he would not be seeking another term of office. Robert F. Kennedy was murdered three months later, and the Democratic nomination, during a rancorous convention in Chicago, fell to Vice President Hubert H. Humphrey. But the Democrats were mortally wounded, and Alabama governor George Wallace stole the South, leading to Richard M. Nixon's becoming the nation's thirty-seventh president on January 20, 1969.

He had a brilliant National Security Advisor in Henry Kissinger. He brought in one or two clever and original Democrats such as Daniel Patrick Moynihan. His speech-writers, who included William Safire, Pat Buchanan, Ray Price, David Gergen and Lee Huebner, were probably the best team of its kind ever assembled. Nixon and Kissinger between them developed the first clear geopolitical strategy for America since the retirement of Eisenhower.... In four years, [Nixon] reduced American forces in Vietnam from 550,000 to 24,000. Spending declined from $25 billion a year under Johnson to less than $3 billion. This was due to a more intelligent use of US resources in the area. They became more flexible, being used in Cambodia in 1970, in Laos in 1971, in more concentrated bombing of North Vietnam in 1972, all of which kept the determined men in

[412] John J. O'Connor, *A Chaplain Looks at Vietnam* (New York: World Publishing, 1968), 15–16.

Hanoi perplexed and apprehensive about America's intentions.... [Nixon] also did something neither Kennedy nor Johnson had dared: he exploited the logic of the Sino-Soviet dispute and reached an understanding with China. It was Nixon's California background which inclined him toward Peking. He saw the Pacific as the world arena of the future.[413]

None of this should suggest that Nixon's time was easy: Protests abounded and opinions on the war's morality shifted, with even as staunch an anti-communist as retired Archbishop Fulton J. Sheen questioning the morality of remaining any longer in Southeast Asia. If the American press had opposed Johnson's Vietnam policy, their vitriol was poured on his successor with a particular vengeance. Nixon's fights with the press had been legendary, and their total opposition to the war drove them to extreme degrees of criticism. In the end, however, with the Paris Peace Accords of January 1973, Nixon's strong desire for peace with honor was achieved in Vietnam.

Had he been in a stronger position politically, the peace might have lasted. Instead, the Watergate scandal drove him from office on August 9, 1974, weakening American foreign policy throughout the world and gutting the initiatives his administration had begun. Less than two years after Gerald Ford had assumed the presidency, North Vietnam began yet another series of attacks against the South. By the beginning of 1975, Ford warned that "American unwillingness to provide adequate assistance to allies fighting for their lives could seriously affect our credibility throughout the world as an ally." Congress paid little attention. Another warning to Congress followed in March, and again it fell on deaf ears. In late April, the Vietnamese government abdicated; Americans

---

[413] Johnson, *A History of the American People*, 741–742.

were evacuated from the U.S. Embassy in Saigon; and "an image of flight and humiliation [was] etched on the countless Americans who watched it on TV."[414]

The Church and the War

Many Catholic voices were heard throughout the war years, both for and against American policy. Perhaps the staunchest defender of the policies of the Johnson administration was Cardinal Francis Spellman of New York. His many years as military vicar of the armed forces allowed him to view firsthand the courage of generations of American fighting men and gave him quite a negative view of the communists they were fighting. Spellman was described as a superpatriot by many, especially by those who disagreed with him. Considering the prestigious positions he held in the Church, though, his voice was clearly heard and surely carried weight among many American Catholics.

Not all bishops held the same views as the archbishop of New York. In May of 1967, an organization called Negotiation Now! was founded, demanding a political settlement of the war. Many prestigious names were to be found on the membership list, including Archbishops Paul Hallinan of Atlanta and James Peter Davis of Santa Fe; James P. Shannon, auxiliary of Saint Paul, Minnesota; John J. Dougherty, auxiliary of Newark and chairman of the Bishops' Committee on World Justice and Peace; Victor J. Reed, bishop of Oklahoma City; and Joseph P. Donnelly, auxiliary of New Haven.[415]

---

[414] Ibid., 758.

[415] Thomas Francis Ritt, "The Bishops and Negotiation Now," in *American Catholics and Vietnam*, ed. Thomas E. Quigley (Grand Rapids, MI: William B. Eerdmans, 1968), 112. James P. Shannon, at odds with the teaching Church for years, eventually left the episcopacy and the priesthood and civilly married.

Catholic newspapers varied in their approach to the war. The Los Angeles *Tidings* and the *Guardian* of the Diocese of Little Rock were both hawkish. The latter publication often spoke of the "holy war" being waged against atheistic communism. The editorials of the Archdiocese of Chicago's *New World* were analyzed by one writer who found that they contained a peace message interwoven with "qualifiers and rationalizations."[416] Irish-born Father Patrick O'Connor covered Vietnam for the National Catholic News Service and was described as being "so anti-communist and pro-American that his writings have the ring about them of U.S. State Department propaganda."[417] The *National Catholic Reporter* was the only Catholic newspaper whose editor, Robert Hoyt, sent a correspondent. Michael Novak went to Vietnam in 1967 to report on the efforts of American Catholic Relief Services to support the popular forces of South Vietnam; in Hoyt's view, the Novak mission was totally worth the effort.[418]

Conservative Catholic reporting seemed to come under closer scrutiny and came in for far more criticism:

It is hardly an accident of fate that the conservative answer to *The National Catholic Reporter*, the new independent weekly, *Twin Circle,* should have drawn its two principal personalities from *The Register* and the *Visitor*: Frank Morriss and Daniel Lyons, S.J. Morriss was news editor and a reactionary columnist at *The Register*; Father Lyons, a hawk who could outfly all hawks, appeared as a columnist in *Our Sunday Visitor*. After Vietnam mushroomed, he became to *Visitor* readers what Father Richard Ginder was to readers

---

[416] John G. Deedy Jr., "The Catholic Press and Vietnam," in Quigley, *American Catholics and Vietnam*, 122–123.

[417] Ibid., 126.

[418] Ibid., 127.

of the McCarthy era. With Lyons and Morriss gone from *Our Sunday Visitor* and *The Register*, observers are genuinely hopeful that both publications will take new directions.[419]

The Brothers Berrigan

Perhaps the most famous exemplars of the Catholic left in this era were a pair of brothers: Philip Berrigan, a Josephite priest who later left the priesthood and married, and his brother Daniel, a Jesuit priest until his death. As early as 1963, Daniel and some friends had formed a group called the Catholic Peace Fellowship. At the same time, the Trappist Thomas Merton was also becoming involved in the peace movement. He invited to his retreat at Gethsemani, Kentucky, a number of Catholics and Protestants, nearly all of whom would go on to play substantial roles in the Catholic left. In August 1965, Roger LaPorte, a member of the Catholic Worker Movement, employed a tactic used by Buddhist monks and burned himself to death in the UN Plaza in New York. Daniel Berrigan's local superior had forbidden him to involve himself in any such activity following LaPorte's death, but he appeared to disregard the directive, giving a well-publicized talk in which he compared the death of LaPorte to the death of Christ. At the time, Berrigan was involved with a publication called *Jesuit Missions*. His superiors decided to send him on a fact-finding junket for the magazine, which was actually busywork meant to give him a chance to cool off and to remove him from the country for a while. When the news got out, one thousand of his supporters signed a petition in the *New York Times* demanding his recall.

---

[419] Ibid., 128–129. Lyons later left the priesthood and married; Ginder was involved in numerous homosexual acts with young men and adolescents.

Toil and Transcendence

Meanwhile, his brother Philip was involved in similar activities in the Baltimore area. He broke into a Selective Service office and poured blood on many of the files—a favorite tactic used around the country. A second raid in suburban Catonsville included his brother Daniel and this time involved dousing files with napalm and kneeling in the office in prayer until they were arrested. It is not hard to see how such activities aroused the ire of FBI director J. Edgar Hoover, who often successfully planted informers within the left's ranks—including the Berrigans' operations—and secured much valuable information.

In the end, the Berrigans had little impact on American Catholic opinion:

> A *Newsweek* poll in 1971 supports the view that across-the-board impact of the anti-Vietnam actions was small. To adult American Catholics, pornography, abortion, and racial discrimination were more appropriate targets for a public stand by the church than Vietnam. Of those polled 69 percent did not believe that Catholics who raided draft boards to protest the war were acting as responsible Christians. Six years after Daniel Berrigan's "exile" and four years after Philip Berrigan poured blood on the Baltimore records, 62 percent of Catholics surveyed had no idea who the brothers were.[420]

Perhaps Navy chaplain John J. O'Connor, a future cardinal archbishop of New York, was closer to the Catholic feeling on the war in the 1960s when he wrote:

> One group of priests I know in a large city [in Vietnam] is forthright in describing what they are convinced will happen

---

[420] Hennesey, op.cit., 320.

if free-world troops leave their city under present circumstances. They say the streets will run red with the blood of
those who in any way consorted with free-world troops and
that such people have already been warned to this effect in
various ways by unidentified V[iet] C[ong].

I talked for an hour or more with a South Vietnamese
Catholic Bishop in another city—a man I had come to know
rather well during my earlier years in the country—and
asked him what he thought would happen if American forces
withdrew right now. His answer was immediate. "Every
Catholic would be killed by the Viet Cong."[421]

While the protesting Catholic left could invariably count on
good press from the mainstream media, the majority of Catholics
through the long years of the conflict were generally inclined to
support American efforts—be they Johnson's or Nixon's.

Catholic Identity

An episode of enduring importance for American Catholics un-
folded in Land O' Lakes, Wisconsin, in 1967: a meeting of Catholic
educators that changed the face of Catholic higher education.
The meeting was convened by Notre Dame's legendary president
Father Theodore Hesburgh, C.S.C., to prepare a position paper for
the International Federation of Catholic Universities scheduled
to meet the following summer. The working paper that emerged
from this session was titled "The Nature of the Contemporary
Catholic University." At least one scholar has described the final
product as "the classic doctrine on how modern Catholic universities were to be defined primarily by their membership in the

---

[421] O'Connor, *A Chaplain Looks at Vietnam*, 42.

modern educational establishment, sharing the same autonomy, academic freedom, functions, services, disciplines, public and norms of academic excellence."[422]

Though the Land O' Lakes statement had no authority, its psychological and practical effects were enormous. It reflected a desire for institutional autonomy, which led many previously Catholic institutions drastically to alter their mode of governance in the late sixties. The participants at Land O' Lakes were a diverse yet ideologically unified group of comrades:

> Jesuit heads of Boston College, Fordham, Georgetown and Saint Louis joined Notre Dame's leader in the contingent of university presidents. The American assistant general of the Jesuits, Vincent T. O'Keefe (himself a former president of Fordham), came with Fathers Lalande and Kenna to represent the religious orders. [Paul] Hallinan [of Newark] and [John J.] Dougherty [auxiliary of Newark] flew the flag for the hierarchy, while the Canadian contingent included Monsignor Alphonse-Marie Parent and Fathers Lorenzo Roy from Laval and Lucien Vachon from Sherbrooke. Fr. Theodore McCarrick, then president of the Catholic University of Puerto Rico, represented schools from the Caribbean. A small number of laymen were present including George Schuster and the newly named chairmen of the boards of trustees of Notre Dame and Saint Louis, Ed Stephan and Daniel J. Schlafly. Rather surprisingly, Hesburgh invited John Cogley, a onetime editor and columnist for *Commonweal* and later the religious news editor at the *New York Times*, who in 1967 was associated with the Center for the

---

[422] Cited in Wilson D., Miscamble, C.S.C., *American Priest: The Ambitious Life and Conflicted Legacy of Notre Dame's Father Ted Hesburgh* (New York: Image, 2019), 121.

Study of Democratic Institutions. No women were present, although it must be said one particular woman had forced her way into Father Ted's thinking prior to Land O'Lakes: Miss Jacqueline Grennan.[423]

Hesburgh and his colleagues at the meeting had two fundamental questions to answer: What makes a modern university Catholic, and how does a modern university act Catholic? They left Land O' Lakes confident they had answered each successfully. They held, with Hesburgh surely in the forefront, that a Catholic university "must be a university in the full modern sense of the word, with a strong commitment to and concern for academic freedom." At the same time, "Catholicism should be perceptibly present and effectively operative on these campuses."[424] Not surprisingly, the

---

[423] Ibid., 123. Theodore McCarrick went on to become auxiliary bishop of New York, bishop of Metuchen, archbishop of Newark, and cardinal archbishop of Washington, D.C. As a result of numerous incidents of sexual perversion, he resigned from the College of Cardinals and was finally reduced to the lay state. John Cogley, Chicago-born and parochial school–educated, became executive editor of *Commonweal* in 1949. In 1955, he joined the center for the Study of Democratic Institutions and, in 1960, served as church-state adviser in the Kennedy campaign, playing a leading role in briefing Kennedy prior to the address to the Houston ministers. He eventually became religious news editor at the *New York Times* and was a syndicated columnist for the *National Catholic Reporter*. In later years, he left the Catholic Faith and joined the Episcopalians, becoming a deacon in that church but not living long enough to be ordained a "priest." Jacqueline Grennan was a Sister of Loretto who served as president of Webster College in Saint Louis. She oversaw her college's transformation into a lay, secular institution, was herself laicized, left her religious order, and was married some years later. She firmly believed that, for an institution of higher learning, any connection to the Catholic Church was incompatible with the norms of American higher education.

[424] Ibid., 124.

call for autonomy and academic freedom in Catholic higher education was widely covered in the American secular press. Hesburgh's
biographer gives a closer insight into his mind:

> For him Catholic universities had to be seen as independent
> from Vatican authority and from their founding religious
> congregations so they could be genuine universities first.
> Yet he denied vigorously that there was any intention to
> follow the great majority of once Protestant universities and
> colleges down the secularization path. "We didn't intend to
> be that way," he held, "and we said that right in the opening
> statement, but at the same time we had to operate in that
> milieu [of the American academy] ... and if there was any
> thought at all that a Catholic university would be under the
> thumb of some Monsignor in Rome who wouldn't know a
> university from a cemetery, we would lose our credibility
> and we would have no influence."[425]

Yet, according to his biographer, "he never effectively reconciled
how the very entity that supposedly did the church's 'thinking' was
somehow independent of the body it supposedly thought for."[426]
The effect was that, when government agencies, private accredit-
ing agencies, and so on, interjected themselves rather forcefully,
these same university leaders acquiesced willingly so as not to lose
financial and political support for their institutions. Thus, Land O'
Lakes set Catholic higher education on a trajectory of secularization, and, with no more than a half dozen exceptions, "Catholic"
colleges and universities today throughout the United States bear
the imprint of Land O' Lakes. Father Ted, according to his biographer, "never fully appreciated the contradiction"; in fact, any

[425] Ibid., 125.
[426] Ibid.

suggestion that he and his collaborators had "severed the branches from the very vine that ultimately secured their Catholic integrity made him angry."[427]

Hesburgh's idea of the modern Catholic university has been challenged by modern scholars, including David L. Schindler, one-time provost and dean at the Pontifical John Paul II Institute for Studies in Marriage and Family at Catholic University of America. Schindler questions if a Catholic university, to be a university in the full sense of the word, must do so on the terms of the academy. Must all the critical methods proper to secular institutes be adopted?

> My thesis is that it would be destructive, if not ultimately fatal, for the Catholic university to accept this presupposition. Catholic universities may have theology departments that are faithful to the teaching of the Church, dormitory life that is a model of morality, campus chapels that are full of prayerful worshippers, and community organizations that energetically serve the most vulnerable and most afflicted in our society. All of these things are indispensable for a college or university that would be vibrantly Catholic. But the point is that none of them yet informs us what specifies a Catholic institution *as a university*. To have a Catholic university, in other words, it is necessary (also) to develop a Catholic *mind*.[428]

A Catholic mind, for Schindler, means thinking through and carrying out the implications "*for the mind* of the call to holiness."[429] That call, which the Second Vatican Council accentuated for all

[427] Ibid., 126.

[428] David L. Schindler, *Heart of the World, Center of the Church: Communio Ecclesiology, Liberalism, and Liberation* (Grand Rapids, MI: William B. Eerdmans, 1996), 147.

[429] Ibid., 149.

believers, further raises the question of whether the component parts of holiness, especially the sacraments and the life of prayer, may hold specific implications for the "methods and content of rationality. Or does such a suggestion represent merely a confusion of categories?"[430] Put another way, "why is it wrong," Schindler asks, "to have a mind that is just like everyone else's?... Why is it wrong to share a public intelligence so long as Catholics, privately, maintain their own morality and religion?"[431] Schindler feels, and many along with him, that having a mind just like everyone else's would be an "unacceptable transformation in the self-understanding of Catholic morality and religion." A Catholic intelligence that would be "public," or "critical" in the modern liberal sense "is just so far already on the road to secularization," and that a secularized intelligence by its very logic would lead to a "voluntarizing" or "fideizing" of Catholic Faith.[432]

> Surely Fr. Hesburgh does not mean by his argument that the Catholic university, by adopting the terms and critical methods of the contemporary academy, is thereby committed to adopting as well all the values and beliefs — the worldviews — that are espoused in the contemporary academy. Quite the contrary, he makes clear that one of the crucial distinguishing features of a Catholic university will be the way it seeks to promote and defend the great moral and religious ideals proper to human nature and destiny. Rather, what Fr. Hesburgh means — what he *can* only mean, it seems to me — is that the Catholic university is nevertheless committed to the *form* of the university *as a university*. This presupposition is that this *institutional form* as such is

430 Ibid., 150.
431 Ibid., 151.
432 Ibid.

neutral relative to the Church. It is neutral in the sense
that, in its pure form, in the form in which it is universally
accepted by university people throughout the world, it is
equally open then to being further qualified as Catholic
or American or Buddhist or whatever. The substantive
noun, having already been constituted, is indifferent to
any and all of these subsequent qualifiers, all of which can
be added without prejudice to the specific content of any
one of them.[433]

If this is the case, it is Schindler's contention that "we must
resign ourselves to achieving what is at best a Catholic version of
a liberal university."[434] All the implications that follow from this
dilute the traditional idea of a Catholic university. What would
result—and did so often result—would be just another university
with Catholicism added on, like a brand, an element which one
would be perfectly free to choose or to reject.[435]

An even more poignant analysis, of Father George William
Rutler, reflected on Land O' Lakes one half century later. He chose
to focus on an adage of William Inge, one-time dean of St. Paul's
Cathedral in London, who, among other things, denied that Saint

[433] Ibid., 155.
[434] Ibid.
[435] Schindler develops his argument at much greater length in the
work cited (pp. 155–176), concluding that "The task of a Catholic
university with respect to the liberal academy, therefore, is twofold:
(1) to show from within each discipline and in the terms proper
to each discipline, how that discipline is being guided by a worldview—in the case of liberalism, by mechanism and subjectivism;
and (2) to show how a Catholic worldview (of the cosmos created in the image of Christ's [Eucharistic] love, hence of a cosmos
wherein order and love are mutually inclusive) leads to a more
ample understanding of evidence and argument, already within
the terms proper to each discipline." Ibid., 171.

John had written the fourth Gospel.[436] For all his liberalism, Inge
made the observation that "whoever marries the spirit of this age
will find himself a widower in the next."[437] Father Rutler recalls
the publication of the final Land O' Lakes document in 1967, a
year "when society seemed to be having a nervous breakdown."
Those who gathered "were fraught with a deep-seated inferiority
complex, rooted in an unspoken assumption that Catholicism is an
impediment to the new material sciences." He went on to cite an
observation of a religious sister, one-time president of a Catholic
college in New York:

> In the 1960s and early 1970s most Catholic colleges severed
> even tenuous ties to the Church.... We became indepen-
> dent and named lay trustees because of accreditation, the
> increased sophistication of higher education as a major en-
> terprise and because of demands of growth.[438]

That same institution was dissolved on the fortieth anniversary
of Land O' Lakes. The Wisconsin meeting "invoked a phantasm
guised as freedom for truth but which was nothing more than liberty to reject truth."

Fifty years later, secular schools have their own orthodoxies, and there are inquisitors ready to arraign anyone who
doubts the dogmas of global warming or "transgenderism."
Where there is no right learning there will be rote learning,
be it that of the fideist or atheist, and the two in fact will

---

[436] G. K. Chesterton, reflecting on the prayer "Matthew, Mark, Luke
and John, bless the bed which I lie on," wondered, in the case of
Inge, if he slept on a three-pronged bed.
[437] Cited in George William Rutler, *Calm in Chaos: Essays for Anxious
Times* (San Francisco: Ignatius Press, 2018), 64.
[438] Ibid., 65–66.

become indistinguishable. Newman taught in the classical sense of liberal education, whose core curriculum is largely abandoned now in schools that have become training centers for future hedge fund managers and computer engineers. "The end [purpose] … of a Catholic University or of any university is 'liberal education'; though its ultimate end may be Catholicism." This was not a declaration of independence from Catholicism but very much a declaration of dependence on that rational thought that provides the system and structure for Catholic culture in all its aspects.[439]

Rutler refers to Saint John Henry Newman's *Idea of a University*, much of which reflected his experience in founding the short-lived Catholic University of Ireland in the nineteenth century. The difference, according to Rutler, was that "in 1854 they thought the life of the mind might wreck the Faith, while in 1967 they thought the life of the mind *was* the Faith."[440] Many of the Irish bishops of those days were conflicted about what constitutes a true university education. Newman said of his contemporaries that "by a careful study of their argumentative basis, of their position relative to the philosophy and the characters of the day, by giving them juster views by enlarging and refining their minds, in one word, by education is (in their view) more than a superficiality or a hobby — it is an insult."[441] Newman, in Rutler's words, "is as grand in thought as those at Land O' Lakes were not." Even more to the point: "Newman still is, while Land O' Lakes never was."[442]

While Father Rutler admits there are a few places where classical liberal education is getting a second wind, the overall wreckage of

[439] Ibid., 67.
[440] Ibid.
[441] Ibid., 68.
[442] Ibid.

Toil and Transcendence

Catholic education around us "witnesses to the harm that wrong thinking and limited imagination can do." He even goes so far as to say Land O' Lakes was "to Catholic education what the Yalta Conference was to Eastern Europe." Most students today have not read, nor are they even aware of, "the most sublime discourse on the art of learning since Aristotle"—namely Newman's *Idea of a University*. Neither they nor those who follow them, Rutler fears, will ever be able to pick up the pieces of the wreckage until respect is given to him who really understood that

> if the Catholic faith is true, a University cannot exist externally to the Catholic pale, for it cannot teach Universal Knowledge if it does not teach Catholic theology. This is certain, but still, though it had never so many theological Chairs, they would not suffice to make it a Catholic University; for theology would be included in its teaching only as a branch of knowledge, only as one out of many constituent portions, however important a one, of what I have called Philosophy. Hence a direct and active jurisdiction of the Church over it and in it is necessary, lest it should become the rival of the Church with the community at large in those theological matters which to the Church are exclusively committed—acting as the representative of the intellect, as the Church is representative of the religious principle.[443]

1968

If the country seemed to suffer a nervous breakdown in 1967, it completely lost its mind the following year: 1968 was a year of

[443] Ibid., 68–69. This specific citation is taken from John Henry Newman, Discourse 9, *The Idea of a University* (London: Longmans, Green, 1907), 214.

turmoil, violence, political disruption, strident protest, and much more. The key players were the "baby boomers," children of the World War II generation who grew up in the prosperity of the postwar era and were not asked to make the sacrifices their parents did. The threat of nuclear holocaust dangled above them like the Sword of Damocles, and many lived life with a corresponding recklessness. Then the assassination of a president who became a folk hero shattered their hopefulness. As the decade continued, television deepened their hatred for never-ending and seemingly never-progressing war in Southeast Asia.

The American intensification of the war had ignited campuses from New England and New York to California. It triggered scores of protest marches and the public burning of thousands of draft cards by students demonstrating their commitment to peace, even at the risk of government prosecution. Many wore their hair long, dressed garishly and messily, and used marijuana or stronger drugs, to the annoyance and often open hostility of their sedate elders and "straight" contemporaries. The nonviolent ones were called "flower children" who preached a version of love as the ultimate answer to every problem.[444]

The two leading public personalities to emerge in these years were: Dr. Martin Luther King Jr., the unquestioned head of the civil rights movement in America whose plea to his fellow African Americans, and to all Americans, was the path of nonviolence; and Senator Robert F. Kennedy, brother of the assassinated president. Kennedy had served as attorney general in his brother's administration, was a staunch foe of his brother's vice president, Lyndon Johnson, and when not chosen by Johnson as his own vice presidential running mate in 1964, left the administration and easily

---

[444] Jules Witcover, *The Year the Dream Died: Revisiting 1968 in America* (New York: Warner Books, 1997), 2.

Toil and Transcendence

won election to the U.S. Senate from New York State. A growing critic of the war, and an even stronger foe of the president, his entrance into the 1968 presidential race seemed to be propelling him to the nomination at the expense of frontrunner Vice President Hubert Humphrey.

Through it all, one journalist has written that Lyndon Johnson "remained the most formidable figure in American public life: tough, commanding, dogged. He was a man who wore power as if it were custom-made for him, and he wielded it with an authority that brooked no argument."[445] At the same time, King was calling for an alliance between the civil rights and peace movements:

> Hundreds of young Americans, white and black, refused induction into the armed forces out of religious conviction or as a personal testimony against what they, like King, considered an unjust war fought disproportionally by American black men. Among them was Muhammad Ali, the heavyweight boxing champion of the world and devout disciple of the Nation of Islam or, as its members were popularly known, the Black Panthers.[446]

In April 1968, Dr. King was assassinated on a balcony of his motel room in Memphis, Tennessee. Only two months later, Kennedy was also gunned down in Los Angeles, after he had won a decisive victory in the California Democratic primary and urged his followers "on to Chicago — and let's win there."[447] For a second time in the decade, figures of popular hope had been felled — this time by the pair. The political temperature was at its highest in

---

[445] Witcover, *The Year the Dream Died*, 9.

[446] Ibid., 5–6.

[447] Chicago was the scene of the Democratic National Convention, where significant protests, arrests, and bloodshed filled the streets near the arena.

at least a generation—and maybe since the Civil War. Rebellion seemed to be everywhere. Much as the Republican candidate Warren Harding had promised the country back in 1920 a return to normalcy after the turmoil of the First World War, so this year's Republican nominee, Richard Nixon, promised the restoration of law, order, and sanity in the streets and on college campuses. His strategy worked, and he was elected by a small but significant margin in November.

Confounding the Experts

This climate of rebellion had its counterpart in the Catholic Church. It was the year in which Pope Saint Paul VI wrote a magnificent defense of human life, *Humanae Vitae*, which caused more turbulence than the Church had known in centuries. Dissenters from Church teaching, from moral theologians to public intellectuals, were concerned with only one aspect of the document: its strong reaffirmation of the Church's opposition to the use of artificial contraception.

Contraception had been part of the landscape of the twentieth century for decades and had been a generally taboo part of human societies for millennia. An inflection point came in 1930, however, when the Lambeth Conference of the Church of England approved the use of contraceptives in a limited way. With that simple statement, the floodgates were opened: Protestant Christianity quickly came to endorse family limitation, not in certain circumstances, but across the board.

In the post–World War II era, meanwhile, society had begun to change considerably. The role of women had begun to change substantially at the end of the First World War with the ratification of the Nineteenth Amendment and the loosening of sexual mores. During the midcentury war years, though, with so many husbands and fathers actively engaged in combat, women took on even greater responsibility for running the household: They began entering the workforce in greater numbers and, in many cases, were earning as much as or more than their husbands. Thousands of returning veterans then took advantage of the G.I. Bill to attend college, and greater incomes were needed to send the "baby boomers" to college and to pay for new suburban lifestyles. Large families began to seem increasingly unrealistic.

Then on June 23, 1960, the Food and Drug Administration announced the approval of Enovid, the first hormonal birth control pill. The news was "met with great enthusiasm as it appeared to give women the opportunity to engage in spontaneous sexual activity without fear of pregnancy. The bond between the procreative and unitive dimensions of the marital act was severed, and only time will tell if it will ever be healed."[448] In *Gaudium et Spes*, the Council fathers recognized the difficult circumstances modern couples found themselves in, when it seemed "at least temporarily the size of their families should not be increased." At the same time, the document taught clearly that

> when there is question of harmonizing conjugal love with the responsible transmission of life, the moral aspect of any procedure does not depend solely on sincere intentions or on an evaluation of motives. It must be determined by objective standards. These, based on the nature of the human person and his acts, preserve the full sense of mutual self-giving and human procreation in the context of true love. Such a goal cannot be achieved unless the virtue of conjugal chastity is sincerely practiced. Relying on these principles sons of the Church may not undertake methods

[448] John Burns, M.Th., *The American Rebellion against Humanae Vitae* (self-publ., 2011), 80.

of regulating procreation which are found blameworthy by the teaching authority of the Church in its unfolding of the divine law.[449]

Pope John XXIII died in 1963 before the Council's conclusion, but just before his death he instituted a commission on birth control to represent the Church in an upcoming conference with the World Health Organization and the United Nations. A member of the Vatican Secretariat of State, Father Henri de Riedmatten, was appointed to be the commission's secretary general. He kept the title until Pope Paul VI named Cardinal Alfredo Ottaviani, prefect of the Congregation for the Doctrine of the Faith, to be the new secretary general. Even so, de Riedmatten maintained control of the commission's work.[450]

> It is not possible to find a published statement that makes clear the purpose of this commission. It is certainly not clear that it was convened with the purpose of discerning whether the Church's prohibition of contraception was justifiable. Its original purpose semed to have been a rather broad study of the Church's teaching on marriage but came to focus on the question of contraception. It seems possible that Paul VI never really questioned the prohibition against contraception but that he did have doubts about the status of the pill and wanted a more updated defense of the Church's teaching in light of contemporary problems, such as population.[451]

---

[449] Walter M. Abbott, S.J., ed., *The Documents of Vatican II* (New York: Herder and Herder, 1966), 256.

[450] Burns, *American Rebellion*, 87.

[451] Janet E. Smith, *Humanae Vitae: A Generation Later* (Washington, D.C.: Te Catholic University of America Press, 1991), 13.

Toil and Transcendence

The original commission consisted of only six nontheologians who met once in 1963 and twice the following year. Paul VI enlarged the commission to fifty-eight members and added theologians and married couples. By the early sixties, public dissent against Church teaching was picking up steam; Dr. John Rock, a Boston physican who had been quite active in the pill's development and enthusiastic about promoting its use, described himself as a Catholic and, in his work *The Time Has Come*, strongly advocated a change in Church teaching. By mid-1963, articles by three theologians—Louis Janssens, W. van der Mark, O.P., and Bishop J. M. Reuss—appeared in various European journals defending oral contraception. By 1966, Richard McCormick, S.J., a noted American moral theologian, who at first was allied with those who would uphold Church teaching, turned around and endorsed the commission's pro-contraception majority report, saying that its points "incorporate most of the important things that have been said on the subject of contraception over the past three or four years, plus a few very interesting and important nuances. The majority report ... strikes this reader as much the more satisfactory statement."[452]

Whatever the original purpose of the commission, the result was a majority report, which called for a redefinition of Church teaching and a minority report, which defended the status quo. One writer has argued that the majority report was hastily drawn up and made public before all members of the commission were able to review it thoroughly.[453] A statement by moral theologian Bernard Häring, C.Ss.R., long an opponent of Church teaching, is telling: Asked to serve as a consultant to the commission, he recalled that he "received from officials on all levels of the Holy Office unequivocal instructions and warnings that I was to keep

[452] Ibid., 8–9.
[453] Burns, *American Rebellion*, 90–91.

precisely within the framework of *Casti Connubii*. However, efforts to restrain freedom of speech were only partially successful."[454]

The reports were meant to be working papers for Pope Paul VI and had no authority whatever, but by the spring of 1967, portions had been leaked to the press, including the Brooklyn *Tablet* and the *National Catholic Reporter*. These leaks fueled speculation that Church teaching was indeed about to be changed. Among American prelates on the commission, Cardinal Lawrence Shehan of Baltimore and Archbishop John Francis Dearden of Detroit were among the majority, while Archbishop Leo Binz of Saint Paul abstained.[455] In the opinion of one moral theologian, the documents exhibit four primary areas of disagreement: They differ on the meaning of the constancy of the Church's opposition to contraception, on the effect that a change in Church teaching would have on Church authority, in their understanding of how contraception violates natural law, and in their assessment of the impact that a change in the Church's teaching on contraception would have on Her teaching on other sexual acts.[456]

It was amid this atmosphere of confusion and, among some, excitement in both the clergy and the laity that the Holy Father issued his encyclical in July 1968. It was a magnificent defense of human life, carefully set forth and immediately divisive. Paul looked at the arguments for artificial birth control coming from an appeal to both conjugal love and responsible parenthood, and he responded that the former realized its true nature and nobility when it considered God as its ultimate source. Thus, marriage was not "the effect of

---

[454] Smith, *Humanae Vitae: A Generation Later* 14. *Casti Connubii* was the 1930 encyclical on marriage by Pope Pius XI that reaffirmed the Church's teaching on artificial contraception after the Anglicans' capitulation at Lambeth.

[455] Ibid., 12–13.

[456] Ibid., 14.

chance or the product of the evolution of blind natural forces; it is a wise institution of the Creator for realizing in mankind His design of love." Furthermore, for baptized persons, marriage "takes on the dignity of a sacramental sign of grace, inasmuch as it represents the union of Christ and the Church."[457] In regard to responsible parenthood, the pope did not for a moment disregard the very difficult decisions parents have to make regarding their family size, but

> in the task of transmitting life, they are not free ... to proceed at will, as if they could determine with complete autonomy the right paths to follow; rather they must conform their actions to the creative intention of God, expressed in the very nature of marriage and of its acts, and manifested by the constant teaching of the Church.[458]

Pope Paul forcefully argued both the unitive and procreative aspects of marriage, and he noted that when both of these are safeguarded, "the conjugal act preserves in its fullness the sense of true mutual love and its ordination to man's loftiest vocation of parenthood."

> God has wisely arranged natural laws and rhythms of fertility which already of themselves bring about a separation in the succession of births. But the Church, calling men back to the observance of the natural law, interpreted by her constant teaching, teaches that each and every marriage act must remain open to the transmission of life.[459]

The Holy Father wrote eloquently of the need for personal discipline nourished by a deep, abiding prayer life and was truly

---

[457] Pope Paul VI, *On Human Life: Humanae Vitae* (San Francisco: Ignatius Press, 2014), 53.

[458] Ibid., 57.

[459] Ibid., 58–59.

prophetic in linking contraception to marital infidelity and the degradation of the marital bond, with the husband seeing in his own wife a mere instrument for his sexual gratification. The pope foretold other consequences that would come to pass:

> Consider also the dangerous weapon that would thus be placed in the hands of those public authorities who have no concern for the requirements of morality. Who could blame a government for applying, as a solution to the problems of the community, those means acknowledged to be permissible for a married couple in solving a family problem. Who will prevent rulers from favoring, and even imposing upon their people, the method of contraception they judge to be the most effective, if they should consider this to be necessary? In this way, men, while wishing to avoid the individual, family or social difficulties they encounter in observing the divine law, would come to place at the mercy of the intervention of public authorities the most personal and most private sector of conjugal intimacy.[460]

A first-class Catholic philosopher explained the sinful nature of the intrinsically evil act of contraception:

> The sin consists in this alone: the *artificial, active* severing of the mystery of bodily union from the creative act to which it is bound at the time. Only in this artificial intervention, where one *acts against* the mystery of superabundant finality, is there the sin of irreverence — that is to say, the sin of presumptuously exceeding the creatural rights of man.[461]

---

[460] Ibid., 68.

[461] Dietrich Von Hildebrand, "The Encyclical *Humanae Vitae*: A Sign of Contradiction," in *Why Humanae Vitae Was Right: A Reader*, ed. Janet E. Smith (San Francisco: Ignatius Press, 1993), 81.

Toil and Transcendence

Confounding the Church

None of this, of course, was a message contemporary society was terribly interested in hearing. Priests disagreed; laity strongly disagreed; and many national hierarchies merely gave the encyclical unenthusiastic lip service. The major focus of dissent was found in the United States, specifically on the campus of the Catholic University of America, where it was led by a tenured professor of moral theology, Father Charles E. Curran. Curran was born in Rochester, New York, in 1934 and was ordained a priest of that diocese in 1958. He had taken his advanced theological studies in Rome, obtaining degrees at the Gregorian University, and a second doctorate in moral theology at the Alfonsianum of the Redemptorist Fathers. Of all his proferrors, Curran stated that Bernard Häring had the most influence on him. Häring, a peritus at the Second Vatican Council and long a dissenter from Church teaching on birth control, supported the "Statement of Dissent" Curran and others presented at Catholic University; in the minds of many, his support lent legitimacy to Curran's protest.

Dissent was not new to Curran: He had been teaching in favor of contraception for some time, and in April 1967, university trustees voted to let his tenure-track appointment lapse rather than reappoint him. In response, faculty organized a strike, joined by students, and the university not only reversed course, but promoted him to associate professor with tenure. After this, Curran returned to real prominence.

The infamous "Statement of Dissent" was issued July 30, 1968, just as *Humanae Vitae* was published, and it initiated an open battle for control of Catholic University between the school of theology and the board of trustees. The battle occupied most of the 1968–1969 academic year and ended with a victory for the dissenting theologians. In late August 1968, the chancellor of the

University, Archbishop of Washington Cardinal Patrick O'Boyle, called a meeting with all those who signed the dissenting statement. One historian of this entire episode, studying the transcript of this meeting, has noted that it "lays out the entrenched battle lines that came to define the American Church," with the dissenting professors convinced that their position was a necessary service to the Church's Magisterium, and the board of trustees, particularly the university chancellor, convinced their position undermined legitimate authority and was detrimental to the faith of many:

> There was a not-so-subtle current of intellectual intimida-
> tion at play in the meeting: the theologians came prepared
> with their technical theological argument justifying dissent
> and the principles of academic freedom as defined by the
> AAUP [American Association of University Professors],
> which they calmly and cooly presented on their behalf.
> O'Boyle, in contrast, gave the impression of being some-
> what disorganized, a bit frustrated, and clearly inferior in his
> knowledge of theology, the statutes of the university, and the
> principles of the AAUP. The result was a long, drawn-out
> meeting in which the dissenters refused to give up an inch
> of their well-defined position and rejected O'Boyle's request
> to submit a simple written statement summarizing the theo-
> logical justification of their position, on the grounds that it
> was much too subtle and complex to be contained in a brief
> statement.... From the beginning of the meeting, O'Boyle
> attempted to restrict the matter to addressing the faculty
> members of the Catholic University who were signers of the
> "Statement of Dissent." Thus, when Charles Curran made a
> motion that the names of all six hundred theologians who
> had joined in signing the statement be added to the minutes,
> O'Boyle objected that these names were irrelevant to the

situation at CUA.... Curran, however, insisted the names
be added ... [and] O'Boyle agreed to append the names of
the six hundred signers to the official record, but said he
considered it "a very liberal concession."[462]

Curran told the Washington cardinal that there was no doubt
whatever of the orthodoxy and faith of all the signatories and that
they intended no disrespect to the papal office or to the Church's
Magisterium. The theologians argued that their dissent should
present no problem to persons familiar with the history of theology, which was always about give and take, and so their dissent was
rendering a valuable contribution to the Church.

At the end of the meeting, Cardinal O'Boyle requested a written
statement of the official position taken by the theologians, which
exposed disunity or trickery among the dissenters. It seemed a simple enough request, but one theologian immediately said he didn't
have time for such a task, while Curran suggested that O'Boyle
should be satisfied with what he had been told in the meeting. The
cardinal had wanted to submit such a statement to the board of
trustees for their review. O'Boyle made clear he was not making any
accusations of anyone present, but it was his belief that the statutes
of the university called for a panel of three bishops to meet with a
theologian whose views were suspect; the difficulty was, O'Boyle
was not able to locate such a provision in the statutes in front of
him, and Curran took immediate advantage of the situation to cite
another article in the statutes that would prohibit such an action.
Once again, O'Boyle "came across as somewhat disorganized and

---

[462] Peter M. Mitchell, *The Coup at Catholic University: The 1968 Revolution in American Catholic Education* (San Francisco: Ignatius
Press, 2015), 154–155. At the meeting, O'Boyle expressed serious
doubts that all six hundred who signed were, in fact, professional
theologians.

uncertain of exactly what he was trying to accomplish. His weakness both theologically and procedurally continued to be exploited by the theologians throughout the course of the meeting and in subsequent interactions."

The August 20, 1968 meeting between Cardinal O'Boyle and the dissenting theologians in many ways determined the course of the Catholic Church in the United States for more than a generation. From the beginning the theologians presented themselves as the ones in the driver's seat—educated, articulate and precise in their knowledge of minute points of doctrine and procedure. O'Boyle, on the other hand, representing the American hierarchy, left the impression of having many holes in his knowledge of theology and of academic matters, of being generally frustrated with the theologians, and of naively hoping that a plea to the good will of the dissenters would somehow lead to a resolution of the dispute. The professors were emphatic that they could not be forced to give a statement of explanation of their position to the Chancellor.... The dissenting theologians emerged victorious from Caldwell Hall on August 20, 1968, confident that they were squarely in control of both the public spin on the controversy and the internal Church response to their actions.[463]

In early September 1968, the board of trustees met.[464] Initially, they discussed what options were open to them: a resolution of

---

[463] Ibid., 164, 168.

[464] Members present were: Cardinals O'Boyle (Washington), Krol (Philadelphia), McIntyre (Los Angeles), and Shehan (Baltimore); Bishops Baum (Springfield–Cape Girardeau, and O'Boyle's eventual successor in Washington), Casey (Denver), Hannan (Washington, auxiliary), Shannon (Saint Paul, auxiliary), Wright (Pittsburgh), and Zaleski (Lansing).

censure for the theologians, an attempt to dismiss them or to close the ecclesiastical faculties of CUA altogether, a drastic move to separate the university from the Church and give it to the District of Columbia, or simply no action whatever. The most aggressive proposal of the entire meeting came from the Los Angeles archbishop, Cardinal James Francis McIntyre. He suggested they offer the dissenters two options: either they withdraw their support for the "Statement of Dissent," or they have their contracts immediately terminated. But the board's legal counsel continually advised the bishops to do nothing that might provoke legal action against the university. So McIntyre's proposal was not accepted, since it would not only risk litigation but "bring censure upon CUA from the American academic community."[465] In the end, the board decided to turn the matter over to a faculty enquiry, which gave "academic freedom" the upper hand. The final agreement included a statement of deference to the Magisterium, but it was understood that this would in no way restrict the freedom of the professors.

And so, in the end, the professors agreed "not to teach contrary to the Magisterium," which meant in practice that they would not speak about *Humanae Vitae* and its teaching at all, which, in turn, meant that at Catholic University, for the duration of the inquiry, there would be nothing said whatsoever about the most widely discussed and controversial theological issue of the day. The university that had been instituted by the American hierarchy to promote and defend the Catholic Faith would be silent at what was arguably the greatest instance of cultural and academic opposition to the Church in the history of American Catholicism.[466] And silence favored the dissenters.

[465] Ibid., 180.
[466] Ibid., 181.

And then the final report of the faculty board of inquiry was a further rejection of the Church's mission, adding insult to injury: Dissent against *Humanae Vitae*, they declared, was an acceptable theological position; the style, mode, and manner of the original statement of dissent was entirely appropriate; the notion of a canonical mission had been abandoned at CUA, and professors were in no way bound by any such restrictions in their teaching; professors did not owe direct allegiance to the Church's Magisterium but were constrained only by the truth itself; more dialogue was necessary to overcome the many conflicting statements emerging from this controversy; and the "Statement of Dissent" in no way violated the "spirit of Catholic University."[467]

Cardinal McIntyre eventually resigned from the board. Cardinal Krol, often charged with being spokesman for the Magisterium at board meetings, evidently felt the tension: When CUA president Clarence Walton wrote to congratulate the cardinal for the superb job he had done at a particular meeting, Krol replied that Walton's letter "helps to continue my resistance to the temptation to stay away from some of the many meetings I must attend, or at least to stay out of the arena of unpleasant controversy."[468]

Many of today's controversies in the Church can be traced to events such as these. During this era, the Church in America increasingly adopted a posture of accommodation to dissent and the secular world, which in many respects continues into the twenty-first century. We still live with the spirit of dissent that developed in the 1960s, but, as with all things in the history of the Church, the real spirit of the Second Vatican Council, emerging beautifully step by step, will arrive at the top of the staircase in due time.

---

[467] Ibid., 191–196.
[468] Cited in ibid., 209.

7

∞

The Century Closes:
The Seventies and the Eighties

Inauspicious Beginnings

The seventies began with the triumphant victory of President Richard M. Nixon for a second term, trouncing his liberal Democratic opponent, Senator George McGovern of South Dakota. Nixon's victory would be short-lived, however: Within a year and a half, in the midst of the Watergate scandal, he would become the first president in United States history to resign from office. Usually defined by dictionaries as a scandal involving abuses of office and cover-ups, Watergate differed from most previous political scandals in that no one benefitted financially — except those who wrote books about it. Nixon remained convinced that the press had contributed substantially and unfairly to bringing him down: They had disliked his Vietnam policy for years; he had defeated a stridently anti-war candidate; and they knew he would owe them nothing for the remainder of his term. When the Watergate scandal was uncovered, however, by Nixon's own admission the press had the big guns — but the administration handed them the ammunition. This culminated on August 9, 1974, with Nixon's resignation; that same day, his vice president, Gerald R. Ford of Michigan, a Congressional veteran of many decades, became the nation's thirty-sixth president.

Toil and Transcendence

Sad as this episode was for the country, a far sadder one for most American Catholics occurred in January of the previous year, when the Supreme Court of the United States legalized abortion in *Roe v. Wade*. It surely remains the most celebrated case of the Warren Burger Court, and it involved a woman from Dallas, Texas, named Norma McCorvey (Jane Roe in court documents) who wanted to terminate her pregnancy. Texas prohibited such procedures, except by a physician to save the life of the mother. Roe sued in a district court against Henry Wade, the district attorney of Dallas County, to have the law declared unconstitutional and to have him enjoined from enforcing it. The lower court did declare the state law unconstitutional but refused to enjoin its enforcement. Roe appealed to the Supreme Court, who heard arguments in 1971 and 1972.[469]

The sexual revolution that began in the 1950s reached full steam in the succeeding decade, fostering increased demand for and access to contraceptives and more women seeking abortions. Illegal abortions were widespread, many of them unsafe, resulting in an unknowable number of women's deaths, and so the women's movement began to make legal abortion one of its highest priorities. At the same time, abortion reform was becoming more common at the state level: Legislatures were relaxing laws, making it easier for women to procure an abortion for the sake of her health, broadly defined. These looser laws usually required the approval of the abortion by a committee of doctors, in addition to the woman's own physican.

Meanwhile, the Supreme Court had been developing for several years a doctrine of personal privacy in sexual matters, most notably in the 1965 case *Griswold v. Connecticut*, which struck down a state law that restricted access to contraceptives. In 1973, *Roe v. Wade*

[469] Regan, *Constitutional History*, 192.

presented a challenge to the restrictive Texas law and to a more modern Georgia law that allowed abortions to be performed in hospitals, when approved by a hospital committee, to avoid danger to the woman's health.

When the case was first argued, Justice Harry Blackmun drafted an opinion that held both statutes to be unconstitutionally vague. Blackmun, a Republican and Methodist, had been nominated by Richard Nixon. Raised in Saint Paul, he was a Harvard Law School graduate and served as legal counsel for the Mayo Clinic in Rochester, Minnesota, for a decade.[470]

> In part because his analysis was clearly unpersuasive and in part because some justices believed that the case had been improperly assigned to Blackmun to write, the case was set for reargument. During the summer preceding the reargument, Blackmun engaged in an extensive study of medical material relating to abortion. After reargument, Blackmun circulated an opinion finding both statutes unconstitutional on the grounds that they violated the woman's right to privacy, which the opinion located in the Due Process clause of the Fourteenth Ammendment. Justice Potter Stewart's concurring opinion properly pointed out that this invocation of substantive due process meant that the Court was enforcing a right not specifically spelled out in the Constitution.[471]

Blackmun's opinion divided pregnancy into trimesters: During the first, the woman had an unrestricted right to an abortion; during the second, states could regulate abortion, in line with the advice of medical experts, to protect the mother's health; only in the third was human life held to be important enough to permit

[470] Ibid., 172.
[471] Hall, *Oxford Companion*, 740.

blanket restrictions on abortion—and even then it must be allowed if the life of the mother were threatened.

> Justices Byron White and William Rehnquist, in separate dissents, criticized the Court for enforcing a right not specified in the Constitution to overturn statutes that were no more restrictive than those widely in force when the Fourteenth Amendment was adopted. In addition, they criticized the Court for the trimester framework, which, in their view, was arbitrary. If the state had an interest in protecting the potential life of the fetus, that interest existed, and was equally strong, through the entire pregnancy. Further, they said, the Court's balancing of competing interests and careful laying out of what Doctors could do in various circumstances resembled a statute.[472]

Three justices appointed by President Nixon joined Blackmun's majority, an outcome that "appears to be inconsistent with the sort of 'strict construction' of the Constitution that they were said to support." This was perhaps best understood as part of the Court's "attempt to respond to and develop support within an emerging constituency, the organized women's movement."[473] Far more disturbing, from the Catholic perspective, was the position of the sole Catholic justice on the Supreme Court, William Brennan, who voted with

---

[472] Ibid., 741. Rehnquist was nominated by President Nixon in 1970. A Republican and a member of the Lutheran faith, he was born in Milwaukee, graduated from Stanford Law School in 1951, engaged in private practice in Phoenix for sixteen years, and served as an assistant U.S. attorney general from 1969 until 1971. Byron White was appointed by John F. Kennedy in 1962. A Democrat and an Episcopalian, he was born in Colorado, was a Rhodes Scholar at Oxford, and graduated from Yale Law School. He was deputy U.S. attorney general in 1961 and 1962.

[473] Ibid.

the majority. Brennan, an Irish Catholic Democrat from Newark, was nominated by President Eisenhower during his 1956 reelection campaign, ostensibly for religious diversity—and maybe to motivate the Catholic vote. In future years, Ike would come to regard this appointment as one of his worst mistakes: Brennan quickly joined the Court's liberal wing and continually argued for individual rights against moral duties, as well as for expanding the power of the federal government. Given his background, it came as little surprise:

> The second of eight children born to parents who had immigrated to the United States in the 1890s, Brennan grew up in a struggling middle-class family and was a first-hand witness to suffering and social unrest in Newark, New Jersey. By his own account, the most influential person in Brennan's life was his father, a coal shoveler in a local brewery who later became a prominent labor leader and municipal reformer. The elder Brennan passed his activist social philosophy on to his son and pushed him to achieve excellence. William junior was an honors graduate of the Wharton School of the University of Pennsylvania and ranked high in his class at Harvard Law School, which he completed through scholarships and odd jobs after his father's death.[474]

Roe became the law of the land, and it changed people's attitudes on a procedure that was once viewed by the overwhelming majority, regardless of creed, as a heinous crime. But legality conferred legitimacy. There were occasional bright moments culturally and poitically,[475] not the least of which was the development and

---

[474] Ibid., 87.

[475] One good example was *Harris v. McRae* in 1980, in which the Court held that Congress did not violate the Constitution when it prohibited the use of Medicaid funds to pay for nontherapeutic abortions.

enormous growth of the country's pro-life movement. Some have viewed the movement as simply an adjunct of the Catholic Church and even conjured up old anti-Catholic tropes, but the movement today is truly ecumenical and interreligious, including even agnostics and atheists who, simply on the basis of the natural law, clearly see abortion as the impermissible direct taking of human life.

The attitude of the Nixon administration toward abortion had been expressed on a few occasions prior to *Roe*. The state of New York had passed a liberal abortion law years before, and it was Patrick J. Buchanan—a long-time Nixon activist, speechwriter, and by now member of the White House staff, as well as a devout Catholic—who shaped administration policy and rhetoric in this area. In April 1971, Cardinal Terence Cooke, archbishop of New York, in his capacity as military vicar for the armed forces, had written President Nixon to direct military hospitals to respect local laws prohibiting abortions. The president complied, stating "that the policy of abortions at American military bases in the United States be made to correspond with the laws of the states where bases were located."[476] Part of the correspondence between the president and the cardinal was a much-circulated statement expressing Nixon's views—a statement written by Buchanan:

> From personal and religious beliefs I consider abortion an unacceptable form of population control. Further, unrestricted abortion policies, or abortion on demand, I cannot square with my personal belief in the sanctity of human life—including the life of the yet unborn. For, surely, the unborn have rights also, recognized in law, even in principles expounded by the United Nations. Ours is a nation with a Judeo-Christian heritage. It is also a nation with serious

[476] Patrick J. Buchanan, *Nixon's White House Wars* (New York: Crown Forum, 2017), 150.

social problems—problems of malnutrition, of broken homes, of poverty, and of delinquency. But none of these problems justifies such a solution. A good and generous people will not opt, in my view, for this kind of alternative for its social dilemmas. Rather, it will open its hearts and homes to the unwanted children of its own, as it has done for the unwanted millions of other lands.[477]

A year later, Buchanan suggested that President Nixon send a letter to Cardinal Cooke commending the Church's campaign to repeal the state's liberal abortion law. John Mitchell, the attorney general, agreed, and the letter was sent; Buchanan then informed the cardinal that the administration would have no objection to the archdiocese's sharing the letter with the press.[478]

Nixon, to be sure, did not think through all possible ramifications as a Catholic would. One biographer recounts discussions held in the White House about issues that were not even on the table for discussion, where Nixon's less honorable qualities came out:

"On abortion—get the hell off it," the president told his aides. "Just say it's a state matter and get the hell off it." ... Abortion encouraged permissiveness, Nixon believed, but "there are times when abortions are necessary—I know that—you know ... between a black and a white," he told Colson. "Or rape," Colson said. "Or rape.... You know what I mean. There are times."[479]

Roe was not the absolute last word on abortion. In addition to the previously footnoted *Harris* decision, the Hyde Amendment,

---

[477] Ibid.
[478] Ibid.
[479] John A. Farrell, *Richard Nixon: The Life* (New York: Doubleday, 2017), 377.

sponsored by Catholic Congressman Henry Hyde of Illinois, "prohibited the use of federal Medicaid funds for abortions except where the life of the mother was at risk, or in cases of rape or incest."[480] It was not until Ronald Reagan's administration years later, though, that opportunities to reshape the Court in a more conservative direction became possible. One of the most infamous episodes in this cause was the president's attempt to nominate Justice Robert Bork, a convert to Catholicism who was remembered for his role in the "Saturday Night Massacre" in Nixon's time, to a post on the nation's highest tribunal. Bork was chosen because of his outspoken criticism of *Roe*, and the very thought of him on the Court evoked strident protests from abortion supporters, leading ultimately to his defeat.

Growing Tensions

As the seventies wore on, and more years elapsed since the close of the Second Vatican Council, division began to grow in the Church. Historian Russell Shaw describes two versions of this division:

> The first version divides the post conciliar era into two parts. The first, starting with the Council's close in 1965 and continuing until late 1978, was marked by turmoil and dissent mirroring the cultural revolution that was then taking place in society. Thousands of priests and religious quit the priesthood and religious life, while new priestly and religious vocations fell precipitously. After the brave gesture of *Humanae Vitae* in 1968 — and the violent reaction against it — Pope Paul VI grew increasingly weary and depressed. The "smoke of Satan" had entered the Church, he declared,

---

[480] Regan, *Constitutional History*, 193.

and it was smothering the Vatican II renewal. Indeed, at times the Church appeared to be rushing toward collapse. But 1978 brought the election of Pope John Paul II, and collapse was averted.

The second version of the story divides the same stretch of time in the same way, but it interprets the two segments very differently. In this view, the years from 1965 to 1978 take on the aura of the golden age for the Church in America. Heroic progressives battled reactionaries over the direction of Church renewal and, except for a few setbacks like *Humanae Vitae*, generally emerged victorious. But then came 1978, and the election, following the month-long pontificate of John Paul I (the "smiling pope" who apparently died of anxiety and stress), of John Paul II. Suddenly Rome's emphasis became thwarting renewal and turning back the clock. This project of restoration is believed to have continued under Benedict XVI.[481]

The American Bicentennial year of 1976 was a case in point. The American bishops had developed a program for the Church's official participation; its chairman was Cardinal John Dearden, archbishop of Detroit, by then a prelate who enjoyed great prestige and influence among his fellow bishops. The heart of the program was titled "Liberty and Justice for All," and nationwide public events were organized, culminating in a national conference in Detroit with the name "Call to Action." The conference drew more than thirteen hundred delegates, though the representation was clearly one-sided:

Proposals included returning laicized priests to ministry, ordaining women and married men, permitting lay preaching,

[481] Shaw, *Catholics in America*, 144–145.

allowing the use of contraception, adopting an open attitude toward homosexuality, and giving Holy Communion to divorced and remarried Catholics whose first unions hadn't been declared null by the Church. Recommendations on social and political issues supported amnesty for Vietnam War resisters and for undocumented immigrants, along with much else.[482]

On the other side, the International Eucharistic Congress held in Philadelphia presented to the nation a more authentic manifestation of the Catholic Faith.[483] At the closing *Statio Orbis* Mass, celebrated by His Eminence Cardinal James Knox, archbishop of Melbourne, Australia, and legate of Paul VI, U.S. President Gerald Ford gave closing remarks, during which he expressed his concern over the growing disrespect in America for human life. He received thunderous applause from the hundreds of thousands gathered.[484]

As the fall presidential campaign progressed, the American bishops had meetings with both President Ford and his Democratic opponent, Governor Jimmy Carter of Georgia. Carter told them that he was personally opposed to abortion, but when pressed to support a constitutional amendment outlawing abortion, he refused. Ford, on the other hand, could point to the anti-abortion plank in the Republican platform and promised his support for such an

---

[482] Ibid., 152.

[483] Such international gatherings are held every four years in different parts of the world and are meant to be public manifestations of faith in Our Lord's Real Presence in the Most Blessed Sacrament. They consist of theme Masses, Eucharistic processions, adoration of the Blessed Sacrament in designated churches, conferences, opportunities to receive the sacrament of Penance, and so on.

[484] Interestingly, some years after leaving office, former President Ford stated publicly that both he and his wife were "pro-choice" on the matter of abortion.

amendment should it ever materialize. Though the bishops, through their spokesman Archbishop (later Cardinal) Joseph Bernardin, were more encouraged with the president's position than with his opponent's, Ford was described, quite correctly by one political commentator, as "mushy on abortion."[485] In the end, Carter narrowly defeated the incumbent president.

The Advent of Reagan

Four years later, Carter would himself be defeated for reelection by Ronald Reagan, former two-term governor of California and an icon of political conservativism known to generations of Americans for his years as an actor in Hollywood, especially for his time as president of the Screen Actors Guild, which fueled his late-in-life entry into politics. At age sixty-nine, Reagan was the oldest man up to that point elected to the presidency.

Ronald Reagan was born in Tampico, Illinois, on February 6, 1911, to an Irish Catholic father and an English-Scottish Protestant mother. After several moves within the state of Illinois, the family finally settled in the town of Dixon, along the Rock River. It was here that the basic values that molded his entire life were formed.

For their part, parents Jack Reagan and Nelle Wilson had married in Fulton, Illinois, in November 1904 in the parish church of the Immaculate Conception. As was customary for mixed-faith marriages in those times, the ceremony was performed in the rectory parlor, and there is no recorded evidence that the Protestant

---

[485] Shaw, *Catholics in America*, 150. Shaw goes on to describe 1976 as "the worst year ever," not only because of all the above but also because of the granting of general absolution by a bishop of Memphis, Carroll Dozier, with absolutely no Vatican approval. The act of disobedience, as would be expected, made national Catholic headlines.

Toil and Transcendence

Nelle had serious objections to it. Her devoutness would emerge later in Dixon, though it was not directed to Catholicism.[486] Paul Kengor, a historian who has studied and written extensively on the subject of Reagan's religion and personal spiritual life, has attempted to figure out some hard-to-find details:

> Jack attended Saint Patrick's Catholic Church at 612 Highland Avenue in Dixon and was a member there. He usually went to Mass with his son Neil, whereas Ronald attended the Disciples of Christ Church with his mother. I was also told that Neil, even though he had been baptized with Ronald at the Disciples of Christ church in the summer of 1922, soon converted to the Catholic Church so fully that he took First Communion at Saint Patrick's Church in 1928. Neil would never regret that move, becoming a devout Catholic whose faith only intensified in the decades ahead. . . . I also learned that both Neil and Jack were active together in the Knights of Columbus. In fact, Jack had been involved with the Knights in Tampico, Illinois, the little town where Ronald was born. A member of the Dixon Council of the Knights told me that contemporaneous newspaper accounts confirm Jack's presence at Knights events. As for Neil, the Dixon Council retains records proving that Neil was a formal member and in fact an officer (or "warden"). The Dixon Council forwarded my inquiry on Jack to the National Office of the Knights of Columbus in New Haven, Connecticut, which told me that it could find no record of Jack's being a formal member. Regardless . . . Jack was at least involved with the Knights in his local parishes. Several Dixon sources over the years have described Jack's Mass attendance to me

[486] Some Reagan biographers have claimed that Nelle did have serious objections to the perceived strictness of Catholic morality.

as "irregular," though their sources are word of mouth.... Ronald Reagan himself in his post-presidential memoirs said that his father's "attendance at Catholic Mass was sporadic," whereas his mother "seldom missed Sunday services at the Disciples of Christ Church in Dixon."[487]

Nelle chose the Disciples of Christ, or, as they were often called, the Christian Church. Church origins could be found in Western Pennsylvania, Ohio, and Kentucky, and it was there, in the Blue Grass State that they were unified into one cohesive body in 1832. In that decade, Illinois proved fertile soil for the growth of the church, a body described by one historian as "the voice of democracy, of individualism in the religious sphere."[488] In the early 1900s, Nelle joined the Disciples. In Dixon,

> the group first met in the basement of the town's YMCA until it could raise funds for a building. The new First Christian Church opened at 123 South Hennepin on June 18, 1922. Nelle became a pillar in the local church.... She wore multiple hats, including directing the choir and the missionary society. The vigorous congregation boasted more than a dozen Sunday school classes each week, with Nelle's True Blue class the largest. It was said that if Nelle had had the education she would have taken the pulpit.... Nelle's thoughts and works were fixed heavenward. She was a firm believer in the power of prayer.... "Lemme tell you", one

---

[487] Paul Kengor, *A Pope and a President: John Paul II, Ronald Reagan, and the Extraordinary Untold Story of the 20th Century* (Wilmington, DE: ISI Books, 2017), 46–47. In fact, Reagan also stated in his memoirs that, prior to his death, Jack Reagan had returned to Catholic Mass attendance.

[488] Cited in Paul Kengor, *God and Ronald Reagan: A Spiritual Life* (New York: HarperCollins, 2004), 10.

Dixon resident commented, "Nelle was a saint" That was not a rare sentiment. "If there is such a thing as a saint on earth, it is Nelle Reagan", said another.... From his mother Reagan learned the power of prayer and the desire to seek it at any time, from childhood to adulthood, from a seat at the dinner table to the seat of world power.... She gave him a solid foundation in Christian faith, one that never left him.[489]

Reagan attended Eureka College in Eureka, Illinois, affiliated with the Disciples of Christ, and became a sports radio announcer in the Midwest before heading to Hollywood to find his fortune. There, he joined the Hollywood Beverly Christian Church, run by the Disciples. He and his first wife, Jane Wyman, taught Sunday School there, and their children, Michael and Maureen, attended.

Remarkably, over four decades later, long after Reagan had ceased attending the church and joined another congregation, the current pastor reported that Reagan was still technically a member and contributed financially. For a time, Nancy Reagan

---

[489] Kengor, *A Pope and a President*, 48. In later years, Nelle's son Neil, who did not share his mother's Protestant beliefs, remembered her weekly Sunday schedule: "Sunday school Sunday mornings, church Sunday morning, Christian Endeavor Sunday evening, church after Christian endeavor, and prayer meeting on Wednesdays." Kengor, *God and Ronald Reagan*, 28. Many decades later, when Reagan was president, two of his closest Catholic friends, William Wilson, whom he appointed first ambassador to the Holy See, and Judge William Clark, who became his national security adviser, frequently tried to convince the president he should convert to Catholicism. "Reagan would listen politely and then ask questions, but he'd already made his decision on that long ago." Peggy Noonan, *When Character Was King: A Story of Ronald Reagan* (New York: Viking, 2001), 109.

continued to send a monthly check to Beverly Christian Church in their names.[490]

Reagan had been a staunch Democrat in the time of Franklin D. Roosevelt, a president for whom he always had admiration. This allegiance held true during the Truman and Eisenhower years, though he supported the latter still as a Democrat. In the early sixties he switched parties, shortly before making a famous speech, "A Time for Choosing," to boost the candidacy of Republican nominee Barry Goldwater in 1964. By then he had clearly moved from a New Dealer to a free-market conservative: "It was during his Hollywood years that Reagan first became fed up with the high tax rates, intrusive regulations, and burgeoning welfare state he associated with the Democratic party."[491] Even as early as 1952, his view of the United States and its destiny was clear, and it was a view that, in future years, he could easily incorporate with his political agenda. Delivering the commencement address at William Woods College, another Disciples of Christ school in Fulton, Missouri, Reagan said:

> I, in my own mind, have thought of America as a place in the divine scheme of things that was set aside as a promised land.... I believe that God in shedding His grace on this country has always in this divine scheme of things kept an eye on our land and guided it as a promised land.

[490] Kengor, *God and Ronald Reagan*, 49. Reagan and Wyman divorced in 1948, and four years later, Reagan married Nancy Davis, with whom he had two children, Patty and Ron. Kengor relates a story from the late 1950s when fourteen-year-old Michael came to visit his father and his new family. Ronald left him at home while the rest of the family went to church, and when Michael later complained, his father responded that he did not want to offend Michael's mother: Jane Wyman had converted to Catholicism in 1953 and apparently did not want her son attending Protestant worship. Ibid., 50.

[491] Ibid., 53.

This is one of his earliest known speeches. By 1990, in Carmel, California, his views had not changed at all:

> You may think this a little mystical, and I've said it many times before, but I believe there was a Divine Plan to place this great continent here between the two oceans to be found by peoples from every corner of the Earth. I believe we were preordained to carry the torch of freedom for the world.[492]

This was the sort of message he would carry to the American people for years, especially through his national radio broadcasts and his syndicated column. It would take him to the Republican National Convention in Detroit, which nominated him for the presidency in 1980, and at which he concluded his acceptance speech with a moment of silent prayer. And, ultimately, it would take him to the White House in January 1981.[493]

Catholic Counterpart

Two years prior to Reagan's election to the presidency, the first non-Italian pope in four and one-half centuries was elected. Karol Wojtyla, the cardinal archbishop of Kraków, Poland, was fifty-seven

---

[492] Ibid., 95.

[493] Judge Wiliam P. Clark, President Reagan's national security adviser, once remarked that praying was so important to Reagan that he did it on a daily basis. Edmund Morris, one of Reagan's biographers, feels that Clark was the only one in the administration who had "any kind of spiritual intimacy with the president." Clark himself told of being on an airplane with Reagan when word was received that Martin Luther King Jr. had been shot. "He expected some comment from Reagan but heard nothing. Clark stepped away; when he turned back he found Reagan in prayer, looking down at his knees, lips moving in silence." Ibid., 123.

years of age and would begin a reign of nearly twenty-eight years, the third-longest in Church history, following Saint Peter and Pope Pius IX. Born in Wadowice, Poland, in 1920, Wojtyla had lost his entire family by the time he was twenty-one and trained for the priesthood underground, due to German military occupation. During this time, the young Wojtyla helped many Polish Jews escape the Nazi terror. His ordination to the priesthood occurred on November 1, 1946, followed by graduate work, under the famed Dominican Father Réginald Garrigou-Lagrange, in Rome at the Pontifical Angelicum University, where he won the doctorate in sacred theology for his dissertation, *The Doctrine of Faith in Saint John of the Cross.*

Back in his native land, he began teaching philosophy at Jagiellonian University and later at the Catholic University of Lublin. He wrote a work evaluating the possibility of a Catholic ethic based on the ethical system of Max Scheler, founder of a school of philosophy called phenomenology, which emphasized the study of human consciousness. From this, Wojtyla developed a theological approach called phenomenological Thomism, a system blending the traditional theology of Saint Thomas Aquinas with the ideas of personalism, a philosophical approach deriving from phenomenology. From this new philosophical standpoint, Wojtyla published, in 1960, his influential book *Love and Responsibility*, a defense of and expansion on traditional Church teachings on marriage. The book would be enormously successful.

Within twelve years of his priestly ordination, he was appointed auxiliary bishop of Kraków—at thirty-eight, the youngest bishop in Poland. He took an active role at the Second Vatican Council and made contributions to two of its most important documents: the Decree on Religious Freedom (*Dignitatis Humanae*) and the Pastoral Constitution on the Church in the Modern World (*Gaudium et Spes*). The quality of his philosophical mind was clearly seen

Toil and Transcendence

by many of the Council fathers, and, many years later, he would help to found the *Communio* school of theology, which would offer tremendous insights into what the Council had been trying to convey. By 1964, he was the archbishop of Kraków and, within three years, was a member of the Sacred College of Cardinals. He was elected successor of Saint Peter on October 22, 1978, after the brief thirty-three-day reign of Pope John Paul I. In memory of his predecessor, he chose the name John Paul II.

The world waited anxiously to see what this new pope would be like. At his Mass of Installation, he left little doubt:

> Be not afraid to welcome Christ and accept His power. Help the Pope and all those who wish to serve Christ and with Christ's power to serve the human person and the whole of mankind. Be not afraid. Open wide the doors for Christ. To His saving power open the boundaries of states, economic and political systems, the vast fields of culture, civilization and development. Be not afraid. Christ knows "what is in man". He alone knows it.[494]

It is difficult to say when Ronald Reagan became fully cognizant of the magnitude of the man chosen to lead the Catholic Church. What is certain is that by June 1979, when the Holy Father first returned to his homeland after being elected, and the attention of the world was once again focused on him and the staggering response he received among his fellow Polish citizens, Reagan surely sat up and took notice — and deep interest.

According to the recollection of Richard V. Allen, a foreign-policy adviser to Reagan, the two sat mesmerized at the footage from Poland, especially the enormity of the crowds on hand to

---

[494] Cited in George Weigel, *Witness to Hope: The Biography of Pope John Paul II* (New York: HarperCollins, 1999), 262.

welcome their most famous native son. Allen recalled that Reagan became "intensely focused"; he "remained silent for the longest time ... and then I glanced at him, saw that he was deeply moved, and noticed a tear in the corner of his eye."[495] He went on to observe that Reagan reached the conclusion "that the Pope was the key figure in determining the fate of Poland"—and thus the fate of Eastern Europe and the world. The future president was "overcome by the outpouring of emotion that emanated from the millions who came to see him," and for Reagan, "this helped solidify a deep and steadfast conviction that this Pope would help change the world." Millions listened to Ronald Reagan's radio broadcasts throughout the United States, and, in the immediate aftermath of the pope's Polish visit, he devoted at least two of them to the events of the mission. Perhaps most telling was his commentary that

> for 40 years the Polish people have lived under first the Nazis and then the Soviets. For 40 years they have been ringed by tanks and guns. The voices behind those tanks and guns have told them there is no God. Now with the eyes of all the world on them they have looked past those menacing weapons and listened to the voice of one man who has told them there is a God and it is their inalienable right to freely worship that God. Will the Kremlin ever be the same again? Will any of us for that matter?[496]

Between that moment and their first formal meeting, two assassination attempts occurred—one on the president, one on the pope. In the Holy Father's case, he gave great thanks to Our Lady of Fatima for saving his life on her feast day, May 13, 1981.

[495] Ibid., 192.
[496] Ibid., 192–193.

Toil and Transcendence

One year later, John Paul took the bullet which had entered his body and placed it in the crown of her statue in front of the great basilica at Fatima. In Ronald Reagan's case, he received a visit, after returning from the hospital, from Cardinal Terence Cooke, archbishop of New York. The two had been friends, and during the cardinal's visit to the White House on Good Friday 1981, the president told him that whatever time he had left belonged to God.[497]

Just a few weeks after the attempt on Pope John Paul II's life, Saint Teresa of Calcutta visited the Reagans at the White House. There were no cameras, no media of any sort—just the president, the First Lady, and a few selected guests. At the end of the luncheon, Mother Teresa came right to the point:

> "Mr. President do you know that we stayed up for two straight nights praying for you after you were shot? We prayed very hard for you to live." Humbled, Reagan thanked her, but she wasn't finished yet. She looked at the President pointedly and said: "You have suffered the passion of the cross and have received grace. There is a purpose to this. Because of your suffering and pain you will understand the suffering and pain of the world." She added, "This has happened to you at this time because your country and the world need you." Nancy Reagan dissolved into tears. Her husband, the great communicator, was at a loss for words.[498]

---

[497] Ibid., 341. Some years later, President and Mrs. Reagan visited the cardinal in his residence in New York when he was close to death, after they had participated in a brief prayer service in his chapel. Reagan, in his diary, called the cardinal a "brave and good man," and posthumously awarded him the Presidential Medal of Freedom. Ibid., 341–342.

[498] Ibid., 263–264.

Collaboration and Friendship

The first personal meeting between the pope and the president[499] took place at the Vatican on June 7, 1982. It was assumed by many that, because of their mutual interests, some sort of collaboration would eventually be established. That day, both men shared a "unity in spiritual views, and in their vision on the Soviet empire, namely, that right or correctness would ultimately prevail in the divine plan." That day, too, both felt they had been given "a spiritual mission—a special role in the divine plan of life," and each expressed concern for "the terrible oppression of atheistic communism."[500]

Well before the first formal meeting, operations had been set in motion for what the administration and the president himself knew to be a vital connection with the Church. Richard Allen recalls going to the White House in 1981 for the administration's first diplomatic reception.

> I was at the very end of the line with my wife, Pat.... And the person right in front of us was Archbishop Pio Laghi, who had flown up the day before from Argentina, where he had been ambassador. And now he was going to be [papal] representative to the United States.... And so we stood in line. And you can imagine with the 116 ambassadors and their wives going through the line to meet the president that I had about forty-five minutes or fifty minutes with Archbishop Pio Laghi. And I knew immediately that we had a ten-strike in this man. He had the full confidence of the Pope. I could tell that he wasn't bluffing. He was earnest, down to earth, and that was a source of great joy to me that I discussed with the president later on. And I was then able

---

[499] There would be seven in all.
[500] Paul Kengor, *The Crusader: Ronald Reagan and the Fall of Communism* (New York: HarperCollins, 2006), 134.

to work with Pio Laghi from time to time in an important way to get messages through to the Vatican.[501]

In addition to Allen, the Reagan administration's close relations with the Vatican in general and the Holy Father in particular were handled by three others, all devout Catholics. William P. Clark was born in October 1931, in Oxnard, California, not far from Reagan's home in Hollywood and his ranch, Rancho del Cielo, in the Santa Ynez Mountains above Santa Barbara. He had been born into a California family of "ranchers, cowboys, sherriffs and lawmen." Clark himself was raised a rancher and shepherded livestock in the mountains of central California. After Villanova Prep School in the Ojai Valley, he went on to Stanford and for a considerable time thought of becoming a priest. He did spend some time in an Augustinian Novitiate in New York, but decided against a religious vocation, went into law and politics, and, influenced by early Thomas Merton and Fulton Sheen, became a lifelong crusader against the godlessness of communism.

This path "eventually led him to a California celebrity-turned-politician named Ronald Reagan, who was greatly impressed with Clark—his mind, his faith, his loyalty, his sense of good versus evil, his anticommunism."[502] In his time as California's governor, Reagan appointed Clark his chief of staff, then appointed him to

---

[501] Paul Kengor and Robert Orlando, *The Divine Plan: John Paul II, Ronald Reagan, and the Dramatic End of the Cold War.* (Wilmington, DE: ISI Books, 2019), 150–151. Pio Laghi (1922–2009) became a cardinal of the Church in 1991. He spent many years in the Diplomatic Corps of the Holy See, as well as in the Roman Curia. He served as apostolic nuncio to several countries, as well as prefect of the Congregation for Education. Laghi was John Paul II's secret emissary to the White House and to several presidents. He had a particularly close relationship with Presidents George H. W. Bush and George W. Bush.

[502] Kengor, *A Pope and a President*, 205–206.

a seat on the state's supreme court. In later White House years, he served as deputy secretary of state and finally head of the National Security Council. He was, in effect, Reagan's right hand in matters of national security, foreign policy, and especially relations with the Soviet Union.

Early in his 1980 campaign, Reagan tapped a former Wall Street lawyer and Nixon administration official to take the lead. William J. Casey was a native of Elmhurst, Queens, New York, who had graduated from Fordham University, did graduate work at the Catholic University of America, and obtained his law degree at St. John's University. A Knight of Malta and a very active Catholic, Casey was about to head into a comfortable retirement when Reagan tapped him and, once in the White House, asked him to be director of the CIA.

Finally, there was General Vernon A. Walters.[503] A United States Army officer and diplomat, he served as deputy director of Central Intelligence, as well as U.S. ambassador to the United Nations. He was ambassador to the Federal Republic of Germany during the period of German reunification after World War II and rose to the rank of lieutenant general in the U.S. Army. He is a member of the Military Intelligence Hall of Fame. From the outset, Walters felt a particular attachment to John Paul II:

> For some years I was concerned about the excessive misinterpretation of the documents of Vatican Council II. In his

---

[503] Walters was born in New York City in 1917. His father was a British immigrant and insurance salesman. From age six, he lived in England and France and attended the Jesuit boarding school at Stonyhurst in Lancashire, but he took no higher education. He left school and returned to the United States to work for his father as an insurance claims adjustor and investigator. Walters spoke French, Italian, Spanish, Portuguese, and German fluently. He died in 2002 in West Palm Beach, Florida.

opening statement to the Council of Fathers on 11 October 1962, Pope John XXIII had advised them to try to meet the pastoral needs of the church. The fathers, however, became caught up in a frenzy of change — change for change's sake. When the Council ended in December 1965, under Pope John XXIII's successor, Paul VI, the fathers had executed sixteen documents described simply as having a progressive viewpoint. It would take a strong hand to stand up to those who wanted to throw away a large part of the Catholic heritage of twenty centuries in favor of "modernization," but this Polish Cardinal had stood up to the communists in his native land and I was sure that he had been elected for a purpose. I am more certain of it now than ever before.[504]

Robert McFarlane, Clark's deputy at the National Security Council, recalled that everything that had to do with Poland was handled outside normal State Department channels and went through Bill Casey and Bill Clark. "I knew that they were meeting with Pio Laghi, and that Pio Laghi had been to see the president, but Clark would never tell me what the substance of the discussion was." Further: "Clark and Laghi met regularly to discuss developments in the Polish situation. Crucial decisions on funneling aid to Solidarity and responding to the Polish and Soviet regimes were made by Reagan, Casey and Clark in consultation with Vatican officials." Zbigniew Brzezinski, former president Carter's national security adviser, a Catholic native of Poland and a staunch anticommunist, gave Casey the primary role in the operation: "Casey ran it ... and led it; he was very flexible and very imaginative and not very bureaucratic. If something needed to be done it was done."[505]

[504] Vernon A. Walters, *The Mighty and the Meek: Dispatches from the Front Line of Diplomacy* (London: St. Ermin's Press, 2001), 231.
[505] Kengor, *The Crusader*, 136.

They were a discreet working group, Laghi, Casey, Clark and Walters. They even came up with the code name *cappuccino* for their connection. Named for the Italian coffee that Archbishop Laghi always prepared for Clark and Casey, the two administration officials would phone each other when they had need to speak to the Archbishop, and merely say "would you like to have some cappuccino?", knowing full well their phone lines might be bugged. They would meet the Archbishop at his residence on Connecticut Avenue, and would exchange news of the latest happenings of concern both in Washington and Rome. Clark and Casey briefed Laghi on the administration's position, and he shared with them the extent of the Vatican's knowledge on any number of matters. The Archbishop met with President Reagan at least half a dozen times, always entering through the southwest gate of the White House so as to avoid the press. In both cases, Poland was so often the chief topic of concern.[506]

Vernon Walters would visit the Vatican two or three times a year for about four years. His initial assignment came in 1981, when he received his instructions from Clark while he was serving as deputy to Secretary of State Alexander Haig, himself a staunch Catholic. Walters would meet with John Paul for about forty minutes each time. "He always received me alone," Walters recounted, "and whenever anyone attempted to interrupt the briefing, he would wave them out of the room."[507] As to the subject matter of these conversations:

Basically, I discussed the threat we faced from missiles, from conventional ground forces, and from the Soviet air force

[506] Kengor and Orlando, *The Divine Plan*, 151–152.
[507] Ibid., 154.

and navy. In addition, whenever appropriate, I covered problems in Poland, and once I touched on developments in the concentration camps in the Soviet Union that were then still operating. Sometimes he would tell me what subjects he would like the next time.... The briefings were generally arranged through the nuncio in Washington by Archbishop (now Cardinal) Laghi and our ambassador to the Vatican, William Wilson. I tried to tailor the meetings so that they would not last more than forty minutes, including any questions the Pope might want to ask me. His questions were generally penetrating and insightful.

To these thoughts, General Walters added the insight that John Paul "knows where he is going and will not be turned aside. There is no one in the modern world with the drawing power for crowds that he has."[508] Casey and Walters flew to the Vatican frequently; indeed, more visits were made, apparently, than official records indicated. Both met with the Holy Father privately, and no notes were taken, just as Casey and Clark took no notes during their Washington meetings with Archbishop Laghi. "The CIA director flew to Rome with the president's blessing," Richard Allen observed, "and he kept his Vatican meetings secret by flying in what Allen call[ed] his specially equipped windowless C-141 jet, painted black."[509]

This esteem for the Holy Father and the Church was not something new to President Reagan. Half of his heritage, after all, was Irish Catholic, and though he wasn't raised in the Faith of his Irish forebears, as president he and Nancy visited the ancestral town from which his great-grandfather, Michael O'Reagan, emigrated in the nineteenth century: Ballyporeen,

508 Walters, *The Mighty and the Meek*, 233.
509 Kengor and Orlando, *The Divine Plan*, 156.

County Tipperary. The visit included a brief prayer service in the parish church, with the pastor showing him Michael's baptismal record. And back in the mid-1970s, he began quoting Pope Pius XII's remarks about America at the end of the Second World War: "Into the hands of America God has placed an afflicted humanity. The American people have a genius for splendid and unselfish action." Reagan emphasized, whenever he quoted Pius, that Americans did not seek this leadership role; rather it was thrust upon them by God.[510]

Reagan was also introduced to another part of Catholic tradition: the message of the Blessed Virgin Mary at Fatima in 1917. This came shortly before his June 1987 meeting with John Paul. The president was briefed by Frank Shakespeare, who had been appointed ambassador to the Vatican several months earlier. Shakespeare had been a successful CBS TV executive, serving as president of the network for nearly twenty years. In 1969, President Nixon appointed him head of the U.S. Information Agency, and four years later, he returned to private life, becoming an executive vice president at Westinghouse and later president of RKO General. Ronald Reagan appointed him chairman of the Board for International Broadcasting, where he oversaw operations for Radio Free Europe. Finally, the president appointed him ambassador to Portugal.

"I talked to Reagan about Fatima on this trip [to Rome], in the plane and the car." He had Reagan's complete attention. Shakespeare could not recall, twenty-six years later, Reagan's exact words in response to his briefing on Fatima. But he remembered the Protestant president's being locked in, highly attentive and engaged: "He listened very, very carefully—very intently. He was *very* interested".[511]

---

[510] Kengor, *God and Ronald Reagan*, 140.
[511] Ibid., 446.

Toil and Transcendence

At the conclusion of his June 6, 1987, meeting with the pope, Reagan once again alluded to something most American presidents would not have brought up. John Paul had designated a Marian Year to begin in the Church that day, the vigil of Pentecost, and though this statement was written by a staff member, it nonetheless conveyed Reagan's sensitivity and goodwill:

> I know that today marks the beginning of a very important time for you personally and for the people of your faith, for it's this day you begin the observance of a year of prayer and devotion to the Virgin Mary with a worldwide prayer for peace. I wish you great joy, happiness and fulfillment in the coming months. And I thank you, your Holiness, and may God bless you.[512]

The two would meet again in three months in Miami, Florida, as the pope undertook a second apostolic journey to the United States. It was a journey that would also take him to South Carolina, Louisiana, Texas, Arizona, California, and Michigan. The two spent nearly six hours together that day, and after a number of afternoon and evening appointments, had another private audience at the Vizcaya Museum on Biscayne Bay. At this meeting, the pope had some remarks on the American form of government, in particular his admiration for the "ordered freedom" found in the United States.[513] It was at this meeting as well that a famous photo was taken of the two leaders: Reagan making a point, the Holy Father listening intently. It caught the attention of Nancy Reagan, who observed that

> the pope is sitting with his head bent, listening, and Ronnie is half way out of his chair and talking to the pope, and his

---

[512] Ibid., 452.
[513] Ibid., 456–457.

hand is out and his finger's out. Obviously he's telling him something. And you wonder, what in the world is Ronnie saying? The pope is listening very carefully to him.[514]

John Paul told Nancy there was a psychological and emotional bond between the two that he had not felt with any other president.[515] And the bond really extended to the whole of the Reagan administration, because it became routine to brief the pope on matters of mutual concern and interest, and to seek out his opinions and recommendations.[516]

The relationship between the two leaders has been the topic of several books and numerous articles and scholarly studies. In the end, the same conclusion is inevitably reached, and it has been well captured by John Paul's leading biographer:

> Both were orphans, at least of a sort; Wojtyla was a genuine orphan before he was twenty-one, while Reagan's difficult experiences with an alcoholic father had given him something of an orphan's sensibility. Both were men of the theater, with shared convictions about the power of words. Both took unconventional routes to positions of eminence that the conventional wisdom assumed they would never hold. Both were what might be called *positive* anticommunists,

---

[514] Kengor, *The Crusader*, 138.

[515] Ibid.

[516] One such occasion was a lengthy meeting between the Holy Father and Vice President George H. W. Bush, in February 1984 in which the pope was briefed on Lebanon, as well as Bush's recent meeting with the Soviet general secretary. The pope's advice was then sought on Poland, and the vice president immediately forwarded his report to the White House Situation Room. Some time later, President Reagan wrote to John Paul of his appreciation for his counsel and his intention to carry out specific recommendations on Poland that the pope felt must be put into effect. Ibid., 137–138.

in that the cause of freedom and the promotion of human rights set the context for their respective critiques of communist theory and practice. As the two men considered the world, neither was locked into the conceptual categories of Realpolitik, as were old-school American conservatives, liberal American arms controllers, and more than a few senior Vatican diplomats. And because of this, both were unafraid of challenging the conventional wisdom and their own bureaucracies.[517]

Reagan and the Hierarchy

If President Reagan had a magnificent relationship with Pope John Paul II, the same was not always true with the bishops of the United States, who often found themselves at odds with him on the question of nuclear arms. The most vocal critic was Bishop Thomas Gumbleton, auxiliary of Detroit, president of the Catholic peace organization Pax Christi and a staunch supporter of George McGovern's presidential campaign against President Nixon in 1972. Reagan's 1980 election and his position on nuclear armaments led Gumbleton to feel "we are getting ever more closer [sic] to the day when we will wage that nuclear war and it will be the war that will end the world as we know it."[518]

Gumbleton had been an active participant in the nuclear-freeze movement and mobilized opposition to Reagan's defense and nuclear programs, unconvinced that the president's tough rhetoric against the Soviets was hardly a provocation to war but an attempt to bring them to the negotiating table so that such arms might be

---

[517] George Weigel, *The End and the Beginning: Pope John Paul II: The Victory of Freedom, the Last Years, the Legacy* (New York: Doubleday, 2010), 127–128.

[518] Cited in Kengor, *A Pope and a President*, 331.

reduced. Many of the country's bishops, though they didn't go as far as Gumbleton, were likewise troubled and took a vocal stance against the administration's tactics. This became evident in the 1983 pastoral letter *The Challenge of Peace: God's Promise and Our Response.*

The Vatican and the Holy Father himself were keenly interested in the progress of this letter, and there were several who offered constructive criticism, including the future Pope Benedict XVI, Joseph Ratzinger, who asked them to consider whether a country's possession of nuclear weapons for the purpose of promoting disarmament could be considered morally acceptable. The Kremlin, for its part, "applauded the clergymen for their open-mindedness and dedication to peace"—that is, to the Soviet position against Reagan's. "Certain bishops," one author has noted, "were proving themselves splendid dupes for political exploitation and propaganda."[519]

The bishops' committee that drafted the document was chaired by Archbishop Joseph Bernardin of Cincinnati, who would later become cardinal archbishop of Chicago. Other members were Gumbleton; Bishop John J. O'Connor, auxiliary of the Military Ordinariate, future cardinal archbishop of New York, and polar opposite of his counterpart from Detroit; Bishop Daniel P. Reilly of Norwich, Connecticut; and Bishop Raymond A. Lucker of New Ulm, Minnesota, a member of Pax Christi.[520] Early in 1983, Bernardin traveled to Rome for a meeting with the Holy Father.

> The pope did not ask for specific changes [to the pastoral letter], but he warned that the Church must not be seen as pacifist or as calling for unilateral U.S. disarmament. The Soviet Union, the pope said, did not subscribe to the same moral principles as the Church. Finally, the pope gave

[519] Ibid., 332.
[520] Ibid.

Bernardin specific responsibility for the pastoral. Bernardin clearly took the pontiff's counsel to heart.[521]

In a series of letters to Bernardin from Bill Clark and Caspar Weinberger, Reagan's secretary of defense, the officials laid out the "peace through strength" approach of the administration. In response, the Archbishop told the *New York Times* in a detailed interview that the administration's position had been greatly clarified and that the bishops had initially misunderstood some of the key points in Reagan's thinking. The State Department said that the bishops' statement had been "substantially improved," and

> the final text, although no endorsement of Reagan's nuclear policies, was more favorable to the president than earlier drafts had been, and it was much less critical of the administration's policies than the nuclear freeze movement and many U.S. bishops actually desired.[522]

Signs of Hope

Although the seventies and eighties continued to witness the fallout from erroneous views of what the Second Vatican Council had tried to accomplish, there were also tremendous fruits of the Council appearing everywhere. Religious communities sprang up and flourished — the closer they hewed to the true spirit of the Council and to Church teaching on the authentic renewal of religious life, the more successful they were. Just a few examples are Saint Teresa of

[521] Ibid., 334.

[522] Ibid., 334–335. Professor Jared McBrady has noted that "the nature of cooperation between the Reagan administration and the Vatican, and the shared goals and level of trust that existed between the president and the pope, certainly colored the way *The Challenge of Peace* was revised." Cited in ibid.

Calcutta's Missionaries of Charity, the Sisters of Life founded by John Cardinal O'Connor, the Ann Arbor and Nashville Dominican Sisters, and the Alma Sisters of Mercy. Yet another influential religious woman was Mother Angelica of the Poor Clares of Perpetual Adoration in Irondale, Alabama, whose initial venture into television gave birth to the Eternal Word Television Network, a global Catholic station now seen on every inhabited continent.

As the laity became more and more involved in the Church, previously untapped spiritual resources began to emerge:

Opus Dei ("the work of God") was founded in Spain in 1928 by a diocesan priest, St. Josemaría Escrivá (d. 1975). Although directed by priests, it was in some ways the most significant lay movement of modern times, embracing over eighty thousand members worldwide, a majority of whom were married but lived under the spiritual direction of priests and under the disciplinary authority of their own bishop. Part of Opus Dei's original significance was the fact that, whereas traditional European Catholicism had always been cool, even hostile, to industrialization, Opus Dei enthusiastically embraced technological modernity and successfully combined it with traditional piety.[523]

Other groups such as Focolare, Comunione e Liberazione (Communion and Liberation), Regnum Christi, the Neocatechumenate, and the Community of Sant'Egidio, primarily devoted to prayer and works of charity, added to the list. The charismatic movement, begun at Duquesne University in Pittsburgh and concentrating on the recovery of the "charisms" described in the Acts of the Apostles, became enormously popular and brought many people into a more intense life of faith. Marian piety also received a boost,

[523] Ibid., 518.

including from the cult of Medjugorje in Bosnia and Herzogovina, where three young people reported apparitions of the Blessed Virgin Mary. Pilgrims flocked by the thousands, and, though pilgrimages were never discouraged by the Church, official approbation has not been given.

With the Council's affirmation that parents were the official teachers of their children, the Catholic homeschool movement began to flourish. Contrasted with the secularism of American culture, represented especially in the system of public education, Catholic parents dedicated to the Church and Her teachings began to see in homeschooling the surest way for their children to be thoroughly grounded in the Faith amid contemporary culture.

Tied Together

One of the most significant events to occur in recent years between the Church and the United States, though hardly noticed at the time or since, was the opening of formal diplomatic relations between the two sovereign nations. The relationship was solidified in 1984, fulfilling, in a sense, the bond that had developed between the pope and President Reagan. The fact that there was so little organized opposition to the news testified to the unquestioned position of Catholicism in the country as the third millennium approached. Of course, anti-Catholicism had been part of the American psyche since the earliest of colonial days and, in all probability, will remain so, no matter how sophisticated national life becomes. Rather than a fear of papal dominion, it is a fear of truth itself that motivates anti-Catholicism in a society in which the dictatorship of relativism prevails. When Holy Mother Church speaks in the name of Her Lord, the world reacts—usually quite negatively.

And so there were some negative reactions to the establishing of closer ties with the Holy See. The Reagan Library in California's

Simi Valley has preserved many individual letters of protest, commemorating both old Protestant fears and secularist anxieties:

> Joseph P. Folds, director of missions for the South Florida
> Baptist Association, wrote President Reagan a letter refer-
> encing an article in ... *Church and State* magazine reporting
> that the Reagan administration had used $78,000 in public
> funds to send a delegation to Alaska to meet with Pope
> John Paul II. Folds said he was "very anxious" and "terribly
> upset," telling Reagan that this was "absolutely wrong" and
> "immediately violates the spirit of the First Ammendment."
> "If the officials of the Roman Catholic Church wanted to
> meet their Pope," he wrote, "that would be their business."
> This kind of opposition would continue well after Vatican
> recognition. In May 1986, when Bill Wilson announced
> that he was stepping down as U.S. Ambassador, conserva-
> tive Protestants such as Robert P. Dugan, Jr., director of
> the Reagan-friendly National Association of Evangelicals
> (which had hosted Reagan's Evil Empire speech), and B. E.
> Pitts, Jr. of the Southern Baptist Convention wrote letters
> urging their president "in the strongest terms" to "not fill the
> vacancy" (Dugan's words). Oddly, Dugan and Pitts stood on
> the same side as leaders of left-wing secularist groups, such
> as Dr. Robert L. Maddox, executive director of Americans
> United for Separation of Church and State, and John V.
> Stevens of the Church State Council.[524]

Plans for official recognition proceeded on schedule. The event,
after all, had been a long time in the making. In 1867, on hearing
a rumor that the pope was going to forbid American Protestants to
hold services within Rome's city walls, the U.S. Congress had passed

---

[524] Kengor, *A Pope and a President*, 354.

Toil and Transcendence

a resolution saying that no federal funds could be used to maintain a diplomatic mission in Rome. Then FDR had (unofficially) sent Myron Taylor; Harry Truman had attempted to appoint Mark Clark; and Presidents Nixon, Carter, and Reagan had all had personal envoys to the pope prior to the opening of formal diplomacy. By 1984, aside from cranky private individuals and groups, there was little opposition from Congress or the courts. And so William A. Wilson was appointed by Reagan as the first American ambassador to the Holy See. For its part, the Holy See named Archbishop Pio Laghi as the first apostolic nuncio (equivalent to ambassador) of the Holy See to the United States.

Bill Wilson and his wife had been close friends of Nancy and Ronald Reagan for years.[525] Born in Los Angeles in 1914, Wilson received a B.S. and an M.S. from Stanford University and during World War II had served as a captain in the Army Ordnance Corps. His wife, Elizabeth "Betty" Johnson, was a Catholic, and Wilson converted to the Faith. He became one of Ronald Reagan's early supporters and advisers, urging the former actor to run for governor of California. Upon assuming office, Reagan appointed his friend to the state university's board of regents. Some years after leaving his ambassadorial post, Wilson joined the board of trustees of Thomas

[525] One of Reagan's biographers has written that "Reagan's 688-acre ranch in the Santa Ynez Mountains northwest of Santa Barbara was found for him in 1974 by millionaire investment counsellor and fellow [horseback] rider William Wilson.... The ranch nestles on a mountaintop that, at 2,250 feet, is often bathed in sunlight while fog shrouds the Pacific Ocean below. The view and the re-moteness appealed to Reagan at first sight. He named it Rancho del Cielo ("heavenly ranch") and after the end of his second term as governor in 1974 threw himself into clearing trails and brush, and remodeling the old one-story adobe house to make it comfortable for Nancy Reagan." Lou Cannon, *President Reagan: The Role of a Lifetime* (New York: Public Affairs, 1991), 464–465.

Aquinas College in Ventura County, a bastion of Catholic orthodoxy. Chairing the institution's finance committee for a number of
years, the ambassador was instrumental in introducing the college's
top administrators to John Paul II, Cardinal Ratzinger, and other
Vatican officials. Wilson died at his home in Carmel, California,
in December 2009 at age ninety-five.

The End, for Now

The opening of formal diplomatic relations between America and
the Holy See seems an appropriate place to conclude this study of
the history of U.S. Catholicism in the late nineteenth and twentieth centuries. We are now thirty-six years from this consummation,
and to continue much further would bring us into a contemporary
narrative too susceptible to subjectivity and whose contours are
still changing as we speak.

The story of the Church in these years has been one of growth
and development, of assimilation of countless Catholic groups into
the American scene, of patriotism in war and opposition to war, of
strong episcopal leaders and devoted lay Catholics. It has been the
story of anti-Catholic bigotry and the effective and hopefully enduring transcending of that bigotry, of labor and capital, of Americanism as either a phantom heresy or a real threat to ecclesiastical
unity (or both). The Church's story has included presidents of the
United States and their shifting relationsips with Catholic voters
and hierarchy, tremendous Catholic patriotism, adaptation to the
world-changing Second Vatican Council, Catholic educational
growth followed by secularization and decline. It is the story of the
gallant fight for human life in this land, of three sainted pontiffs
and their relations with the American Church, and of a pope and
a president and the role they each played in the final defeat of
international communism.

Toil and Transcendence

More than any of these particulars, though, it has been the story of the Mystical Body of Christ unfolding in a particular place and a particular period of time, the story of a small portion of that Body's journey to eternity. It has been the story of the men and women God raised up to shepherd, guide, and direct His Church in uncertain times. Finally, it has been the story of the spreading and sharing of God's grace, on and for individuals and the Church Herself. That story, the story of Providence, whenever or wherever or by whomever it is told, must be a glorious one, because it is always a story of God and His people.

Bibliography

Abbott, Walter M., S.J., ed. *The Documents of Vatican II*. New York: Herder and Herder, 1966.

Ahlstrom, Sydney E. *A Religious History of the American People*. 2 vols. Garden City, NY:, 1975.

Berman, Ronald. *America in the Sixties*. New York: Harper & Row, 1968.

Beschloss, Michael R. *Kennedy and Roosevelt: The Uneasy Alliance*. New York: W. W. Norton, 1980.

Boucher, Arline, and John Tehan. *Prince of Democracy: James Cardinal Gibbons*. Garden City, NY: Doubleday, 1962.

Brinkley, Douglas. *Parish Priest: Father Michael McGivney and American Catholicism*. New York: HarperCollins, 2006.

Browne, Henry J. *The Catholic Church and the Knights of Labor*. Washington, D.C.: Catholic University of America Press, 1949.

Buchanan, Patrick J. *The Greatest Comeback*. New York: Crown Forum, 2014.

———. *Nixon's White House Wars*. New York: Crown Forum, 2017.

Buckley, William F., Jr. *A Torch Kept Lit: Great Lives of the Twentieth Century*. New York: Crown Forum, 2016.

———. *Nearer, My God: An Autobiography of Faith*. New York: Doubleday, 1997.

Buckley, William F., Jr., and Brent Bozell. *McCarthy and His Enemies: The Record and Its Meaning*. New Rochelle, NY: Arlington House, 1954.

Budenz, Louis Francis. *This Is My Story*. New York: McGraw-Hill, 1947.

Burns, John, M.Th. *The American Rebellion against Humanae Vitae*. Self-published, 2011.

Cannon, Lou. *President Reagan: The Role of a Lifetime*. New York: Public Affairs, 1991.

Cargas, Harry J. *I Lay Down My Life: Biography of Joyce Kilmer*. Jamaica Plain, MA: Daughters of Saint Paul, 1964.

Chaput, Charles, O.F.M. Cap. "The Vocation of Christians in American Public Life." Address at Houston Baptist University, March 1, 2010. EWTN. https://www.ewtn.com/catholicism/library/vocation -of-christians-in-american-public-life-3681.

Connelly, James F., ed. *The History of the Archdiocese of Philadelphia*. Philadelphia: Archdiocese of Philadelphia, 1976.

Connor, Charles P. *Classic Catholic Converts*. San Francisco: Ignatius Press, 2001.

———. *The Spiritual Legacy of Archbishop Fulton J. Sheen*. New York: Alba House, 2010.

Coughlin, Charles E. *Am I an Anti-Semite?: 9 Addresses on Various "Isms" Answering the Question*. Royal Oak, MI: Shrine of the Little Flower, 1939.

———. *An Answer to Father Coughlin's Critics*. Royal Oak, MI: Shrine of the Little Flower, 1940.

———. *Why Leave Our Own?* Royal Oak, MI: Shrine of the Little Flower, 1939.

Crosby, Donald F., S.J. *God, Church, and Flag: Senator Joseph R. McCarthy and the Catholic Church, 1950–1957*. Chapel Hill: University of North Carolina Press, 1978.

Daughters of St. Paul, comp. *Richard Cardinal Cushing in Prose and Photos*. Jamaica Plain, MA: St. Paul Editions, 1965.

Delaney, John J., ed. *Dictionary of American Catholic Biography*. Garden City, NY: Doubleday, 1984.

Dulles, Avery. *A Testimonial to Grace*. New York: Sheed & Ward, 1946.

Bibliography

Ellis, John Tracy, and Robert Trisco. *A Guide to American Catholic History*. Santa Barbara: ABC-Clio, 1982.

———. "American Catholics and the Intellectual Life." *Thought* 30 (Autumn 1955): 351–390.

———. *Catholic Bishops: A Memoir*. Wilmington, DE: Michael Glazier, 1983.

———. *Documents of American Catholic History*. Milwaukee: Bruce, 1956.

———. *The Formative Years of the Catholic University of America*. Washington, D.C.: American Catholic Historical Association, 1946.

———. *The Life of James Cardinal Gibbons, Archbishop of Baltimore, 1834–1921*. 2 vols. Milwaukee: Bruce, 1952.

Farber, David. *Everybody Ought to Be Rich: The Life and Times of John J. Raskob, Capitalist*. New York: Oxford University Press, 2013.

Farrell, John A. *Richard Nixon: The Life*. New York: Doubleday, 2017.

Felzenberg, Alvin S. *A Man and His Presidents: The Political Odyssey of William F. Buckley Jr*. New Haven: Yale University Press, 2017.

Finn, Brendan A. *Twenty-Four American Cardinals*. Boston: Bruce Humphries, 1947.

Fogarty, Gerald P., S.J. *The Vatican and the American Hierarchy from 1870 to 1965*. Collegeville, MN: Liturgical Press, 1982.

Gallagher, John P. *A Century of History: The Diocese of Scranton: 1868–1968*. Scranton: Diocese of Scranton, Pennsylvania, 1968.

Gallagher, Louis J., S.J. *Edmund A. Walsh, S.J.: A Biography*. New York: Benziger Brothers, 1962.

Gannon, Robert I., S.J. *The Cardinal Spellman Story*. Garden City, NY: Doubleday, 1962.

Garraty, John A. *The American Nation: A History of the United States*. 2 vols. New York: Harper & Row, 1966.

Gibbons, James Cardinal. *The Church and the Republic*. Brooklyn: International Catholic Truth Society, 1909.

———. *A Retrospect of Fifty Years*. 2 vols. Baltimore: John Murphy, 1916.

Gibbs, Nancy, and Michael Duffy. *The Preacher and the Presidents: Billy Graham in the White House*. New York: Center Street, 2007.

Glazier, Michael, and Thomas J. Shelley, eds. *The Encyclopedia of American Catholic History*. Collegeville, MN: Liturgical Press, 1997.

Golway, Terry. *Frank & Al: FDR, Al Smith and the Unlikely Alliance That Created the Modern Democratic Party*. New York: St. Martin's Press, 2018.

Graham, Robert A., S.J. *The Vatican and Communism during World War II: What Really Happened?* San Francisco: Ignatius Press, 1996.

Griffin, William D. *The Book of Irish Americans*. New York: Random House, 1990.

Hagan, Edward A. *To Vietnam in Vain: Memoir of an Irish-American Intelligence Advisor, 1969–1970*. Jefferson, NC: McFarland & Company, 2016.

Hall, Kermit L., ed. *The Oxford Companion to the Supreme Court of the United States*. New York: Oxford University Press, 1992.

Hannan, Archbishop Philip. *The Archbishop Wore Combat Boots: Memoir of an Extraordinary Life*. Huntington, IN: Our Sunday Visitor, 2010.

Hamilton, Nigel. *Commander in Chief: FDR'S Battle with Churchill, 1943*. Boston: Houghton Mifflin Harcourt, 2016.

Harcourt, Felix. *Ku Klux Kulture: America and the Klan in the 1920s*. Chicago: University of Chicago Press, 2017.

Hayward, Steven F. *The Age of Reagan: The Fall of the Old Liberal Order: 1964–1980*. New York: Three Rivers Press, 2001.

Hennesey, James S.J. *American Catholics: A History of the Roman Catholic Community in the United States*. New York: Oxford University Press, 1981.

Hicks, John D. *Republican Ascendancy: 1921–1933*. New York: Harper & Row, 1960.

Hitchcock, James. *History of the Catholic Church from the Apostolic Age to the Third Millennium*. San Francisco: Ignatius Press, 2012.

Hollis, Christopher. *The Achievements of Vatican II*. New York: Hawthorn Books, 1967.

Hoover, Herbert. *The Memoirs of Herbert Hoover: The Cabinet and the Presidency: 1929–1933*. New York: MacMillan Company, 1952.

Hudson, Winthrop S. *Religion in America: An Historical Account of the Development of American Religious Life*. New York: Charles Scribner's Sons, 1965.

The Influence of the Catholic Church on the Eisenhower Administration's Decision to Directly Intervene in Vietnam — Soviet Communist Containment, South Vietnamese Policy, Indochina, Southeast Asia. Washington, D.C.: U.S. Government, U.S. Military, Department of Defense, 2015.

Jeansonne, Glen. *Herbert Hoover: A Life*. New York: New American Library, 2016.

Jenkins, Philip. *The New Anti-Catholicism: The Last Acceptable Prejudice*. Oxford, UK: Oxford University Press, 2003.

Jeffries, John W. *A Third Term for FDR: The Election of 1940*. Lawrence, KS: University Press of Kansas, 2017.

Johnson, Paul. *A History of the American People*. London: Weidenfeld & Nicolson, 1997.

Kengor, Paul. *A Pope and a President: John Paul II, Ronald Reagan, and the Extraordinary Untold Story of the 20th Century*. Wilmington, DE: ISI Books, 2017.

———. *God and Ronald Reagan: A Spiritual Life*. New York: HarperCollins, 2004.

———. *The Crusader: Ronald Reagan and the Fall of Communism*. New York: HarperCollins, 2006.

Kengor, Paul, and Robert Orlando. *The Divine Plan: John Paul II, Ronald Reagan, and the Dramatic End of the Cold War*. Wilmington, DE: ISI Books, 2019.

LaFarge, John, S.J. *A Report on the American Jesuits*. New York: Farrar, Straus and Cudahy, 1956.

Lane, Christopher. *Surge Of Piety: Norman Vincent Peale and the Remaking of American Religious Life*. New Haven: Yale University Press, 2016.

Leuchtenburg, William E. *Franklin D. Roosevelt and the New Deal: 1932–1940*. New York: Harper & Row, 1963.

Lichtman, Allan J. *Prejudice and the Old Politics: The Presidential Election of 1928*. Chapel Hill: University of North Carolina Press, 1979.

Link, Arthur S. *Woodrow Wilson and the Progressive Era: 1910–1917*. New York: Harper & Row, 1954.

Marlin, George J. *The American Catholic Voter: 200 Years of Political Impact*. South Bend, IN: St. Augustine's Press, 2004.

Massa, Mark, S.J., ed. *American Catholic History: A Documentary Reader*. New York: New York University Press, 2008.

McNamara, Patrick. *A Catholic Cold War: Edmund A. Walsh, S.J. and the Politics of American Anticommunism*. New York: Fordham University Press, 2005.

Mindszenty, József Cardinal. *Memoirs*. New York: Macmillan, 1974.

Miscamble, Wilson D., C.S.C. *American Priest: The Ambitious Life and Conflicted Legacy of Notre Dame's Father Ted Hesburgh*. New York: Image, 2019.

Mitchell, Peter M. *The Coup at Catholic University: The 1968 Revolution in American Catholic Education*. San Francisco: Ignatius Press, 2015.

Morris, Richard B. *Encyclopedia of American History*. New York: Harper & Row, 1953.

Morris, Sylvia Jukes. *Price of Fame: The Honorable Clare Boothe Luce*. New York: Random House, 2015.

Mowry, George E. *The Era of Theodore Roosevelt and the Birth of Modern America: 1900–1912*. New York: Harper & Row, 1958.

Moynihan, James H. *The Life of Archbishop John Ireland*. New York: Harper & Brothers, 1953.

Muller, Jerry Z. *Conservativism: An Anthology of Social and Political Thought from David Hume to the Present*. Princeton, NJ: Princeton University Press, 1997.

Bibliography

Mulligan, James J. *The Pope and the Theologians: The* Humanae Vitae *Controversy.* Baltimore: self-published, 1968.

Nichols, David A. *Ike and McCarthy: Dwight Eisenhower's Secret Campaign against Joseph McCarthy.* New York: Simon & Schuster, 2017.

Nixon, Richard M. *Six Crises.* New York: Doubleday, 1962.

Noonan, Peggy. *When Character Was King: A Story of Ronald Reagan.* New York: Viking, 2001.

O'Connell, Marvin R. *John Ireland and the American Catholic Church.* Saint Paul: Minnesota Historical Society Press, 1988.

O'Connor, John J. *A Chaplain Looks at Vietnam.* New York: World Publishing, 1968.

O'Connor, Richard. *Heywood Broun: The Life and Career of the Most Famous and Controversial Journalist of His Time.* New York: G. P. Putnam's Sons, 1975.

O'Connor, Thomas H. *Boston's Catholics: A History of the Church and Its People.* Boston: Northeastern University Press, 1998.

Pegram, Thomas R. *One Hundred Percent American: The Rebirth and Decline of the Ku Klux Klan in the 1920s.* Chicago: Ivan R. Dee, 2011.

Pollard, John F. *The Unknown Pope: Benedict XV (1914–1922) and the Pursuit of Peace.* London: Geoffrey Chapman, 1999.

Pope Paul VI. *On Human Life: Humanae Vitae.* San Francisco: Ignatius Press, 2014.

Powderly, Terence V. *The Path I Trod: The Autobiography of Terence V. Powderly.* New York: Columbia University Press, 1940.

Quigley, Thomas, ed. *American Catholics and Vietnam.* Grand Rapids, MI: William B. Eerdmans, 1968.

Reeves, Thomas C. *America's Bishop: The Life and Times of Fulton J. Sheen.* San Francisco: Encounter Books, 2001.

Regan, Richard J. *A Constitutional History of the U.S. Supreme Court.* Washington, D.C.: Catholic University Press, 2015.

Rutler, George W. *Calm In Chaos: Catholic Wisdom for Anxious Times.* San Francisco: Ignatius Press, 2018.

Schlesinger, Arthur M. *The Rise of the City: 1878–1898.* New York: Macmillan, 1933.

Schindler, David L. *Heart of the World, Center of the Church: Communio Ecclesiology, Liberalism, and Liberation.* Grand Rapids, MI: William B. Eerdmans, 1996.

Schmuhl, Robert. *Ireland's Exiled Children: America and the Easter Rising.* Oxford, UK: Oxford University Press, 2016.

Schoen, Douglas E. *The Nixon Effect: How Richard Nixon's Presidency Fundamentally Changed American Politics.* New York: Encounter Books, 2016.

Shaw, Geoffrey. *The Lost Mandate of Heaven: The American Betrayal of Ngo Dinh Diem, President of Vietnam.* San Francisco: Ignatius Press, 2015.

Shaw, Russell. *American Church: The Remarkable Rise, Meteoric Fall, and Uncertain Future of Catholicism in America.* San Francisco: Ignatius Press, 2013.

———. *Catholics In America: Religious Identity and Cultural Assimilation from John Carroll to Flannery O'Connor.* San Francisco: Ignatius Press, 2016.

Smith, Janet E. *Humanae Vitae: A Generation Later.* Washington, D.C.: Catholic University of America Press, 1991.

———, ed. *Why Humanae Vitae Was Right: A Reader.* San Francisco: Ignatius Press, 1993.

Spalding, John Lancaster. *An Address Delivered at the Laying of the Cornerstone of the Catholic University at Washington, D.C., May 24, 1888.* Peoria, Illinois: B. Cremer & Bros., 1888.

———. *The Religious Mission of the Irish People and Catholic Colonization.* New York: Catholic Publication Society, 1880.

Spalding, Thomas W. *The Premier See: A History of the Archdiocese of Baltimore, 1789–1989.* Baltimore: Johns Hopkins University Press, 1989.

Spellman, Francis J. *The Road to Victory: The Second Front of Prayer.* New York: Charles Scribner's Sons, 1942.

Spitz, Bob. *Reagan: An American Journey.* New York: Random House, 2018.

Tansill, Charles Callan. *America and the Fight for Irish Freedom*. New York: Devin–Adair, 1957.

The Influence of the Catholic Church on the Eisenhower Administration's Decision to Directly Intervene in Vietnam: Soviet Communist Containment, South Vietnamese Policy, Indochina, Southeast Asia. Washington, D.C.: Progressive Management Publications, 2015.

The Whittaker Chambers Reader: His Complete National Review Writings. New York: National Review, 2014.

Tucker, Todd. *Notre Dame vs. the Klan: How the Fighting Irish Defeated the Ku Klux Klan*. Chicago: Loyola Press, 2004.

Tull, Charles J. *Father Coughlin and the New Deal*. Syracuse: Syracuse University Press, 1965.

Von Hildebrand, Dietrich. *Love, Marriage, and the Catholic Conscience: Understanding the Church's Teaching on Birth Control*. Manchester, NH: Sophia Institute Press, 1998.

Walters, Vernon A. *Silent Missions*. Garden City, NY: Doubleday, 1978.

———. *The Mighty and the Meek: Dispatches from the Front Line of Diplomacy*. London: St. Ermin's Press, 2001.

Wayman, Dorothy G. *Cardinal O'Connell of Boston: A Biography of William Cardinal O'Connell: 1859–1944*. New York: Farrar, Straus and Young, 1955.

Weigel, George. *The End and the Beginning: Pope John Paul II: The Victory of Freedom, the Last Years, the Legacy*. New York: Doubleday, 2010.

———. *Witness to Hope: The Biography of Pope John Paul II*. New York: HarperCollins, 1999.

Williamson, Chilton, Jr. *The Conservative Bookshelf: Essential Works That Impact Today's Conservative Thinkers*. New York: Citadel Press, 2004.

Wish, Harvey. *The American Historian: A Social-Intellectual History of the Writing of the American Past*. New York: Oxford University Press, 1960.

Toil and Transcendence

Witcover, Jules. *The Year the Dream Died: Revisiting 1968 in America*. New York: Warner Books, 1997.

Wolfskill, George. *The Revolt of the Conservatives: A History of the American Liberty League*. Boston: Houghton Mifflin, 1962.

Woolner, David B., and Richard G. Kurial, eds. *FDR, the Vatican, and the Roman Catholic Church in America, 1933–1945*. New York: MacMillan, 2003.

Zwierlein, Frederick J. *Theodore Roosevelt and Catholics: 1882–1919*. Saint Louis: Central Bureau of the Central Verein, 1956.

∞

About the Author

Fr. Charles P. Connor, S.T.L., Ph.D., is a professor of systematic theology and Church history at Mount St. Mary's Seminary in Emmitsburg, Maryland. He has previously authored books on several topics, such as *Classic Catholic Converts, Defenders of the Faith in Word and Deed, Meditations on the Catholic Priesthood, The Saint for the Third Millennium: Thérèse of Lisieux, The Spiritual Legacy of Archbishop Fulton J. Sheen, John Cardinal O'Connor and the Culture of Life, Pioneer Priests and Makeshift Altars: A History of Catholicism in the Thirteen Colonies,* and *Faith and Fury: The Rise of Catholicism during the Civil War.* He has co-produced dozens of series for EWTN and is actively engaged in preaching retreats for priests and laity throughout the United States. A priest of the Diocese of Scranton, Pennsylvania, he served in diocesan parishes for eighteen years, including as rector of St. Peter's Cathedral in Scranton. Fr. Connor holds a B.A. and an M.A. in U.S. history from the University of Scranton, a Ph.B. from the Institute of Philosophy at the Catholic University of Louvain in Belgium, a doctorate in U.S. history from Fordham University in New York City, an S.T.B. from the Gregorian University in Rome, an M.A. from the Angelicum University in Rome, and an S.T.L. from the Pontifical John Paul II Institute for Studies on Marriage and Family in Washington, D.C.